W9-BUJ-972

The praise continues . . .

"Farley Granger was there during that golden time when Hollywood sparkled in the light of such stars as Bette Davis, Charlie Chaplin, Judy Garland, Elizabeth Taylor, Jimmy Stewart, David Niven, Hedy Lamarr—and thrown into the mix were Leonard Bernstein, Aaron Copland, and Jerome Robbins. You will be there, too, when you read Farley's fascinating book. Don't miss this one."
—Barbara Cook

"Farley Granger has written with a clear eye and much love about the golden age of Hollywood and Broadway. He paints vivid pictures of his travels in Europe, as well as his work with Hitchcock and Visconti. He pulls no punches in describing his passionate bisexuality: He had affairs with Arthur Laurents, Ava Gardner, and the conductor Leonard Bernstein, among others. At the same time, Granger succeeds in conveying, in these pages, a stubborn integrity and an indomitable charm that give his life the force of legend. I can't remember when I've read a book that I've enjoyed as much as Farley Granger's *Include Me Out*."
—Patricia Bosworth, author of *Diane Arbus: A Biography* and *Marlon Brando: A Biography*

"Farley Granger, youthful, strikingly handsome, and distinctly talented star of a series of brilliant films of the 1940s and '50s, is a rare and truly free spirit in the annals of Hollywood personalities. A highly intimate firsthand account of golden-age stardom, *Include Me Out* recalls Farley Granger's colorful, independent-minded life—the creative triumphs and pitfalls; the glamour comrades, legendary directors, and maddening moguls; his friendships, love affairs, and sexual adventures—with candor, insight, and enormous likability."
—Lee Server

Include Me Out

My Life from Goldwyn to Broadway

FARLEY GRANGER
WITH
ROBERT CALHOUN

St. Martin's Press New York

 For information, address St. Martin's Press, 175 Fifth Avenue, New York, N.Y. 10010.

www.stmartins.com

Frontispiece photograph courtesy of Farley Granger

Library of Congress Cataloging-in-Publication Data

Granger, Farley.
Include me out : my life from Goldwyn to Broadway / Farley Granger with Robert Calhoun.—1st ed.
p. cm.
Includes index.
ISBN-13: 978-0-312-35773-3
ISBN-10: 0-312-35773-7
1. Granger, Farley. 2. Actors—United States—Biography. I. Title.

PN2287.G669A3 2007
791.4302'8092—dc22
[B]

2006050194

First Edition: March 2007

10 9 8 7 6 5 4 3 2 1

In memory of my beloved Ethyl

There is only one success . . . to be able to spend your life in your own way.

CHRISTOPHER MORLEY

Currently embroiled in my own "Golden Age," I've done my best to assemble the facts of my private and professional life accurately. If at one time or another, the wrong person shows up at the wrong party, forgive me. Everyone mentioned was with me at one party or another, at one time or another. It's my movie and it changes with every passing day.

FARLEY GRANGER

CONTENTS

Special Acknowledgment

To Lawrence Malkin, whose generosity of spirit, intelligence, good humor, and willingness to share his expertise as a professional writer made this collaboration possible.

Acknowledgments

To Diane Reverand, our editor, who missed nothing: our excess of, or lack of, information, opinion, style, continuity, and taste.
To Philip Spitzer, our agent, who patiently resumed his efforts on our behalf after a twelve-year hiatus and found, with his usual dispatch, the right people.
To Jay Julien, our lawyer/manager, who has been our rock and the repository of our trust for thirty years.
To Frederick Kaufman, whose personal and professional opinion has been cheerfully given, eagerly sought, and happily received.
To Shirley Kaplan, who has never wavered in her enthusiastic support for this project.
To Linda and Patrick Pleven, who assisted on every how-to problem, willingly, cheerfully, and lovingly, every time we called upon them.
To Neila Smith Kennedy, who has been there with and for us from day one, twelve years ago.
To Eddie Muller and the San Francisco Film Noir Festival.
To Regina Scarpa, our associate editor, whose unflappable good humor and good sense saved many fraught moments from descending into disaster.

Special Thanks

To Samuel Goldwyn, Jr.
To Jane Klane and the Museum of Television and Radio; to the New York Public Library for the Performing Arts and its staff at Lincoln Center; and to the Academy of Motion Picture Arts and Sciences.

Include Me Out

Prologue

In December 2004, I was invited to a Visconti retrospective to see a newly restored print of his 1954 film *Senso,* at the Brooklyn Academy of Music, one of New York City's most respected arts organizations. The print included some scenes that had been cut from the film. As the house lights dimmed, I felt a hint of the familiar tightness in my stomach that always accompanied viewing myself on screen. The film opens with a scene from Verdi's *Il Trovatore* being performed on the stage of La Fenice, Venice's jewel box of an opera house. Italian partisans stealthily infiltrate the audience composed of groups of officers from the occupying Austrian Army, Venetian aristocrats, and ordinary citizens to pass out materials for a public anti-Austrian demonstration. I was so swept up by the beauty and drama of the moment that I didn't even notice my character's first appearance. I continued to be that absorbed by the film up to the final scene of the Countess running like a broken bird through crowds of drunken Austrian soldiers in the streets of Verona at night after she has had her lover, Franz, executed. As the audience applauded at the film's conclusion, I found myself applauding with them. Not only had I enjoyed *Senso* as much as they had, but I was also proud of the performance of that young actor playing Franz Mahler.

I had only seen a version of the film that had been butchered to fit into a ninety-minute television format, released in the United States in 1968 as *The Wanton Contessa.* For the first time in my life, I realized that in the time I had spent making films between my first movie, *The North Star,* in 1944, and *Senso,* in 1954, I had become an actor.

Seeing *Senso* that evening in Brooklyn flooded my mind with memories of my days as a film actor. I realized how important those years had been, how they had helped mold whatever talent I was able to develop. I'd been lucky enough to work with some legendary directors and to appear in several classic films. It was a fascinating time in film history. The more I thought about it, the more I realized how important those days were to all of us. They were the foundation of my life as an actor, and they also represented a time that shaped an entire generation of post–World War II Americans.

I never liked looking at myself on screen. I found it disquieting in the same way as hearing your voice on an answering machine for the first time. It doesn't sound the same as you hear yourself and therefore seems disconnected from you. When watching a performance of mine, I've never been able to relax and enjoy it as a member of the audience, because my focus was always on the choices I or he, the character, made for the scene. For example, in a confrontational scene, was I too controlled, which could seem calculating, or too aggressive, which could seem out of control? In a love scene, was I too eager, which could come across as needy and immature, or too smooth and relaxed, which could be interpreted as narcissistic and self-absorbed? No matter what the demands of a scene—comic or tragic, naturalistic or operatic—watching myself just gave me another chance to worry that maybe I'd missed the acting choice that could have made the scene deeper, more moving, more exciting, more fun, or simply more honest. I was never satisfied with what I saw. It was painful to see my performance blown up on screen, so much larger than life.

Interviewers would sometimes ask me if I didn't feel lucky because of my looks. I never thought about my looks at all. They were a given, neither an accomplishment nor something I could work on to get better parts. At times how I looked felt like a handicap in terms of casting. Leading men are much more liable to be typecast. Character actors get to play a wider range of parts, which is more challenging and more fun.

One of the benefits of getting older, aside from the experience and technique acquired along the way, is that now it is easier for me to look objectively at that young actor up there on the screen. I have become a much less demanding self-critic. Since I am frequently requested to attend events honoring Alfred Hitchcock, I most often see my younger self as Guy, the tennis pro in the 1951 classic *Strangers on a Train.* This film, which after several flops reestablished Hitchcock as Hollywood's master of suspense, is so good that after many years and viewings, I can finally sit back and appreciate my contribution to it.

I have only made two other films that inspire the same sense of pride. One is Nicholas Ray's *They Live by Night;* the other is Luchino Visconti's *Senso.* Nick's film is a small, tight story of two doomed young lovers on the run in small-town middle America during the Depression.

Visconti's film is a lush, sprawling epic in which two doomed lovers play out their fate against the backdrop of the Risorgimento, Italy's struggle for independence and political unification in the mid-nineteenth century. The locations were Venice; a Palladio villa in Vicenza, a small town in the mountains north of Venice; and a sound stage in Rome. Making *Senso* was a unique and sometimes thrilling experience for me, but not always an enjoyable one.

I had not been happy making films in Hollywood. I wanted to move to New York, learn how to act, and work in the theater. Mr. Goldwyn had refused to—

using his own malapropism—include me out of the last two years of my seven-year contract. He finally agreed, provided I pay him a sum based on what he got for me when he loaned me out to other studios. This was approximately ten times what he paid me. I paid. I was free. I was broke.

My agent got me the deal to make *Senso* in Italy. The salary was what Goldwyn got for me on loanout. If the film did not finish in three months, it doubled. I was making good money, but I got frustrated when we hit the eight-month point with no end in sight. It seemed as if I was never going to get to New York and the theater.

Act I

Discovered

It was 1943. America was at war. I was a healthy seventeen-year-old high school student, halfway through my senior year. My future was clear: I would graduate and when I turned eighteen in July, I would join whatever branch of the armed forces most of my buddies were choosing. That's exactly what happened, with one exception: I became a movie star first.

As a clerk in the unemployment office in North Hollywood, my dad was used to seeing actors when they came in every week to collect their checks. There was the occasional grand one like Adolphe Menjou, who arrived in a chauffeured limousine each week to pick up his check, but most of them were just ordinary out-of-work actors waiting for their next paying job to come along. Dad became friendly with an actor who was far from ordinary. It was Harry Langdon, who had been one of the "Big Four," Hollywood's most beloved stars during the silent film era, along with Harold Lloyd, Buster Keaton, and Charlie Chaplin. Chaplin was the only one of the four who survived the transition to talkies. The others had fallen on differing degrees of hard times. Keaton and Lloyd eventually survived more successfully than Mr. Langdon. My dad had great admiration for his new friend, and eventually felt free enough with him to ask his advice about my dream of becoming an actor.

After mulling it over for several weeks, Langdon told Dad about a small showcase theater on Highland Avenue in Hollywood that was run by Mary Stewart, a little-known actress with a lot of money and some talent. There was no permanent company, no set schedule. Each production that Miss Stewart managed to put on consisted of a pickup group of actors, most of them amateurs who would work for nothing in order to get the experience, and the credit, not to mention an opportunity to live the dream of being discovered.

She was currently seeing young actors for *The Wookie,* an English play about Londoners during the blitz in World War II. At dinner that evening, my dad told us about it, and my mom agreed to take time off from her job at the five-and-ten-cent store to drive me to the theater the next day to find out how to go about trying out for a part.

The next afternoon, Mom got off early and picked me up at school, and off we went. The theater was a nondescript auditorium with folding chairs, much like many of today's Off-Broadway theaters. Lucky for me, they were having an open audition, one to which amateurs, actors who were not yet members of Actors' Equity, were welcomed. The stage manager gave me some pages from different scenes and told me to go study them and come back in an hour. I returned to read for Miss Stewart and the director using a Cockney accent, which had to be awful, because it was something I'd just made up after reading the scenes. I had no frame of reference for the accent other than the few English movies I'd seen. There was a long silence after I finished, and then what sounded like a whispered argument between Miss Stewart and the director. After what seemed like an eternity, Miss Stewart came to the edge of the stage to congratulate me on getting the part. Even though in my naïveté I had felt since childhood that it was my destiny to be an actor one day, I was in a state of shock when it happened.

At our first read-through of *The Wookie,* I met the rest of the cast, including Percival Vivian, our English director, who was also playing the leading man. We all, with the exception of Miss Stewart and Mr. Vivian, had to double and triple parts. Three of the actors were old-timers who had been extras in the movies for years and regulars in Mary Stewart's productions. There was a young boy who was a brand-new member of Actors' Equity. The last two members of the company, a pretty young redhead named Connie Cornwall and I, had never set foot on a real stage before.

Miss Stewart was grand, but she could not have been nicer to everyone. Percy, the director, often seemed as if he had it in for me. I had no idea why. Since he said he had been in London during the blitz, I hung on his every word as if they were graven in stone.

After three weeks of rehearsing scenes, it was time to add the costumes, lighting, and sound effects. Technical rehearsals were very exciting, with the sounds of bombs going off and sirens and shouting all over the place. I had to run on and off, change coats, and return to the stage as someone else. It was exhilarating. After the final tech rehearsal, Percy called me over and said, "Good show, young man. Be at the dress rehearsal tomorrow a wee bit early, would you?" Before I could reply, he turned and walked off. I was so pleased by his compliment that I didn't ask why. I couldn't wait to comply.

At the call for the dress rehearsal, I was in my costume, waiting outside his dressing room, when he arrived. He said he wanted to show me how to make up. I was very excited to get this chance to learn something professional. He did a full character makeup with heavy lines for age and big dark circles under my eyes. I thought I looked just terrific. He had turned me into a character man! My favorite actors were always people like Frank Morgan and Bert Lahr in *The Wizard of Oz,* never the young leading men. After thanking him profusely, I ran back to my dressing room so that everyone could admire the new me. No one even looked up.

The dress rehearsal went reasonably well except for a number of explosions in the wrong place, lots of collisions in the wings and backstage as we all tore on and off, and people forgetting their lines and or entrances. I, with my greasepaint, was letter- and traffic-pattern perfect. After we staged the curtain calls, Miss Stuart grabbed me by the hand and marched me back to her dressing room. She closed the door, turned to me, and, with a surprising lack of grandness, said, "Who put all that crap on your face!?" I told her that Percy had taught me how to do my makeup. She shook her head for a minute and started to laugh, "You tell that son of a bitch that if he ever lays another one of his dainty fingers on your face again, I'll cut them all off at the wrist! He just doesn't want anyone to be prettier than he is onstage. Now, go and scrub it all off. Do not wear *any* makeup tomorrow night. The last thing I want you to do is hide that face."

Backstage the following evening, I thought I saw Percy scowling at me. When I went over to apologize to him for not wearing makeup, he gave me a pat on the back and a tight little smile as he said, "Break a leg, laddie." The house was filled with friends and admirers of Miss Stewart, and of all of us in the cast. What nobody knew was that an up-and-coming young talent agent named Phil Gersh was there with Bob McIntyre, the casting director for Samuel Goldwyn.

Meeting Mr. Goldwyn

My father had already left for work when our phone rang the next morning. It was Phil Gersh. After explaining who he was, he asked me if I could come in and see him as soon as possible about a movie. I thanked him and said of course I could. I was fairly calm about it, because I knew (same old naïveté) that it was fate in action, but my mother was hysterical. She called my father, who had just arrived at work, and insisted that he come home immediately. Somehow he managed to get away from work. After I finished cleaning up and dressed in my best blazer, shirt, and good-luck tie, we headed for Mr. Gersh's office at the Goldstone Agency in Hollywood. My father told me to just keep quiet and listen. He would do all the talking.

Mr. Gersh's secretary buzzed us into his office. He made us comfortable and got right to the point. He told us that he and the casting director for Sam Goldwyn had seen me in *The Wookie,* and thought I might be right for a part in a new movie that Mr. Goldwyn was producing. Would I be interested in trying out for it? "I sure would!" popped out of my mouth before my father could speak.

Mr. Gersh laughed, and my father said, "We would certainly be interested in talking about it, Mr Gersh." They excused my mother and me, and a short time later came out beaming.

Mr. Gersh said; "Welcome to the fold, Farley. I'm sure we'll be doing great things together." He then apologized for having another appointment and not being able to come with us. He promised that Mr. McIntyre would take good care of us at the studio, and that he would see us again soon.

When we were out of earshot, I turned to my father. "What was he talking about? What studio? Where are we going? What did you talk about in there?"

"I think he's a good man, Sonny, so I signed with him to be our agent." I resented the "our" and not having been a part of the conversation even more than I resented that nickname, something he had known for years, but I was too excited to spoil the event with an argument.

We arrived at the Goldwyn Studio, and my name was at the gate. The guard directed us to the casting office. The studios were disappointingly drab and industrial-looking, mostly two-story gray stucco buildings with signs indicating what was inside. We found the casting office with no problem. There the secretary had me take a seat and politely told my eager stage parents that they would have to wait outside, which secretly delighted me. Bob McIntyre came out and took me into his office. He was a nice-looking older man, dressed like Robert Donat in *Goodbye, Mr. Chips.*

After we sat down, he talked about seeing me in *The Wookie* the night before and how good he thought I was. When he asked me if I would like to act in a movie, I said, "You bet!"

He smiled and asked me how old I was. When I told him seventeen, he said that the movie was about the life of a boy my age during the last forty-eight hours of peace and the first forty-eight hours of World War II in a Russian village called North Star. He gave me a couple of pages of a script and told me to go into the outer office and read it over. The part I was reading for was Damian. The scene was a very emotional one in which Damian was saying goodbye to the girl he loved because he was going off to fight with the resistance. She understood his decision, but was afraid he would be killed. After about ten minutes, Mr. McIntyre came out and asked if I was ready. I took a breath and nodded. He said we were going to a conference room to meet the three people I was going to read for: Mr. Goldwyn; Lillian Hellman, the writer of the movie; and Lewis Milestone, the director. By the time we got there, I was no longer calm.

We entered a big room with nothing in it other than a long table with a lot of chairs around it. Three people were seated at the far end of the long table.

Mr. McIntyre introduced me and quietly left. Mr. Goldwyn was tall, ramrod-straight, and healthy-looking, impeccably dressed in a steel-gray suit. He was bald with black eyebrows and ball-bearing eyes. He stood, nodded, and, in an incongruously thin, high-pitched voice said, "Mr. Granger." Miss Hellman, an ugly little lady wreathed in clouds of cigarette smoke, said nothing. Mr. Milestone, a friendly-looking, stocky middle-aged man, smiled at me and winked. He asked if I had any questions about the scene. I was afraid to ask anything, so I said, "No."

As if on cue, a pretty young girl around my age appeared to read with me. Mr. Milestone introduced us and asked us to begin. We finished and no one said a word except Mr. Milestone, who came over, shook my hand, and thanked me for a job well done.

I went back to Mr. McIntyre's office to find out what to do next, but he was in a meeting. His secretary told me, "Don't call us, we'll call you," and showed me the door. I was thrilled. They said they would call me, which echoed over and over in my head as I ran down the hall and out the door to inform my waiting parents, "They're going to call me!"

More than a month, and a mild case of scarlatina, went by as my discouraged parents began to give up hope. I never doubted that the call would come, and thought the fact that it was taking so long was fate providing me with time to get over my rash. How was I to know that Lillian Hellman had spent that entire month trying to talk Montgomery Clift into leaving a Broadway play for the part of Damian in *The North Star*? Luckily for me, Monty was very happy on Broadway, and now the movie was ready to go into production. They had to have someone for the part. My call did come.

I was back in the same conference room. The same three people were there along with another man introduced to me as Benno Schneider, an acting teacher from New York. He was the dialogue director for the film. He asked me to sit down with him to read the scene. I pulled out my tattered pages and we began.

Something was wrong—our lines didn't fit together. Miss Hellman jumped up waving her cigarette and yelled, "Stop, stop! That's not the new script, goddammit! Get him the right script and let him go look at it." They did, and told me to come back to Mr. Schneider's office in an hour.

I took it to a nearby drugstore, ordered an ice cream soda, and studied the new script. It was confusing because I had worked so hard on the other lines, and although some lines were the same, many of the others were a little bit different. When I returned, the guard directed me to Mr. Schneider's office. He was waiting for me. Mr. Schneider was a small middle-aged man with a slight European accent. He was courteous and very soft-spoken. He was also patient and kind.

He asked me if I knew anything about the story of *The North Star* or the character of Damian. I said, "No, nobody told me anything." He filled me in on all of it and asked me just to sit and read the scene with him. The scene was a rewritten version of the one from my first audition, in which I explained to my girl why I had to go and fight with the partisans. After we finished, he said, "Come with me."

We went to Bob McIntyre's office and Mr. Schneider said to him, "This is the boy." Mr. McIntyre replied, "Don't tell me, I'm the one who saw him in that play."

We went back to the conference room and I read the scene again with Mr. Schneider for Mr. Goldwyn, Mr. Milestone, and Miss Hellman. When we finished, Mr. Goldwyn said, "Do a screen test on this boy as soon as possible."

The next day I was walking into a soundstage on the Goldwyn lot when a voice from somewhere yelled out, "Hey, Farley, what the hell are you doing here?" I looked around and spotted Glen Lambert's father up on the seat of a boom microphone. Glen was my best friend and a member of The Daredevils, an adventure club that Glen and I and four of our friends had founded. His father was a sound man in movies. I yelled back, "I'm here to test for a part in the *The North Star* movie, Mr. Lambert." Just as he burst out with "No shit!," Mr. Milestone walked over to me with a glamorous young woman who was going to do the test with me. Her name was Constance Dowling. She was a contract player at the Goldwyn Studio whose career never took off.

The girl I had read with the first time was sweet and pretty, but she didn't look at me much during the scene, which made it hard for me to feel anything about her. When Connie looked at me and spoke, I felt as if I had known her all my life, and what a difference that made. To read the scene with someone who could act and was able to feel it emotionally helped me to feel it, too. We ended up crying in each other's arms.

This was the first time I was aware of what actors need to do for one another when working together. That, combined with what Mr. Schneider had told me about the story and the boy's life, made it possible for me to imagine that I really was Damian.

Phil Gersh called that same evening. Mr. Goldwyn wanted me for the part in *The North Star*. Mr. Gersh explained how happy he was to be representing me. Since I would be eighteen before too long, he wondered if I would mind signing the agreement, too. I was giddy with excitement, but managed to sound calm, because I didn't want to say anything stupid. I knew that my destiny had finally arrived and that Mr. Gersh was a part of it. I said I was very happy he would be representing me, and I would be glad to sign the agreement for myself. At this point my father demanded that I hand him the phone while my mother smothered me with a huge hug.

Indentured

The next morning, dressed once again in my Sunday best, we drove first to Mr. Gersh's office, where my father and I both signed an agreement. From there, we all drove to the Goldwyn Studio to sign a seven-year contract for $100 a week. The seven years did not include any time I spent in the armed forces. That would automatically be added on to my contract. It never occurred to my parents or me to have a lawyer look at anything we eagerly signed that day.

Mr. Goldwyn's office was much fancier than anything else I had seen at the studio. It was wood-paneled with windows and big bookcases. His desk seemed almost as big as the conference table in the room where I had read for him. He was warm and courteous to my father and me, calling me "my boy," and he was absolutely courtly with my mother. We learned that my mother had to be with me on the set every day because I was still only seventeen. They asked me to wait in the outer office for a few minutes.

I was sitting there thinking about my mother accompanying me to the set every day. This development had taken the edge off my excitement. I wasn't a child anymore, damnit! A chirpy voice penetrated my thoughts and wiped the frown off my face. "I said, aren't you excited, Farley?" It was Mr. Goldwyn's secretary. "Yes, I'm very happy," I said quickly and then added, with little false bravado, "but I always knew it was going to happen." And I did, ever since I was five.

Childhood Memories

One of my happiest childhood memories was of a Christmas play at the Mariposa School, a progressive private school that I attended as a child in my hometown, San Jose, California. In the first and third acts, I played an elf in Santa's workshop at the North Pole. The second act was set in an imaginary classroom. On the night of our performance, I was drafted to go on as a pupil in the second act, a last-minute replacement for a mumps victim. Not only was I letter-perfect in my own lines, but I also remembered all of my stricken classmate's lines. Truth be told, I think I knew every line in the play. My proud parents stood and led the bravos. I was so happy that I refused to remove my costume after the show. I lived in it for two days until my patient mother finally coaxed me out of it for a well-needed bath. From that moment on, I knew as a certainty that it was my destiny to be an actor.

The other memories of my early childhood were also happy ones. My father was well off, and he and my mother were social leaders in San Jose, California. We had a lovely new house on the edge of town as well as a beach house in the nearby seaside town, Capitola. I was an only child, born after thirteen difficult years of miscarriages. My parents lived for my every whim.

My father's beloved world-traveling sister, Edith Pomtag, lived with her husband, their only son, Jack, and her three daughters from an earlier marriage in a beautifully restored farmhouse on hundreds of acres in the countryside near San Jose. Jackie, who was a year younger than I to the day, was my closest friend and companion. They had a beach house next to ours in Capitola where Jackie and I and our dogs Mick and Beau spent magical, sun-drenched, waterlogged summers.

In 1929 my father lost everything in the crash. He had to sell the beach house and the house in town. He turned the second floor of his Willys-Overland regional automobile dealership in downtown San Jose into a large apartment where we lived for the next two years as he struggled to stay afloat. My parents' busy social life was replaced by their increasingly heavy drinking at home.

Unhappy cooped up in our new apartment, I would sneak down to the showroom, where I had a grand time meeting people. My dad didn't seem to mind. In fact, I think he enjoyed showing me off. When my mother realized what was going on, she raised the roof. She had always been very protective, but now that we lived in town, she was becoming obsessive about not letting me out of her sight.

My first really frightening memory is of the night when, locked in my bedroom, I heard everything that we owned being auctioned off in the main part of our apartment. I didn't understand what was going on, but I knew it wasn't good.

I now realize what shame and humiliation my parents must have felt when they bundled me into the back seat of the last car my father salvaged from his dealership in order to sneak off in the middle of the night. I felt that I must have done something very bad. I drifted in and out of sleep as we drove all night to Los Angeles. Neither of them ever explained why we left San Jose. It was never mentioned again.

Hello, Hollywood

We lived in a small courtyard apartment in a run-down area of Hollywood. I attended the closest public school, and my folks took various temporary jobs to keep food on the table and booze in the cupboard. Their drinking, which inevitably led to fighting, had become a part of our lives. Now I am able to appreciate how difficult this time must have been for them. As a child, after the freedom of my young life in San Jose and Capitola, I just felt isolated, frightened, and trapped.

When she had time between temporary jobs, my mother got busy chasing our dream. She had never forgotten how carried away I had been by my childhood stage triumph as Santa's elf, which explains her well-intentioned effort (along with untold thousands of other mothers in the heyday of Shirley Temple) to turn me into a tap dancer. She enrolled me as a member of the Meglin Kiddies, a popular performing group of the moment. After school, she would drive me to tap class two afternoons a week. I hated it! But she loved sitting around and talking with all the other would-be stage mothers and hearing all the latest show business gossip. Our reward for completing the course was a public performance at the Shrine Auditorium in downtown Los Angeles. The dream was that "people in the business" would be there to discover a new star. The Shrine was a mammoth theater, and the audience barely filled the front and center part of the orchestra. I felt like an ant with two left feet on that huge stage, but we all got through the program without anyone being knocked down. Considering the bumpy rehearsal, that was a triumph. My mother called the school for weeks to see if any scouts or agents had called to ask about me. Much to her chagrin, no one ever did. The dream was dropped for a while.

Adolescence

After several years, good luck arrived on our doorstep in the form of a long-overdue government bonus check for veterans of "The War to End All Wars." My father, who had enlisted and had risen through the ranks to become a captain in World War I, had been injured in the trenches in France and discharged.

At almost the same time as the veterans' bonus arrived, Dad got a permanent job as a clerk in the North Hollywood branch of the California Department of Unemployment.

This unexpected windfall enabled him to put a down payment on a small house in Studio City, an outpost of the urban sprawl that was creeping into the orange groves of the San Fernando Valley. The house was simple but nice, and the area was beautiful, with big old pepper trees, and an open-air vegetable stand at the nearby intersection of Laurel Canyon and Ventura Boulevard. As we made a real home, my parent's drinking and fighting tapered off a bit. My folks enrolled me in nearby North Hollywood Junior High and gave me a bicycle. That was the happiest moment of my life. In California, with its wide-open spaces, a bike meant I finally had some freedom. Things were looking up.

Our next-door neighbors were a big raucous Irish family of circus performers turned vaudevillians, the O'Connors. One of their sons was my age and already a movie star. Donald and I became friends, but I didn't see a lot of him because he was always working and went to the school at whatever studio he was working for at the time. He was an incredibly talented young man who had appeared in a string of low-budget musical films for Universal Studios in the early 1940s. Donald went on to star for MGM in what many, including me, consider to be one of the best films made during Hollywood's Golden Age of Musicals, *Singin' in the Rain.*

Once we had settled into our new life, my parents and I found something we could enjoy doing together as a family—going to the movies. There was a big movie theater in nearby Sherman Oaks. Best of all, we were close enough to Hollywood to go to the grandest movie palaces of them all—Grauman's Chinese, the Egyptian, and the Pantages. The Chinese was a real treat, not only because it was the most colorful, with a starry sky as the ceiling, but also because it had the handprints and footprints of all the big movie stars in cement out front and I could put my hands and feet in the impressions made by my favorite stars.

Sometimes I would get on my bike and head for Sherman Oaks to see a double feature in the afternoon. After an early supper, at which I would act out all the best parts for my parents, we would all get in the car and drive to Hollywood to see another movie in the evening. The parts I loved acting out were never the hero or the leading man; I much preferred the villains and the character men like Peter Lorre, Eric Blore, and Sydney Greenstreet, to name just a few of my favorites.

A Player

As soon as my seven-year contract with Mr. Goldwyn was signed, I was taken out of school and handed over to the studio machine—wardrobe, makeup, and publicity. My contract was for seven years, at one hundred dollars a week, exclusive of any years spent in military service. The studio provided a private tutor who was in touch with my teachers at North Hollywood High. Since I was in the last quarter of my senior year, my studies were not at all demanding. It was easy to schedule sessions with the tutor around preproduction for *The North Star*.

The publicity department wanted me to change my name. They were afraid people might mix me up with the British actor Stewart Granger, whose real name was Jimmy Stewart. They gave me a list from which to choose. The names were all interchangeable, like Gordon Gregory and Gregory Gordon. I didn't want to change my name. I liked Farley Granger. It was my father's name, and his grandfather's name. They kept bringing me new combinations, and finally I offered to change it to Kent Clark. I was the only one who thought that was funny. They just increased the pressure. I went to tell Mr. McIntyre about my dilemma and to seek his advice. He asked if Mr. Goldwyn had said anything about my name. I told him, "Not that I know of, just the people in the publicity department." He suggested that I lay off the jokes and quietly keep promising to make up my mind by tomorrow. Publicity had to go out very soon, and suddenly it would be too late for any name change. He liked my real name, too.

He was right. Three days later, the studio put out a story that Sam Goldwyn had placed an ad in the paper looking for a young man for his next production, *The North Star*. Farley Granger, a senior at North Hollywood High School, had answered the ad and been discovered. Even though I was delighted about my name, I thought that was a really dumb story. The truth was much more interesting.

The Gorgons

The studio publicity department called to tell me that I had been summoned to audiences with the two reigning Queens of Hollywood, Louella Parsons and Hedda Hopper, bitter rivals on rival newspapers. Their patronage in their daily columns could make or break careers. They were in league with the heads of the studios, who did not hesitate to use them to keep their actors in line, a tactic used on me in the early 1950s when my fights with Mr. Goldwyn increased in intensity.

My first appointment was with the thrice-married Miss Parsons, whose column was syndicated in Hearst newspapers, with which she had an unprecedented, unexplained lifetime contract. The rumor was that as a guest aboard Hearst's yacht in 1924, she had witnessed the shooting of Thomas Ince, a pioneering mogul of silent films. When Hearst caught his mistress, Marion Davies, kissing Charlie Chaplin, he had tried to shoot Chaplin, but missed and instead killed Ince . . . hence, Louella's lifetime contract.

She was known to be a tippler, along with her current husband, "Docky," a urologist and studio physician for MGM. Tippler may be too mild a word to describe this man's use or misuse of booze. Infamous as "clap (STD) doctor to the stars," Docky could be trusted by the studio heads to keep their stars' afflictions a dark secret.

They lived in a big Spanish house in Beverly Hills. When I rang the bell, a nondescript young man, her assistant, answered the door. He showed me into the living room. It was crammed with silver picture frames, cigarette boxes and lighters, porcelain figurines, crystal vases, radios, designer handbags, and cases of wine and Jack Daniel's, said to be her favorite. I learned later that this was all swag given to her at Christmastime by actors, producers, agents, and studio executives, anyone who had benefited or hoped to benefit from a positive mention in her column. After a few minutes she swayed into the room, a pudgy, middle-aged woman.

She plopped down on the sofa next to me, enveloping me in an overpowering cloud of perfume and alcohol, and spoke in a slow sighing manner, smiling vaguely all the while. "Young man, you must tell me all about yourself. Now, who are you?" Her assistant whispered in her ear and she sighed, "Oh yes. You're Sam's new boy. Now tell me everything. There wasn't any want ad, was there?"

I told her everything about my life, which was a very short story, but still long enough for her eyes to glaze over. She hauled herself up from the sofa, still smiling, and moved off, saying to no one in particular, "Oh dear . . . the Niven party tonight, or is it the Rathbones'?"

"The Colmans'," her assistant sang out. She was almost out of the room when she turned to give me a final hazy smile. "Nappy time," she sighed and was gone.

My boss, Mr. Goldwyn, supposedly said of her: "Louella Parsons is stronger than Samson. He needed two columns to bring the house down. She can do it with one."

Hedda Hopper called her home in Beverly Hills "The House That Fear Built." She was very different from her rival; younger, and completely focused, she had a reputation for being sadistic. Married only once, to the actor DeWolf Hopper, she had started as an actress and still played small parts in films on occasion. She was tall, and imposingly attractive. Her penchant for wearing wild hats made her seem even taller and more formidable. The one she was wearing the day of my interview looked like a chef's toque with feathers. "So, you're Sam's new boy," she said from behind the desk of her small Hollywood office. "Take off your jacket and sit down. I want to hear all about *The North Star*. Christ, it's hot in here!" she exclaimed.

Before I could say anything, she whipped off her blouse, revealing her naked shoulders and a white bra. I had never heard a woman, except my mother, swear before, especially one in her bra, with a hat like that, sitting behind a desk. "What the hell is Sam doing making a damn Commie movie?!!" she suddenly shouted at me.

I glued my eyes on the ceiling while trying to get out something about the Russians being our allies, but she would have none of it. I sat silently, sweating, looking out the window, while she went on at length about the evils of sex, drink, smoking, "going Hollywood," and, of course, communism. Then I was dismissed. I stood, eyes on the floor, turned, and headed for the door. She stopped me by shouting, "Tell Sam that want-ad story was the goddamned dumbest thing I ever read!" I looked back at her and laughed as I scooted out the door.

When their columns came out, they were both very flattering, but reading them was like reading about someone I didn't know. Louella Parsons was sugary sweet about the wonderful Sam Goldwyn's latest discovery. Hedda Hopper's approach was a little less respectful, and she made a crack about the discovery story being both untrue and unimaginative.

Millie

As a youngster with no real acting experience, I had no way of knowing how lucky I was to have the great Lewis Milestone direct me and shape my performance in my first two movies. Milestone had won his first Oscar in 1927 for best comedy direction of *Two Arabian Knights*. In 1930 he scored again, winning the best director Oscar for his film about the futility of war, *All Quiet on the Western Front*. That was immediately followed by another Oscar nomination for directing *The Front Page*. In the thirties his superb work continued with *The General Dies at Dawn* and *Of Mice and Men*.

A director's vision not only can make a good film, it can make the difference between a good performance and a bad one.

The North Star, Goldwyn's first film after Pearl Harbor, was a big movie about the horrors of Hitler's invasion of a small town in Russia. In the winter of 1942, when the news from the Russian front was very bad indeed, Goldwyn received a message from President Roosevelt through Lowell Mellett, the chief of the Bureau of Motion Pictures of the Office of War Information, that America needed a film about our Russian allies. As soon as he was able to assemble the creative team of Lillian Hellman as writer and Lewis Milestone as director, with Aaron Copland composing the score, Goldwyn rushed *The North Star* into production. The ensemble cast was led by Dana Andrews, who may best be remembered as the detective in *Laura;* Teresa Wright, who had just won an Oscar as Greer Garson's daughter in *Mrs. Miniver*; Walter Brennan, a three-time Oscar winner; Walter Huston, a superb actor and father of John Huston; Ann Harding, Ruth Nelson, the great Erich von Stroheim, Jane Withers, and me. Although some of these names may now be forgotten, they were all terrific actors drawn from the pool of regulars developed by each of the major studios in the golden age. These character actors were appreciated by moviegoers with almost as much pleasure as the stars. Some of them, Humphrey Bogart and Jimmy Cagney, for example, went on to become big stars in their own right.

I was starting my film career in the very best company. Each actor had his own beautifully honed technique, and every one offered something from which I could learn. Before each scene, Mr. Milestone, or Millie as everyone called him, would explain to those involved what was happening and how he expected them to react. He would then shoot the scene as many times as he had to in order to get a finished product that satisfied him. For the first few days, I went up to him after every scene to find out how I was doing. After the third time he took me aside and explained that I didn't need to check with him after each scene. He would let me know when he wanted me to do anything different. Up until now he was very happy with my work. I was pleased as could be, but I also got the message not to bother him.

During my first day on the set of *The North Star,* a tall, spectacled gentleman with a raspy voice came up to me and introduced himself. "I'm Aaron Copland, and I just saw your screen test. I think you will be wonderful in the film." I thanked him and asked if he was working on the film. When he said that he was, I asked, "Doing what?" He said, "Oh, Ira Gershwin and I are writing a few songs for it." I recognized Gershwin's name, but, as a not very sophisticated seventeen-year-old, I hadn't a clue who Aaron Copland was. I said, "That's nice," and a call to the set for rehearsal saved me from putting my other foot into my mouth.

A couple of days later I found a record of "El Salon Mexico" in my dressing room with a note from Mr. Copland wishing me luck. I took it home that night, listened to it on the phonograph I had bought with my first paycheck, and was overwhelmed by the vitality and splendor of the music. I did not see Aaron Copland again until right after I finished the film. As I was leaving Bob McIntyre's office, I ran into Mr. Copland in the hall. I told him how much I loved the record he had given me. He asked if I had time to listen to some of the music he had composed for the film. I said, "You bet!" He laughed, and we went down the hall to his studio, where he spent about a half-hour playing music that he had composed and explaining how it worked in the film. I felt privileged to be exposed to that part of the process of putting a film together.

Who needed a dressing room to wait in? I never left the set. I was intrigued by everything: how the cameras worked; how special effects made bomb explosions look real; what fake blood was made of; where and how Milestone put the cameras and what he saw through the lens. I was a kid, and it was my first movie. In truth, everything was an adventure.

I was like a puppy trying to be liked by everyone. Two of the people I tried hardest with were Anne Baxter and Dana Andrews. Anne, who was Frank Lloyd Wright's granddaughter and an up-and-coming young actress at 20th Century-Fox, was a last-minute replacement for Teresa Wright, whose pregnancy got her out of the film. I had been looking forward to working with Teresa, but one look at Anne and I was a goner.

When a picture of the two of us became the cover of *Look* magazine, I was convinced that we were destined to be together. The fact that she was a couple of years older than I and had experience on the New York stage made her even more glamorous in my eyes. She was fun, she was sexy, she was great to work with, and she was very sweet to me, but my crush went nowhere. She treated me like a kid brother—something Dana never did even though I was playing his kid brother.

I tried my best to become friends with Dana, but it was not easy. He was taciturn by nature. Early each morning, when we were all in wardrobe and makeup, he was downright grumpy. On set he was always line-perfect and always there for me, but I never felt a connection to him as I would with a brother who loved me. Of course, I thought that it was my fault.

The great character actor Walter Brennan had been under contract to Goldwyn since 1935. This was his thirty-fifth picture under that contract, but only his sixth for Goldwyn, who rarely made more than one movie a year. The other twenty-nine films had been made on loanout to other studios for large fees. This made a great deal of money for Goldwyn, who only had to pay Walter his contractual wage.

Walter was warm and supportive and had become a sort of mentor to me. When I asked him what I was doing wrong with Dana, he said, "Nothing, kid, and stop worrying about it. You're doing fine. Dana's just hungover and trying to get it together each morning, and it don't help that you're the good-looking new kid on the lot, either." That made me feel a little better, because there was nothing I could do about either of those things.

One memory from *The North Star* that still tickles me is a trick Walter played for my benefit. He got a kick out of making me laugh, and he knew I was a pushover. One afternoon in his dressing room, he picked up his phone and, in a pitch-perfect imitation of Goldwyn, commenced firing people at the studio—the head of accounting, the motor pool chief, and the entire makeup department. Before too much chaos spread, he called back with outrageous explanations and rehired everyone. His practical joke was cruel, but his performance was very funny.

My mother was thrilled with her new role in show business. There were a lot of young children in the film, so there were plenty of stage mothers present. Mom bonded instantly with Jane Withers's mother. Jane, who was about my age, had become a popular child star in the 1930s as the brat everyone loved to hate. Her mother knew all the tricks of the stage mother's trade, which she generously shared with my mother. I liked Jane. I did not like the fact that my mom was embracing stage motherhood so enthusiastically. I intended to exercise my right to be free of parental supervision on my approaching eighteenth birthday, and knew the fight would be epic.

Late in the film, we had gone on location to the Fox ranch in Malibu Canyon to shoot a battle scene with lots of horses and extras that was too big for the soundstage. Milestone had only finished one setup when it clouded over. We stopped. After waiting an hour or so for the sun to return, we broke for lunch. Jane and I got permission to take two of the horses for a ride after lunch. We were instructed not to go far, and to come back immediately if the sun came out. By midafternoon, with still no sign of sun, we returned to find everyone packing up to go. I saw my mother sitting and laughing with some of the grips. When she headed toward me, I knew that my worst fears had come true. She'd been drinking.

We shared a car back to the studio with Dana and Anne. My mother was far too garrulous, going on about her life in San Jose society, her golf trophies, and how smart she had been to enroll me as one of the Meglin Kiddies. No one else could get a word in, not that anyone tried. Teenagers are always easily embarrassed by their parents. I felt like I was trapped in the longest ride of my life.

During the last few days of work on *The North Star,* I began to experience the onset of a chronic malady that is a part of every actor's life: the "will I ever work again syndrome." In my case it was compounded by the fact that in a month I would turn eighteen. My country was at war, and I wanted to do my part. On the last day of shooting, Mr. Milestone pulled me aside to say how proud he was of the work I had done, and then told me something I had to keep secret. His next film was being done at Fox and there was a part in it that he wanted me to do. Dana was going to be in it, because he had a split contract between Goldwyn and Fox, but Milestone needed to convince both studios in order for me to be cast. I was very proud that he wanted to use me again. It meant he liked my work. When I reminded him that I was soon to be eighteen and anxious to enlist, he assured me that the studio could get me a temporary deferment until the film was finished, because the film he wanted me for, *The Purple Heart,* was also important to the war effort.

At first Mr. Goldwyn refused to loan me out to 20th Century-Fox. He had never been happy about Dana's split contract, and since I was an unknown, he could not get a lot of money for me. He would have preferred to be the first to exploit his new discovery, but he had no projects ready for me to work on, and he was aware of my impending military service. Fox was not eager to cast me, either. The studio had its own stable of juveniles under contract and was not keen on paying for and promoting anyone under exclusive contract to the tight-fisted Sam Goldwyn.

Happily, Milestone got his way. As a celebrated director of such war movies as *All Quiet on the Western Front,* still one of the greatest antiwar movies ever made, his special talent was essential to the studio bosses' role in Hollywood's war effort. It was wise to defer to his wishes. Later, in 1945, he directed *A Walk in the Sun,* one of the most honest and penetrating studio films ever made about GIs in combat.

The New York Premiere

Goldwyn had arranged a gala premiere opening in New York for *The North Star.* Never one to leave anything to the whims of fate when he could take charge, he decided to call in a few paybacks in order to stack the critical odds in his new film's favor. This gambit was not entirely successful. As soon as *The North Star* opened, it became the center of a controversy that involved William Randolph Hearst, Henry Luce of Time-Life Inc., Sam Goldwyn, and various other members of the press on both sides of the political spectrum. Hearst was such a rabid anticommunist that the most Goldwyn had gotten from him was an agreement not to prejudge the film. Henry Luce was much more amenable. After its lavish opening, he called the film a "Cinemilestone!" Hearst's major New York paper, the *New York Journal-American,* came out on the morning after the premiere with a very positive and enthusiastic review. Goldwyn and everyone else connected with *The North Star* were thrilled. Hearst was decidedly not. That morning's review had slipped by him. He made sure that the next edition of the *Journal-American* reversed its positive review. It also made the outrageous suggestion that the film was not only Red propaganda but Nazi propaganda. Hearst's evening tabloid headlined its review, "UNADULTERATED SOVIET PROPAGANDA." Other reviews across the country were mixed except in the Hearst papers, where they were unanimously bad.

Despite an extensive advertising campaign, the picture never made its money back. Some years later, after it had been sold to television in the early 1950s, in an effort not to catch the attention of any Red-baiters gearing up for the high times of the McCarthy era, its name was changed to *Armored Attack.* Any indications that the film was about Russia were erased as completely as possible, including most of Aaron Copland's wonderful score, into which he had incorporated some stirring Russian folk songs. The new promotional material said that the whole movie took place in Hungary.

Turning Eighteen

My second film was the first that Darryl F. Zanuck produced for 20th Century-Fox after his discharge from the Army Signal Corps. *The Purple Heart* was a small film about the first American plane shot down over Japan in World War II. The crew was captured, tortured, tried, and executed by the Japanese. Aside from the Asian-American actors playing the Japanese, the cast consisted solely of the seven members of the bomber's crew, featuring Dana Andrews; Richard Conte, a brooding Italian-American leading man of the 1940s and 1950s; Sam Levene, a marvelous Jewish character actor from New York, who was equally at home onstage and before the cameras, and me. I was the kid—a sort of mascot—on the film. I had turned eighteen shortly after the film started shooting, which meant that I would be enlisting in the armed forces as soon as we wrapped. Although no one ever mentioned it, I'm sure everyone was aware of it.

Millie felt that it was important for us to bond as a group. When he arranged for us all to share one large dressing room adjacent to the soundstage, no one complained even though a few wary looks were exchanged. Every actor cherishes his own private bit of space. It was fine with me. I was eager to bond with anyone. Again, I made a concerted effort with Dana. He warmed up a bit more on this, our second film together, particularly as the day wore on. As usual, Millie was right. We quickly became a band of brothers. I was the youngest. Sam Levene became my father and Dana Andrews my big brother.

Halfway into the film, my Japanese captors cut out my tongue—remember, this was a wartime film, with every propaganda stop pulled out. Whenever I started to speak or ask a question after this barbaric incident, I was shushed by both Millie and/or the other actors. Frustrating, yes, but they made sure I got into my character's head and stayed there.

A Real Movie Studio!

Working at 20th Century-Fox was far more exciting than working at my studio, because Goldwyn only did one film at a time, and often no more than one a year. At 20th they turned out pictures like products on an assembly line, so a whole cast of great Hollywood characters paraded before my wide and inexperienced eyes. While we were filming *The Purple Heart* on the Fox lot, Betty Grable, who along with Rita Hayworth was every GI's favorite pinup during World War II, was shooting *Pin Up Girl.* Roddy McDowall (*How Green Was My Valley, Lassie Come Home, The White Cliffs of Dover*) was finishing *My Friend Flicka;* Orson Welles and Joan Fontaine, who was so good in Alfred Hitchcock's *Rebecca,* were working on *Jane Eyre,* which included a young and very beautiful Elizabeth Taylor and a wonderful young actress, Peggy Ann Garner. Dana was getting ready to start *Laura* with Gene Tierney as soon as we finished our film.

It was an adventure just having lunch in a commissary filled with actors and extras decked out in splendid costumes, a bit like eating at a spectacular masquerade ball. Betty Grable, usually in feathers or sequins or both, may have been the studio's biggest star, but she came equipped with the soul of a chorus girl who relished a good dirty joke. She supposedly had it stipulated in her contract that Freddy Ney, an outrageously funny chorus boy from New York, was always directly behind her in big musical numbers. His filthy, stage-whispered running commentary kept a big smile on her face at all times. Elizabeth Taylor looked like a perfect porcelain doll in her mid-nineteenth-century costume from *Jane Eyre,* but even at that early age she was an earthy, no-nonsense young lady. Gene Tierney in modern dress was breathtakingly lovely and equally warm and gracious. The young and then trim Orson Welles was an overpowering presence. With his piercing gaze and a voice that reverberated throughout the dining room, I found him too intimidating to approach.

The first star I met in the commissary was "The Brazilian Bombshell," Carmen Miranda. Even in her ten-inch wedgies, she was tiny, a dynamo with a great big laugh, dressed like an oversized fruit salad. She was constantly in motion. With all her baubles, bangles, and beads, you could hear her coming a block away. It was easy to see how she almost stole every Betty Grable movie in which she appeared doing her "Souse American" song and dance numbers.

I particularly loved the 20th Century-Fox musicals, because their colors seemed brighter than those of the other studios and because nobody aged in them. In *Alexander's Ragtime Band,* Don Ameche, Tyrone Power, and Alice Faye looked just as young at the end of the movie, when they were all supposed to have aged forty years, as they did at the beginning. The same youth and beauty principle held fast for Betty Grable, June Haver, and John Payne in *The Dolly Sisters.* Maybe the women had their hair in pigtails at the beginning of the movie and in a bun at the end, and maybe the men's sideburns got a touch of gray as they aged, but that was about it. Perhaps we should lay the blame for America's obsession with youth and beauty at the feet of Darryl F. Zanuck.

At every major studio there was always a next-in-line being groomed to replace a star who got too big for the ruling mogul's comfort. For example, at MGM, Louis B. Mayer had Deborah Kerr ready to step into Greer Garson's lovely pumps; at Columbia, Harry Cohn began grooming Kim Novak when Rita Hayworth seemed irreplaceable; and at Fox, Betty Grable was brought in to be ready when Alice Faye decided she had had enough. The situation was the same for the men, just not as obvious.

Except for some sporadic dating in high school, I'd never had a real social life. During my first week at 20th, I met June Haver, a very pretty little blonde whom I liked and dated for a while. That word still signified a very chaste encounter in 1943. June, who was being groomed by the studio to replace Betty Grable if or when that became necessary, although lovely and talented, did not possess the wattage of Betty's star power. She later quit movies and became a nun. Later still, she left the convent, married an older actor, Fred MacMurray, and never returned to films.

I liked June, but dating her exposed me to the hyped-up world of the studio publicity machine that manufactured fake love lives of their young hopefuls for the fan magazines. They went into overdrive for us. Everywhere we went we were met by and pursued by photographers. We were featured in every fan magazine and every gossip column in Hollywood. YOUNG LOVE BLOSSOMS AT 20TH!, or FARLEY & JUNE MEANT FOR EACH OTHER!, or HOLLYWOOD'S NEWEST YOUNG LOVERS! the gossip columns and fan magazines shouted on a very false note. It didn't matter that we didn't even know each other that well. June had already done several movies and was not surprised by the commotion, but I was in shock. I don't think she liked it any more than I did, but she was not caught off guard the way I was. I hated it and never learned how to be comfortable with it.

There was a schoolhouse on the lot and any actors under eighteen were required to attend classes whenever we were not being used on set. The actors in our group included Elizabeth, Roddy, Peggy Ann, and several other young girls and guys whose names I don't remember. One name that none of the boys could ever forget was Linda Darnell. She was making a movie called *Summer Storm.* Whenever she appeared in class in her costumes, which emphasized every traffic-stopping curve, lessons went right out the window for the guys. I don't think Linda realized the effect she had. She was as shy and sweet as she was voluptuous. School on the lot was so much fun that I continued there even after I turned eighteen.

Before starting work at 20th, I had informed my mother that she would no longer be driving me to the studio and staying on set with me as my chaperone. Since I was about to be eighteen, I no longer needed to be accompanied at work by a parent. That was an unexpected blow for her and a furious fight ensued, but I refused to back down.

Neither she nor my father was happy with what they considered my premature declaration of independence, but my salary was easing our financial worries, and that helped me get my way. The only negative was that I would have to drive the funny family car. The beige Willys Overland with aquamarine fenders was all that remained of a more prosperous time in San Jose. I never saw another car like it. Early in the war, Willys had stopped making cars and started making Jeeps. Our car looked so odd that people pointed and cracked jokes. I was mortified. Looking back, I can see what an ungrateful, insecure, self-absorbed kid I was . . . in other words, a typical teenager.

Aside from a crash landing in a rice field, our scenes in *The Purple Heart* were staged in a studio mockup of a Japanese courtroom. Sam Levene took me under his wing and taught me some tricks of the trade. For example, he explained how not to fall into the inexperienced film actor's trap of listening only when you are also speaking in a scene. Listening intently to everyone at all times put you in the moment in every scene.

When I got home at night, all I talked about was how much fun the studio was, and how funny, kind, patient, and helpful Sam was. I must have carried on about him a bit too much, because one night at dinner, my father suddenly shouted, "At least you could get a white man for a friend!" At first, I didn't know what he meant, and then I got it.

In a flash of anger, I threw my water in his face and stormed out. With the drinking, the fighting, and the neighbors calling the police, things were spinning out of control on Maxwellton Road. The truth was, my parents had never accepted the comedown from their grand life in San Jose, were unable to make any real friends in Los Angeles, and, like so many who are forced to stare failure in the face and are ashamed to do so, turned to mutual recrimination, arguments, and alcohol.

Roddy McDowall and I became friends at the studio. He was a few years younger than I and a smart, decent kid. He invited me to his home for dinner one night, and I accepted gladly.

Roddy's family had moved to Hollywood from England before the war and lived in a big old house near the Fox studio, where Roddy was under contract. His father was off to war in the Royal Navy, his sister in high school in Beverly Hills. His mom, a large, warm, enveloping type, welcomed me as family. At dinner, we all laughed a lot, and when she asked if I would like to spend the night I jumped at the invitation, because the whole experience was so different from the drinking and fighting during meals at my house. I called my parents and asked permission to stay at Roddy's. I told them we both had early calls, and that I was practically next door to the studio, which would save my mother from getting up at 5:00 A.M. to make my breakfast. Roddy's mother got on the phone and confirmed the arrangement. This was the first of many nights of fun and laughter there while I was shooting *The Purple Heart.*

I had turned eighteen before the film finished, and my temporary deferment expired as soon as we wrapped. It was time for me to really say goodbye. I said my farewells to everyone on the set at 20th. Dana could not have been warmer. Hardest of all was saying goodbye to Millie, because I felt he had put himself on the line for me. When I went to talk with Sam, he said, "Forget it, kid. You ain't getting rid of me that easy. You call me and let me know what day you're leaving because Roddy and I are coming to see you off." I gave him a big hug and got out of there before he could see my tears.

The next day I went to tell everyone at my studio that I was going to enlist. I couldn't get in to see Mr. Goldwyn, so I just said goodbye through his secretary. Then I cleared out my dressing room and went to find Mr. McIntyre. He wasn't there. There was nothing filming at the studio, so I was not surprised to find it somewhat deserted. I walked through the soundstage where I had done my first movie. It was empty and dark. I couldn't even conjure any ghosts of the small Russian town of North Star. It was disconcerting to leave the studio to which I was under contract with no real farewell. I felt as if I was just fading away.

Actor Aweigh

I went downtown to the induction center with a couple of my high school buddies. We'd decided to join the Navy because they heard that it was the best branch of the service. We were herded upstairs for physicals, and then I was sent before the chief petty officer in charge. I gave him my papers. He asked, "You want regular Navy?"

Unaware that there was any other kind, I said, "Sure." He stamped my papers, gave me a copy, and sent me downstairs to rejoin my friends. One asked what I'd signed up for. "Regular Navy," I said.

"Are you crazy? Things are finally starting to go our way. The regular Navy is six years. You should have just signed for the duration. With any luck, we will get out a lot sooner than that."

I raced back upstairs, arriving just as the petty officer was covering his typewriter. I grabbed him. "Please, please, I've just made a terrible mistake!" He was understanding, thank goodness, and changed my papers.

I received a call from the studio publicity department at 20th. They had obtained a two-week extension for me to do publicity on *The Purple Heart* before I had to report for duty. This meant that my high school friends shipped out before I did. That made me a little apprehensive. I would be taking this next step in my life all alone.

Two weeks later, when I said goodbye to my parents, my mother, through her tears, promised hand-on-heart that they would stop drinking and fighting and would make a happy home for me when I returned. I knew my dad was angry because I told him Sam Levene and Roddy were driving me to Union Station to see me off. Even in the short time I knew them, I felt closer to them than to my parents. It seemed forever until my train arrived, but Sam managed to keep Roddy and me in stitches while we waited. I finally made them leave, but watching them disappear through the crowd was the loneliest moment of my life.

I don't know how much time passed before the loudspeaker summoned us aboard. I woke up later in a bunk still in my clothes. I had no idea how I got there. Suddenly a voice announced: "Lights out, NOW!" Someone in a nearby bunk began to strum a guitar and sing softly. For the next couple of days, I felt lost in a strange world. I supposed everyone else felt the same way. I made no effort to make any friends. I just stared out the window watching the countryside pass by. I'm not sure how many days it took to reach boot camp in Farragut, Idaho, landlocked in the desolate white-and-gray landscape near the western Canadian border.

When the train finally jerked to a stop, we dry-land sailors were herded into a single line that stretched as far as the eye could see. In an hour or so, I entered a small cafeteria, picked up a metal tray, and went down the line without knowing or caring what was being dumped into its compartments. When I emerged, I just kept going. I must have bumped into somebody or something. When my loaded tray hit the floor, I still just kept going. I followed the flow to a big building that looked like a soundstage. Inside men from the train were setting up cots to sleep on. I set one up, fell on it, and had my own lights out.

I was awakened by all kinds of loud noises—loudspeakers, people yelling, and bright lights. Everyone was running outside even though it was pitch black, like some crazy jailbreak. I followed the others and came to a mess hall. I had no idea what I was served, but it was hot, I ate it, and I felt a little better. An announcement blared over the loudspeakers for all new recruits to assemble on the parade ground "ON THE DOUBLE!!!" It was just getting light as we ran outside, milling around in confusion until several petty officers formed us into some rough sort of order. We were then sent off in alphabetical order to a supply tent where they issued our gear and sent us off to our barracks, where we were then assigned bunks.

I sat on my bunk wondering what was going to happen to me next. Three sailors whose stripes meant they were already more than recruits introduced themselves to me. They were obviously friends and obviously gay. They recognized me from *The North Star* and enthusiastically offered to look after me, show me the ropes. One of them worked in the barbershop, and the others were in the medical department. They said that anytime I needed anything, I should look them up and I would be taken care of. They had connections. Everything they said seemed loaded with innuendo. I didn't know what to say or do. I was a pretty green eighteen-year-old. I stammered my thanks and got very busy stowing my gear. With effusive goodbyes and don't-forget-to-look-us-ups, they disappeared into the crowd. I looked around to see if anyone had taken any notice, but everyone seemed to be too busy trying to figure out what to put where. As it turned out, those guys were always there to help me through the rigors of boot camp and sought no favors in return, sexual or otherwise.

As new recruits, we were a mixed crew, fresh-faced eighteen-year-olds like me and family men of forty. Washington had extended the draft age because of the desperate need for replacements as the war dragged on. Not only were we a strange assortment, so was our equipment. We had no guns. We marched in the snow with brooms. Just beyond the barracks was a large lake where we practiced launching lifeboats. It seemed like an exercise in futility, since the lake was frozen solid, but we slid around launching our boats, trying not to let them collide and to avoid hurting each other. The base was windy and bitterly cold. In some perverse way I enjoyed it. It was so different from everything in my native California. The surrounding snow-covered mountains were beautiful. I kept to myself, and made no real friends. There was even a showing of *Purple Heart,* but most of my dry-land shipmates gave me a wide berth. I think they were too shy, or maybe they just didn't know what to say. The exception of course was my three gay buddies. They thought the movie was fabulous and wanted to know all about Dana Andrews. They thought he was fabulous as well.

Finally it was time for graduation, a sorry affair that had us marching with our broomsticks to strains of "Anchors Aweigh" piped in on loudspeakers in the midst of a blinding snowstorm. We stumbled through it and received orders for our next assignment and a bus ticket for our last leave. I had a ten-day layover in Los Angeles before I was supposed to ship out, so I decided to splurge and bought a first-class air ticket. At the airport a young ensign behind me said, "Aren't you in the wrong line, swabbie?" I looked him straight in the eye, smiled, took a long beat, and replied, "Don't worry about me—SIR. I can afford it—SIR." It was my first trip on an airplane.

Back home my parents were on their best behavior—only one drink before dinner—and the hateful fighting had diminished to minor bickering. My mom thought I was much too skinny and cooked up a storm. I spent some time with Roddy and his family and saw some of my high school pals and of course Sam Levene—this time with no comment from my father.

I went to the studio, but Mr. Goldwyn was again in conference, too busy to be seen. I went to the casting office and found Bob McIntyre, who couldn't get over the fact that I was in uniform and ready to ship out. He made me promise to stay in touch and told me that great things were going to happen when I got back from the war. If I hadn't seen him, it would have been as if my being in the movies had never happened.

At Sea

When my leave was up, I reported to the naval base in Long Beach at the crack of dawn. This time, at my request, no one saw me off. I was put on a bus for San Francisco with a middle-aged father. It seemed strange, only the two of us, but just before we left Long Beach, we stopped at the brig to pick up about twenty prisoners. I guess the Navy was really getting desperate. Instead of being punished for whatever they had done, the detainees were being released back to active duty—and did they ever raise hell on that bus!

The sun was setting when we arrived at Treasure Island, where the cruiser that was to serve as our troopship was docked. We were ordered up the gangway, checked in, and directed down to the cargo deck, a big empty space with no lights containing a freestanding upright piano, a bunch of burlap sacks lashed to the bulkhead, and a lot of unassembled cots piled in the center of the hold. Somehow, with the help of a few flashlights and a lot of cooperation, we managed to assemble our cots in the darkness. I tossed my seabag on mine, and made my way back up topside. The officer on deck said that we could have one last night free before setting sail for Hawaii, but that we had to be back on board no later than 6:00 A.M. I was down the gangway like a shot to grab a cab and head straight for the USO in downtown San Francisco. I found the entertainment desk, asked what was going on in town, and the hostess gave me a ticket to the ballet. I must have looked skeptical, because she smiled sweetly and told me to give it a try, I might like it. In any case, it was the only free ticket she had left. So I found my way to the San Francisco opera house, an impressive place, and saw my first ballet.

The first half of the evening's program was *Rodeo,* with music by Aaron Copland and choreography by Agnes de Mille. Not only did I love it because I knew Copland and thought his music was great, but I had never seen dancing like this. I had expected girls in tutus and men in tights—no way. The cowboys on the stage were masculine and athletic, and their dancing was spectacular. No other world existed for me at that moment. I didn't want it to end. When it did, I found myself cheering and whistling as if the home team had just won the football championship. It seemed impossible to top that—until the second half. *Fancy Free* is a tale of three sailors on their last night's leave in New York before shipping out. Their adventures on this final night, their mishaps and mixups, their search for love and their heartaches, were set in dance by Jerome Robbins to a wonderfully jazzy score by Leonard Bernstein. It was as if they were doing my story. This was also *my* last night before shipping out. I was so involved with what was going on onstage that I didn't even let it get me down that, unlike the sailors in the ballet, I had no buddies with me on the town, and no beautiful girl to kiss goodbye. I practically danced all the way back to the USO. At 5:00 A.M. everyone who had slept there was awakened and herded onto a bus to the Navy Yard and our ship . . . dreams over, back to reality.

I went below to find my bunk and some shuteye, but I couldn't sleep and I felt starved of air. Somehow I made it topside and gulped in some cool air. As I looked around, I realized quite a number of sailors from our bus seemed to be missing. Half the men from brig seemed to have jumped ship. I did find the middle-aged father, and we talked. He had five kids and not a lot of money. The call-up was hard on him and his family, but it was 1943 and we were fighting on two fronts. Everybody was being called up.

With a shudder, the ship began to move. It wasn't long before we passed under the Golden Gate Bridge. I walked forward. My mind was a jumble: Where was I going? Would I come back? Would my parents continue their good behavior, or would they eventually destroy each other? Would anyone ever want me to make another movie? Would I ever get laid?

I felt lightheaded and threw up all over the deck. I just walked away from it. I had no idea how to get back to my bunk and was too dizzy to search around, so I just lay down on the deck and curled up. I don't know how much time passed before I felt a gentle kick. A chief petty officer told me I couldn't sleep there but had to go below to my assigned quarters with the others. I explained my predicament, and he guided me to the right hatch with instructions to proceed to sick bay if I didn't feel better in a few hours. I thanked him and went below, where I stumbled around in the dark until I found the cot with my seabag on it.

I was out again until I heard the call for chow; even the thought of food made me queasy. I returned to the deck for fresh air, and after my stomach calmed a bit, I tried to find the doctor. As soon as I went below I was sick again. Throwing up combined with the dry heaves continued sporadically for the rest of the voyage, which took seventeen days because of the ship's evasive antisubmarine maneuvers. I never found the sick bay, and I was never able to keep down more than a little clear broth and that only on calm days.

In heavy seas one night, the burlap sacks broke loose from the bulkheads, spilling clouds of white flour that dusted us all. The piano broke loose, sailors were run over, and half a dozen had bones broken. Somehow I stayed in one piece during that hellish night, but when we finally docked at Honolulu, I had to be carried off the ship. I had lost twenty-three pounds during our seventeen days at sea. The receiving officer took one look and sent me straight to the hospital. After several days of rehydration, the Navy decided that my war would best be spent on shore duty in Hawaii.

Hawaii

I was assigned to the cleanup crew at an enlisted men's club, a Quonset hut with an open-air bar at the end of Waikiki Beach. About eight men served there, plus a small band. We also doubled as the short-order cooks. We served soft drinks, 3.2 beer—the infamous low-alcohol beverage served by the military at enlisted men's clubs—hamburgers, and hot dogs. The band played evenings to entertain the troops. There was a dance floor but no girls. After enough 3.2 beer, some of the sailors would clown around and jitterbug with each other. Every now and then a couple of WAVES, the Navy's name for female sailors, would show up, and we all would trip over each other trying to dance with them, but that was it. The beer ended up being the only boost to troop morale, and some of the drunken brawls were terrific.

One part of my job was magical. It was being in charge of the garbage detail. Every day or two, we would load up the garbage truck, and I would drive it through pineapple fields to the dump. It was my quiet time, the only time I was totally on my own, and it was when I fell completely in love with the beauty of Hawaii. It rained every afternoon. If I was able to time it correctly, I would see two beautiful rainbows sparkle to life over Diamond Head just as the sun reappeared. My buddies at the club called me a nutcase for being so enthusiastic about the garbage run, but I preferred to take the heat rather than risk competition for my own private rainbow detail.

After about six months, I was reassigned to a unit in Honolulu that worked with Army Special Services. Almost immediately, I managed to get myself out of the Navy barracks I had been assigned to and into one assigned to the musicians. They were the most fun, in part because they paid the least attention to the rules and regulations—what the enlisted men call "chickenshit." I'd gotten to know some of them at the enlisted men's club in Waikiki, so I had a couple of friends. Those guys knew every out-of-the-way bar and club in Honolulu. If you felt like a good steak or a pair of silk stockings for a special date, they knew where to go, and they were also experts on where the prettiest girls hung out. Even better, their barracks was filled with music all the time. They had records of all the latest Broadway shows as well as classics and the best jazz and popular music. It was there that I heard Mozart for first time, and Dinah Shore singing with the Lower Basin Street Society, and Benny Goodman recorded live at Carnegie Hall. It was also the first time I ever heard a recording of a Broadway show, Rodgers and Hammerstein's *Carousel.* I was so caught up by its lyrical beauty and emotional power that I didn't know whether to laugh or cry. I think I did a little of both. The nice thing was that I didn't have to hide my reactions from the musicians. Even the most hard-boiled of them understood that kind of reaction to a terrific piece of music.

The Army Special Services Unit was under the command of the great classical actor Maurice Evans, who put together and arranged entertainment for all the troops in the Pacific. These entertainments varied from comedians like Bob Hope, who toured with a band, a girl singer, and sometimes Bing Crosby, to pinup girls like Rita Hayworth and Betty Grable or glamour queens like Marlene Dietrich and Hedy Lamarr. They, like other great patriotic stars, some of whom came from Broadway with a complete cast, would tour just behind the battlefronts.

The Navy had no Special Services unit of its own, so were completely dependent upon the Army. On the other hand, the Army had to depend on us to help coordinate the movement and scheduling of these entertainments. That was where my superior and I came in.

Our unit consisted of a resentful Navy lieutenant, Chuck Garvin, and me. We shared an office that had been set up in a small Quonset hut down the hill from the much larger Army Special Services Unit. Scheduling these shows wasn't made any easier by my mucho macho boss. He thought what we were doing was a big waste of his and the Navy's time and energy. He didn't believe that "a bunch of fags prancing around on a stage" had anything to do with morale-building, and he especially hated taking orders from Maurice Evans, "a fucking Army actor, no less!" Garvin told me, "When you have to go up there to the fucking Army, just do what you have to and get out of there like your ass is on fire! They are all fucking pansies up there, and I don't want any of that rubbing off on you." In all my work with Evans's unit—and I was up there several times a day—no one ever said or did anything remotely suggestive, although I have to admit that the sergeant serving as Major Evans's private secretary did wear a lot of makeup.

Maurice Evans—Major Evans, as he then was—had some great talent working for him. One with whom I became friendly was Carl Reiner. Carl was only a couple of years older than I. He was then still just a performer, but his wonderfully skewed take on life indicated a talent that would go far. He did not disappoint. From the mid-1950s to the mid-1960s he won eight Emmy Awards as writer, performer, and producer. One of his best productions is his gifted son, Rob.

I recently saw Carl for the first time since those days in Hawaii, and he was still as warm and funny as I remembered. It was at the opening of *Mr. Goldwyn,* a one-man show in New York featuring the comic legend Alan King playing my old boss. It had a running bit with Goldwyn's secretary buzzing him repeatedly in the course of the evening to say: "Mr. Goldwyn, Farley Granger is on the phone again. He says he wants out of his contract." Alan, with perfect comic timing, built Goldwyn's reactions from annoyance to exasperation to an explosion that brought the house down. I was there on opening night and somehow he got word that I was in the audience. During his curtain calls he called for the spotlight to find me and introduced me to the audience as "my co-star—who has finally gotten out of his contract!" Later, at a cast party at the Lambs' Club that was attended by everyone from Billy Crystal to Walter Cronkite, I saw Carl again and we were able to reminisce a bit more about Hawaii.

I kept busy in my little hut working, scheduling, and watching the scorpions skitter by. After an endless nine months, Lieutenant Garvin was transferred and replaced by Lieutenant Bill Militich. He was a good man who thought we were doing important work, but his real passion was golf. He left all of the scheduling details up to me, which I didn't mind, but paperwork and details were not my strong points, resulting in several near-disasters. I once put an extra day on the calendar in November ("Thirty days hath September, April, June, and . . . ???"). I booked three shows in different areas of the Pacific on November 31st. I caught my mistake just in time. Militich even left the golf course and jumped in to help. Aside from a few other similar last-minute near-misses, it was mostly tedious and lonely in my little hut with just me and the scorpions.

My dream of getting away from my desk job by somehow getting myself officially involved as an actor with any of the performers or troupes passing through didn't look like it was going to happen.

Gertrude Lawrence had toured the South Pacific in her one-woman show singing Nöel Coward songs. She was a unique performer best known in her native England as a farceur and light comedienne, but she was not that well known in the United States. Her strong point was a brittle sophistication, which had lot to do with British class distinction and nothing to do with sex appeal—all in all, not the best choice for the troops. Coward's songs are charming, but I don't think there was a soldier, sailor, or marine in the entire Pacific who gave a rat's ass whether or not "Mad Dogs and Englishmen Go Out in the Noonday Sun." Gertie bombed, but Miss Lawrence was not stupid. She quickly realized her mistake and regrouped. She came back to Hawaii and decided to put on Noël Coward's brilliant comedy *Blithe Spirit* for a short run in Honolulu. Major Evans brought in most of the cast who had performed it on Broadway to support her, and gave it a smashing production. The troops loved it, and she was redeemed. Evans's crew, against all advice, then put on a modern version of *The Mikado*. Much to everyone's surprise, it was a huge success. Seeing the troops forget the miseries of their wartime existence for a few hours, hearing them laugh and cheer, confirmed my feelings about what a wrongheaded jerk Lieutenant Garvin had been.

Sex, Sex, Sex, Sex . . .

I was thinking about sex all the time. I was twenty and still a virgin. My hormones had long ago gone ballistic, and I was ready to join them. Something had to be done soon! One of the musicians, Ray, the horn player, seemed to know everyone in Honolulu. A young, single man, he was sympathetic to my situation and knew of an estate on the outskirts of town that was being run by the domestic staff as a private club catering to a select few for "special entertainment." Ray said it was a beautiful place, far off the beaten path, a well-kept secret and therefore very safe. The girls were all well educated, spoke English, and were also under the supervision of a Navy M.D. It was frequented mostly by officers and a few well-placed civilians. No questions were asked as long as you could pay the bill and behaved like a gentleman. The wealthy owners had returned to the safety of the continental United States, and their trusted staff remained to care for the estate. The staff was doing its job and at the same time putting the manicured property to patriotic good use. Only a few customers were allowed every evening, because the man in charge wanted to keep the operation very low-key for obvious reasons. It was a perfect setup: many bedrooms, an open bar, and a pool house with bar.

All I had to do was pick the night, said Ray, and he would make all the arrangements for me. He recommended the pool house, because I could enter through a garden gate at the back of the estate, which would help narrow the chances that I would run into anyone who would recognize me.

The big night finally arrived. I headed out by taxi to become a man at last! Even in the bright moonlight, I could see nothing from the road except tropical foliage and a gated driveway. I walked around to what looked like a service road and continued several hundred yards until I saw an archway. A Hawaiian dressed like a houseman stood in the shadows under the oleander. I approached him and identified myself, and he politely asked me for "the membership dues." I paid him, in cash as Ray had instructed me, and he led me down the garden path to the pool house. He pointed out the fully stocked bar, showed me where to change, told me that my hostess would be down from the house in a few minutes, and disappeared into the night.

I looked around for a bathing suit, but all I could find were several clean thick terrycloth robes. I was beginning to feel a little nervous, but I got out of my uniform, put on one of the robes, which felt and smelled great, and walked past the bar out to the pool. The moonlight sparkling on the water made it look very inviting. I decided it would be a good idea to work off some of my nervous energy with a quick swim. I dropped the robe and dove in. The water felt great and smelled as if it had been scented with sandalwood. I swam several quick laps, then turned on my back and floated for a few minutes, feeling like a million. Then I swam back toward the pool house and climbed out. My robe was gone.

I was looking for it when a soft voice from the shadows called out, "I have it here, Mr. Farley." Walking toward me and holding out my robe was an absolutely ravishing young Hawaiian woman. She had on a simple white silk dress, and her skin looked like pale golden brown velvet. I was speechless. I instinctively covered my nakedness with my hands. She laughed softly, instructed me to turn around, draped the robe over my shoulders, and whispered into my ear, "You must not be so bashful, Mr. Farley. Here in Hawaii we are very comfortable with our bodies, and yours is very beautiful." I stammered out my thanks for this compliment. She laughed again and said, "Why don't we go have a drink?" She turned and walked to the bar while I quickly tied on my robe and followed her. As she walked behind the bar she asked, "What would you like, Mr. Farley?" I said that I would like her to call me Farley and that I would have whatever she was having.

"All right, Farley," she replied, "then you must call me Liana, and I will make us a rum and Coke." She did, and we just sat and talked through a couple of drinks.

She came from an old island family, was well educated, and had no idea who I was. Maybe it was the rum, maybe it was Liana, probably it was both, but suddenly I felt quite relaxed. She must have sensed this, because she stood up, took my hand, and said, "Come with me." I went with her into the bedroom.

I was only in a robe, and her silk dress was little more than a slip, so I was ready to tear into action. Liana stopped me before I could do anything. She made me remove her clothes, one article at a time, very slowly; first her shoes, then her belt, then her dress, one shoulder strap at a time until the whole thing slid off her. It was incredibly erotic. She did the same with my robe, one shoulder at a time, then the belt, and it dropped off. I slipped off her panties and pulled her down on the bed with me. We kissed, then I rolled her over and underneath me, ready for my big moment. She made me stop and slow down to follow her instructions.

That night, in the several hours I was with her, this beautiful Hawaiian girl taught me a great deal about women and about how to make love to them. I did not absorb it all at once, but the first time was wonderful for me, and I hoped the second time was wonderful for us both. She said it was.

After we made love the second time, I fell asleep in her arms. When I woke up about an hour or so later, Liana was gone. I decided on another swim before going back to the base. Robeless and proud of myself, I walked out to the pool and dove in. I felt as if I could swim back to California. Finally I climbed out and walked toward the pool house to get dressed. As I neared the veranda, I saw the glow of a cigarette. A deep voice said, "Mr. Granger, I think you are out of uniform." That stopped me for a moment. Then I walked closer, resisting the impulse to cover up again. A very handsome lieutenant commander stood up in the shadows and held out his hand. His shirt collar was opened, his tie was loosened, and his white jacket was draped over the back of his chair. He looked so much like the actor Sterling Hayden that I must have done a double take. He mistook my confusion and grinned, "Yes, I know, so am I—out of uniform, that is—but you've sure got me beat." I stood frozen in place, not knowing what to do. He grinned and said: "Why don't you get your robe and a drink. It might make introductions a little easier." I went inside, put on my robe, and, following orders, came back out with a drink. He stood again. As we shook hands, he said, "I'm Archie. I know who you are, Farley; I've seen your films. You are a very talented young man." I must have blushed. I had no idea how to answer Archie, whoever he was. He grinned again and said, "You'd better get used to compliments if you intend to stay in movies, because you are growing up very nicely." I think I just stood there in silence until he said, "Why don't you sit down and try to relax." I did, and after we had talked for a while, I actually did begin to relax for the second time that night.

He knew all about Lillian Hellman, Aaron Copland, Lewis Milestone, and *The North Star*. He knew a great deal about the movie business and the arts in general. He was a graduate of the Naval Academy and had been serving as a flight instructor at Edwards Air Force base in Washington, D.C. His request for a transfer to active duty had finally been granted. This was his last night in Hawaii. He was off the next day to take command of a fighter squadron in the South Pacific. When he asked, I told him how I got a contract with Goldwyn and what it had been like making the films. We talked about my last night in San Francisco seeing *Fancy Free* and *Rodeo* and how excited I had been. He said that he had seen them in D.C. and felt exactly the same, but he had been there with some friends who might not have understood if he danced home.

With a nervous laugh, I rose to fix another drink. It was after 1:00 A.M. and I realized it would be hard to find a cab to get back to base. Reluctantly, I said that I'd better get dressed and leave. He asked why I was going so soon, and I told him. Not to worry—he had a car and would drive me to his downtown hotel, where I could always get a cab. I agreed happily and went to make drinks. He followed me, and we continued talking. I mixed two drinks, put his down on the bar in front of him, and started out with mine. He grabbed my arm, took the drink out of my hand, looked into my eyes, and pulled me into his arms. After the first instant of shock and surprise, I struggled for a moment to pull away. Then I realized how excited I was. Before I knew it, we were in the bedroom and out of our clothes. The next three hours passed in what seemed like three minutes. It was almost 5:00 A.M. We scrambled back into uniform, ran out to Archie's car, and sped downtown. He stopped behind his hotel, took me in his arms, and said, "Take care of yourself, kid, because, I promise, I will find you when this mess is over." For a very long time after the war ended, I hoped he would reappear in my life, but I never saw or heard from him again.

It was a while before I was able to sort through my new experiences. I lost my virginity twice in one night. Maybe it was good that I had waited so long. Otherwise, how would I have had the stamina? The way I have lived my life ever since was set on that fateful night in Hawaii. I knew that what had happened between Liana and me was wonderful and right. I was confused by the fact that what had happened between Archie and me felt just as wonderful and just as right. I know most people would not see it that way, but try as I did, I could not feel any sense of guilt. Liana and I had pleasured each other, which made us both happy and had harmed no one. Archie and I had brought each other happiness and pleasure, and we also had harmed no one. What had passed between us was no one's business but ours. I finally came to the conclusion that for me, everything I had done that night was as natural and good as it had felt. The fact that I had to be secretive about Archie was a question of public perception and military policy, not of morals. I didn't care what others might feel or think, but I wasn't stupid. I knew discretion was important then, but I looked forward to the time when I could be myself. And that's how I have lived and still continue to live my life. Fortunately, it has been many years since I felt the need to be secretive.

After several visits to see Liana again, she asked if we could meet in Honolulu like any other couple. Her feelings for me were too real for her to go on accepting payment for us to be together. I felt the same way, and we spent many wonderful nights in her tiny flat in downtown Honolulu before the war ended and I shipped out.

I thought about Archie all the time. I knew his assignment was dangerous, and all I could do was hope that he survived. Although I was still somewhat naïve, I was not stupid. I was in the Navy. I never sought or responded to the opportunity for that kind of male companionship again. At that time, "discretion is the better part of valor" was much more than a cliché, it was a necessity. Now, I am a strong supporter of the Servicemembers Legal Defense Network. The government policy of "don't ask, don't tell" has proven itself to be as unjust as it is unnecessary. And I still wonder why my country, which I was as proud to serve as I am proud to be a part of, is the last major power in the Western world to address this particular social injustice.

I never have felt the need to belong to any exclusive, self-defining, or special group. I find it difficult to answer questions about "gay life" in Hollywood when I was living and working there. There were, of course, gay cliques, but I had no close friends who belonged to any of them, and I had no desire to become involved with any of them.

I was never ashamed, and I never felt the need to explain or apologize for my relationships to anyone. I had many gay friends, but more of my friends were straight and most married with families. The ratio of my gay to straight friends was probably in direct proportion to that of gay to straight people in all aspects of the film business and society in general. I have loved men. I have loved women. I will talk with affection and without guilt or remorse about both in this book.

V-J Day

Franklin D. Roosevelt died suddenly in April 1945. Our president, our commander in chief, was gone. I don't think anyone imagined that could ever happen. I know I thought he would always be there to lead us. The sense of grief was palpable. Harry Truman was sworn in. After FDR, his speeches seemed flat and uninspiring. I wondered if the war would ever end. Then, once again, everything suddenly changed. The atom bombs were dropped on Hiroshima and Nagasaki. Almost immediately, the war in the Pacific ended. We were all elated, but I couldn't avoid also feeling uneasy that now we could destroy an entire city and its inhabitants so easily.

After all the V-J Day celebrations, life on the base remained chaotic because of the heavy transport of troops returning from the South Pacific. I kept hoping that Archie would appear, but there was no sign of him. We opened our last production in Hawaii under the auspices of Evans's unit. Lieutenant Militich, who had come to the end of his tour of duty, was ordered to close down our office.

Our last production was Tennessee Williams's *The Glass Menagerie,* starring Kay Medford. Kay was in her early twenties, only two years older than I, but skilled enough to be playing the part of Amanda, a mother of two grown children, Tom and Laura. Years later, in my mid-thirties, I played Tom in a Broadway revival of the play with Jo Van Fleet, a rather tough Amanda; Hal Holbrook, the best Gentleman Caller I've ever seen; and Carol Rossen, a sweetly vulnerable Laura, whose father was the film writer and director Robert Rossen.

Kay was the first actor from the New York theater I got to know well. We spent all our spare time together, because we found so much in common to talk and laugh about. During the last week of the play's run in Hawaii, the manager and cast were called up to Evans's office. They had expected to go on to perform for troops in the Pacific, but he told them that unless they had any objections, they were being sent to Japan to perform for the occupation troops. None of them refused. I thought, What a great opportunity . . . I've got to get on that tour.

I found Lieutenant Militich all packed and getting ready to leave for his stateside discharge. I begged him as a last act of kindness to send me to Japan with the troupe. He told me to simmer down and come with him to the personnel office. He had a hunch about something. When I started to ask what, he shut me up again and said to bear with him. When we got there, he asked them for my records. I started to say something, and he shushed me again. After what seemed like an eternity, he smiled, waved the papers in my face, and said, "Tokyo, are you crazy? You have enough points to go home—now! Pack your seabag tonight and get down to the transport center first thing in the morning." He promised that one of his golfing buddies, Lieutenant Tom Morrow, who was in charge, would put me on a flight to California for discharge as soon as possible. I stood there dumbfounded and conflicted. I was going home! But I was missing the trip of a lifetime.

Militich clapped me on the back and said, "Wake up! You are legal. Now get the hell out of here or I'll miss *my* plane." He smiled and held out his hand. We shook, and he was out the door. Halfway down the path he turned back to shout, "And look me up sometime; I've got a job teaching English at Beverly Hills High School." By the time I did, a few years later, he was the school's principal.

I ran back to my quarters, packed, and called Lieutenant Morrow, who told me to report first thing in the morning, 8:00 A.M. *sharp!* Then I went to find Kay to tell her why I would not be going to Japan. Reacting to my mixed feelings, she told me to stop being crazy. She understood completely. She promised to see me in Hollywood soon, and I promised to look her up as soon as I visited New York.

I still had one more call to make. Liana didn't hesitate. She wanted me to spend my last night with her as much as I wanted to be with her. It was a wonderful, bittersweet parting. After a quiet dinner, we walked along the beach for hours and talked about our plans for the future. She had already applied to the University of Hawaii and was planning to go into medical research. I promised that we would see each other again, but I think we both knew that the odds were not with us. At dawn, she got me up. I showered, and she had hot strong coffee and fresh pineapple ready for me. We held each other as if we could freeze time by not letting go. When I walked down the path from her cottage, I couldn't look back.

My Escape

I went to the transport center and found it a mob scene. No one knew where Lieutenant Morrow was. No one knew about any travel orders for me, either. I waited for hours with no luck. He didn't show up, and I didn't know what to do. Lieutenant Militich was gone, and I convinced myself that if I went back to the base, I would never get away. I couldn't go back to Liana's after our goodbye. I had no clue which way to turn. Suddenly I remembered my musician friend Ray's girlfriend, Sarah. Maybe she could find out something for me. Sarah, a Navy nurse, had been stationed in Hawaii for the whole war, and she really knew her way around. I hunted her down. She assured me that she would locate my missing transport officer tomorrow. Meanwhile, she would fix us something to eat, and I was to try to get a good night's sleep on her sofa. I tossed, eyes wide open, all night long, but I must have fallen asleep just before daylight. When I did wake up it was almost 11:00 A.M. There was a note from Sarah to stay calm, and to fix myself some breakfast. She would be back as soon as she found out something. I showered and had something to eat, feeling almost normal for a short time.

It was almost 3:00 P.M. when Sarah returned, and I had worked myself back into an anxious lather all over again. She had a mile-wide smile on her face. She had tracked down Lieutenant Morrow. He had almost been run down in the parking lot outside his quarters the day before on his way to work, and in his effort to get out of the way, he had fallen and broken his ankle. He was in the hospital. She told me to phone him—"now!" He said, "Get here to the hospital ASAP." I did and went to his room. It was a nasty break and he was going to be out of commission for a while, but he had my papers with him. He told me to go to the base airport at Pearl immediately. He had cleared me for the evening flight to San Francisco. When I arrived, I was to tell them that I had priority clearance for a connecting flight to San Pedro outside Los Angeles. He said, "Make sure you get on that flight. When you arrive, do not let them send you to Treasure Island under any circumstances. Troopships from all over the Pacific are docking there, and it could be weeks before they get around to processing you. Now get out of here. You have less than ninety minutes to make your flight!" I thanked him and tore out of there.

I made it. The flight was endless. When we finally landed in San Francisco, I found another mob scene. It seemed like everyone was being herded on buses to Treasure Island. I hung back until the crowd thinned out a bit and I spotted a CPO who looked like he was in charge. I showed him my papers, and he pointed out where I should go to wait for the interairport bus outside the hanger. He warned me that most of the buses were for Treasure Island, and not to get on one of them by mistake. I had plenty of time, since the flight for the base in San Pedro was not leaving until the next morning. I thanked him and got out of there.

I sat on my seabag in the shadows and fell asleep. I woke up, dazed and confused, just as it was getting light out. I was afraid that I had missed my bus but saw some other sailors nearby and found out that they were waiting for the same bus. It finally came, and I was off to make the connecting flight to San Pedro. After a couple of days at the center, I got my honorable discharge and was free. It was a great feeling to know that I was home, that the war was over, and that I could pick up my life where I left off with all my newfound knowledge of the ways of the world.

Act II

Picking Up the Pieces

My mom and dad were overjoyed to have me home. Things seemed to be going fairly well between them. There were none of the awful fights I remembered, and they were not drinking as much. My dad would ask occasional questions about the war, but more often than not he would use my answers to segue into his own memories of World War I. I could still remember him showing me his treasured scrapbook from that war when I was a boy. A picture of three young German soldiers hanging by their necks gave me nightmares for months. I could also remember him taking out his violin and playing "The Roses of Piccardy" over and over on those evenings when he had too much to drink.

My mom didn't seem to want to accept that I was now a man. She waited up for me when I had a date, no matter how late I got home. Then she would come into my room after I got in bed to "kiss me good night, and tuck me in" so tightly that I felt a bit like a mummy. To this day I'm not sure what she was trying to accomplish. I guess the simplest explanation was to keep me safe and to keep me there. I determined to find my own place as soon as I got back to work.

After I had settled in and spent my discharge bonus on some new clothes, I checked in at the studio. When Mr. Goldwyn heard I was back, he sent for me immediately. His greeting was warm and effusive. He even got up and came from behind his vast desk to welcome me. He was still a formidable figure of a man. Tall and impeccably dressed, he even seemed to move formally. His thin, high-pitched voice, so at odds with his imposing presence, never failed to take me by surprise. He said that I was like a son to him. It gave me a nice feeling to hear him say that, since my departure from the studio had gone so unnoticed. The problem, I was soon to find out, was that he only felt that way when I was doing exactly what he wanted me to do. When I was not, which became more frequent in the years to come, he referred to me as "that boy," as in "GET THAT BOY IN HERE!"

He told me that he had the part of the young soldier who lost his hands in the war in *The Best Years of Our Lives* written for me, but that they couldn't hold up production until my discharge. Maybe that was true, but I thought that if he had planned for me to be in that film, he must have known when I was due to get out of the Navy. It was nice of him to say it . . . I guess. Anyway, no one could have been better in the part than Harold Russell, a young man who actually had lost his hands in the war. What experience he lacked as an actor was more than compensated for by his life experience.

Mr. Goldwyn said that he had all his people looking for a property that was just right for me, and that they were very close to finding it. Meanwhile he was giving me a one-hundred-dollar weekly raise and starting my salary from the date of my discharge. He wanted me to come in to the studio the next day, because he had a special surprise for me. I thanked him and left his office feeling great. I was now making two hundred dollars a week.

I went down to the mailroom to see if anything was waiting for me, and they welcomed me like a long-lost friend. They told me that while I was away in the Navy, I received more fan mail than anyone else under contract. They also told me that my father had come by periodically to pick it up. I wondered why he had not mentioned it to me.

That evening at dinner I asked my father why he had not told me about picking up my fan mail. After an uncomfortably long pause, I looked at my mother, who avoided my eyes, and Dad finally blustered, "Well, Sonny," that nickname again, which I had asked him not to use for as long as I could remember, "I was just waiting until you got all settled in, and then I planned to surprise you." He went on to explain how proud he was that I received so much more mail than any other actor at the studio. He hated my fans to be disappointed, so he had been answering my fan mail for me. He said that he would not mind continuing to do it if I would like. I was touched by his offer, and since I hated the idea of dealing with fan mail, I agreed. A few years later, on a publicity tour for *Roseanna McCoy,* I learned what a mistake that had been. It seems that he had really gotten into the correspondence with some of my more fervent young female fans. One morning at about 2:00 A.M. in Indianapolis, there was a knock on my hotel room door. I opened it to a young woman. She threw herself into my pajama-clad arms, declared her undying love, and said she knew from my letters that I felt the same way. It took me a few sleepy minutes to figure out what was going on, and a few more wide-awake ones to get rid of her. The next morning, I called to tell my father to cease and desist with the fan mail. As soon as I got back to Hollywood, I arranged for a part-time secretary to handle my fan mail at the studio. My father then started keeping scrapbooks into which he pasted anything he could find that even mentioned my name. I couldn't stay mad at my dad for what he had done. It was just a little sad that he had not made more of his own life after San Jose.

I went into the studio the next day and reported to Mr. Goldwyn's office as directed. His secretary said that he was in a meeting, but that the studio now had an acting coach on staff, and he wanted me to set up a schedule with her. She asked me to check back in after that had been done. I tracked down the acting coach, whose name I can never remember, probably because I never thought she was any good. In her office, I met the young actress who was to be my next leading lady, Cathy O'Donnell.

Cathy was very different from anyone I had ever met. She was lovely, shy, wistful, and ethereal. I felt an instant urge to protect her. We hit it off right away and set up a schedule to work together with the coach.

That accomplished, I dropped in to see Bob McIntyre, the casting director who had been responsible for getting me started at Goldwyn. He had heard I was back and was delighted that I had come to see him. I don't think he was impressed by the acting coach, either, but he was happy that I was going to be doing scene work with Cathy, who he thought was unusually talented. He believed that Cathy and I had a lot of potential as a team and he wanted to see us do some scenes together. We talked about what was currently going on around town, and he suggested that I stop by Republic Studios to say hello to Lewis Milestone, who was shooting *The Red Pony* there. Bob and I made plans for lunch later in the week, and I headed back to Goldwyn's office. He came out this time and boomed, "My boy, you are like a son to me. I am happy to have you back and want you to be happy, too. Now go see the surprise waiting for you at the front gate. Go and enjoy and work hard and we are going to find a great film for you!" Then, shouting orders to his secretary, he strode back to his inner sanctum before I had a chance to say anything. I had a pretty good idea what the surprise was, since Mr. Goldwyn often gave his contract players new cars. That prospect, with all the advantages of independence it offered, made me as happy as I had been when I got my first bicycle in junior high. I hurried to the front gate where Gus, the P.M. guard, presented me with a set of keys to a not-so-new 1940 Ford Coupe. Oh, well, it was wheels, it worked; it set me free—I couldn't complain.

I called Millie at home that evening to tell him I was back. He asked me to come to Republic to have lunch with him the next day.

After straightening out the registration and insurance for the car the next morning, I headed over to Republic to have lunch with Millie. It was great to see him again. I'd forgotten how much he liked to laugh and what a great sense of humor he had. People who didn't know Millie always expected him to be somber and very serious, probably because so many of his films, like *All Quiet on the Western Front, Of Mice and Men,* and *A Walk in the Sun,* dealt with such serious subjects, but he had also done *The Strange Love of Martha Ivers, Anything Goes,* and *The Red Pony* along with dozens of other superb films. The Millie I knew was a charmer who loved life and a good story or joke. Although I never worked with him again, we remained good friends through the years. He and his wife, Kendall, gave an annual Christmas party that was one of the season's social events I actually enjoyed. It was also a prized invitation for many of Hollywood's movers and shakers—until he was blacklisted, a shameful injustice from which he never recovered.

As we were finishing lunch that day, Millie told me that Aaron Copland was in town doing the music for his film. He said that Aaron had heard that I was back, and wanted to see me. Millie gave me his number, and I promised to give him a call.

That night when I called him we arranged to meet at a Chinese restaurant in the valley owned by James Wong Howe. Jimmy, one of the most respected cameramen in Hollywood, had also worked on *The North Star* It would be like old times seeing them both again. The next evening, I put on one of my two new suits, a shirt, and a tie, got into my new car, and, feeling quite the man of the world, set off to meet Aaron.

Jimmy greeted me like a long-lost friend and took me to a booth where Aaron was already seated. He rose to greet me with a big grin. We shook hands, and Jimmy insisted on buying the first round as a welcome-home drink. Aaron ordered a seltzer, and I ordered a vodka martini, extra dry, with a twist, no olive. Then I took out a pack of cigarettes and offered him one, which he declined. I lit up and sat back expansively.

He asked me what the Navy had been like. I told him, and I also told him about seeing *Rodeo* and *Fancy Free* in San Francisco, and how much I loved the productions and his music. He thanked me and asked how I felt about the music for *Fancy Free*. I said that I liked the music and the ballet so much that I had practically danced my way back to the ship. It had been my last night in San Francisco before shipping out to Hawaii, and I had felt like it was my life being danced onstage. He said that was a great compliment and he would love to tell the composer, Leonard Bernstein, a protégé and friend of his, about my reaction, if I had no objection. I was delighted. I ordered another martini and lit up again. Then I asked Aaron if he thought that Shostakovich would ever make it in this country. He gave me a quizzical look, and I said, "You know, will he ever be as popular as someone like, uh, Prokofiev or Stravinsky."

There was a long pause, and he burst out laughing. After a moment, so did I. I was showing off, drinking and smoking and throwing Russian composers' names around. I was trying to show him that I was no longer a kid. He knew what I was up to, and I knew he did. Jimmy came over to recommend dinner and contributed his bit of teasing about my newfound sophistication.

A Gauntlet for Mr. G.

Two days later I was called into the studio to see Mr. Goldwyn. His secretary ushered me into his office immediately. This time, Mr. Goldwyn remained seated behind his vast desk, inscrutable and silent, his ball-bearing eyes hooded and his arms crossed. One of his vice presidents, a twitchy little man with wispy hair whom I had never met, asked me to take a seat. I thought maybe they were going to tell me that they had found that wonderful project Mr. Goldwyn had promised to me. Was I in for a surprise.

The vice president said, "It has come to our attention that you were seen having dinner with Aaron Copland the other evening."

"That's right . . . so?" I said.

He stole a glance at Goldwyn, who was still looking inscrutable, and continued, "Well, I'm afraid that just won't do."

I didn't know what the hell he was talking about. "What won't do?"

He pulled a chair up next to me, sat down, and almost whispered, "Aaron Copland is a known homosexual."

I started to laugh, "So what! He's a very nice man, and I met him for dinner at Jimmy Wong Howe's restaurant. It was great seeing him again. I'm honored that he wanted to see me."

"Don't you see, Farley," he continued, "it's bad for your reputation and the studio's for you to be seen in public with people like that."

I felt the same way I had when my father made his anti-Semitic crack about Sam Levene. I stood up, turned to Goldwyn, and said, "He's talking about one of the most important composers in America, a gentleman I met at this studio when you hired him to do the score for *The North Star*. I'm not going to be told by him"—I pointed to the vice president—"or anybody else, who I can or cannot see in my private life!" With that, I turned and walked out. As I was cooling off, it dawned on me that Goldwyn had not said one word. Even though this was the prelude to many fights I was to have with Sam Goldwyn, he never mentioned this particular incident again.

Getting a Life

I was trying to get a social life going again. I had called and seen most of my old friends. Sam Levene was back in New York working in the theater, and Roddy was working nonstop at 20th. Now that I was twenty-one and had been in the Navy, the discrepancy in our ages was more of a gulf between us than when we were teens. I got a call from Jane Withers, whom I had not seen since we worked together. I didn't get to know Jane all that well during the filming, because my huge, unrequited crush on Anne Baxter dominated all thoughts of the opposite sex. Jane said that she had heard I was back and thought I might like to meet some young people in the business. She invited me to an afternoon party at her home in Beverly Hills.

Jane, who had been cast over and over as Hollywood's obnoxious brat as opposed to Shirley Temple's plucky and adorable child star, had almost grown up. Now she was being cast as the obnoxious, smart-aleck teen as opposed to Deanna Durbin's or Judy Garland's plucky and adorable adolescent.

Jane had a famous doll collection, and now that she had grown up some, she had acquired a soda fountain as well. Her afternoon parties were the subject of many a fan magazine spread. In an effort to get back in the social swim, I went.

Jane hadn't changed a bit, but I had. There were a few pretty girls there, plus a lot of handsome juvenile types who I suspected were mostly gay, not a scene that interested me. Jane carried on about her doll collection endlessly. It didn't take long for me to realize that, sweet as Jane was, this was not the social life that I was looking for; I was ready for a new group of friends.

The next time I saw Jane was in 1990 at a star-studded bash in Hollywood that Shelley Winters talked me into attending. The evening was in honor of Elizabeth Taylor and Michael Jackson, an odd couple, I thought, but as usual the lure of press coverage had hooked Shelley. One of the first people we ran into was Jane Withers. When Jane began carrying on about some crisis that had to do with her doll collection, the feeling of déjà vu was so sharp that I found it hard to keep a straight face.

Meanwhile, back at the soda fountain party, I finally broke away from the doll collection discussion and went behind the soda fountain to search, in vain, for a real drink. A voice nearby chuckled, "Give up. I've already tried" I looked up and standing at the bar was a tall, good-looking guy who was probably a few years older than I. He introduced himself as Ted Reed, an actor currently working at Columbia. We talked for a while. When I agreed that this was a pretty dull excuse for a party, he asked if I wanted to go to an open house that some friends of his regularly threw. They were musicians. The host was a musical director on staff at Columbia, and his wife, a terrific pianist, was a funny, wise, and wonderful person. Musicians had been my salvation in Hawaii, so without hesitation I said, "Let's go." I followed his car to a funny, crumbling old house on Orange Grove Avenue in Hollywood. It looked like one of those castles at the bottom of a fish bowl in Woolworth's.

The family who lived inside this enchanted castle were Ethyl and Saul Chaplin, their young daughter, Judy, and Ethyl's mother and father, Rose and Sam. There was minimal furniture in the living room and a big, gaping hole in the floor in one corner. On the other side of the room was a grand piano. That proved to be more than enough. Ethyl's mother was a great cook, and there was a breakfast nook in the kitchen into which everyone crowded for meals. It was inset into the walls, which were painted black, and the table and benches were fixed. I later nicknamed that nook "the Black Hole of Calcutta." After one evening I knew that this was the home I had wanted all my life, a home filled with laughter, joy, and music, music, music. I loved Ethyl from the first time we talked, and have never stopped. She was beautiful, talented, opinionated, and in every way an original. Saul had a great sense of humor and a mind that seemed to race in at least six directions at all times. I never saw him express a tentative reaction to anything. His opinions, either negative or positive, were all bubbling over the top. His whole world was music, and his knowledge and talent in that world were prodigious. Ethyl welcomed me into their world with breathtaking generosity. She became my mentor, my confidante, my big sister, and my best friend.

Aside from their love for Judy, music was the glue that held everything together on Orange Grove. Their door was always open to friends, and a constant parade of musical talent from New York as well as Hollywood passed through. I spent every spare minute there. Through Saul and Ethyl, I learned about Gilbert and Sullivan, Puccini, Kurt Weill, Rodgers and Hart, Harold Arlen, and countless others, including George and Ira Gershwin.

As a teenager, I was so taken by *Porgy and Bess* and George Gershwin that I had spent my meager salary from the local market on a recording of it as well as one of *An American in Paris*. The only hitch was that we did not own a record player. My parents gave me one that Christmas, but it was on an installment plan and had to go back after the first week. I had read everything I could get my hands on about George Gershwin, and had learned of his tragic death in his thirties. In one of my moments of teen madness, I decided I had to be like Gershwin, to create a masterpiece and die young. I had abandoned that high-minded ambition by the time I met the Chaplins, but it thrilled me to be in the company of people who not only knew him and Ira, but probably knew every note George had ever written. I spent so much of my time at the Chaplin house that my mother got jealous, but it was where I had to be.

Saul and Ethyl's house was not only a magnet for me; everyone connected with any musical aspect of show business in New York showed up there when in Hollywood. At their home I met Betty Comden and Adolph Green, Jerry Robbins, Judy Holliday, Oscar Levant, Phil Silvers, and Leonard Bernstein. These people were savvy, quick, and exciting to be with. They all loved to perform, especially Betty and Adolph. Everyone also loved to play The Game, as charades was then called in Hollywood. If we were not playing that, Saul and Ethyl might be performing Schubert for four hands for Lenny or something else with him. Oscar pounded out George Gershwin's more serious compositions whenever he got his hands on the keyboard. Phil would grab any opportunity to work out some of his special material at the piano with Saul. Frequently, Betty, Adolph, and Saul would work on material for a Broadway musical, *Bonanza Bound,* that they were writing, based on the Alaskan gold rush. Any and every activity was creative and stimulating. I had never been happier.

Saul was working on a musical at Columbia called *Cover Girl,* starring Rita Hayworth and Gene Kelly. Phil Silvers was featured as Gene's sidekick. In those days, we worked six days a week. Saturday was the one night when everyone could get together and blow off some steam. The "old guard," meaning the older established stars and the moguls, had dinner parties that were relatively staid events at which a film was almost always screened. Sometimes, when people were allowed to comment on the film they were viewing, it could be bitchy good fun. But usually everyone had to sit and enjoy or endure the screening in respectful and solemn silence. At a screening of some now-forgotten feature at Jack Warner's house, Van Johnson's wife, Edie, and I got the giggles. Later, as we were leaving, we were taken aside by one of the Warner Brothers executives and scolded for our childish behavior.

Edie had been married to Keenan Wynn. Van was not only their closest friend, but he lived with them. I had gotten to know them all at Gene and Betsy Kelly's house, and we had all become friends. Van had been involved in a terrible automobile accident in 1942 that left him with a steel plate in his head. It also left him untouched by the draft. He became that rare commodity during the war, a clean-cut young leading man. He worked nonstop and soon became the darling of the bobby-soxers, in a series of hit movies made by MGM.

Louis B. Mayer put pressure on Van, who was homosexual, to get married in order to protect his all-American image. I will never understand exactly what happened or how it happened, but Keenan and Edie divorced, she married Van, and they all remained a close as ever. Louis B. must have had his publicity department in overdrive at that time, because all of the people involved came out of that experience relatively unscathed, at least in the gossip columns.

The fun place to be for the younger crowd, especially the musical group, was the weekly Saturday night and Sunday afternoon open house at Gene and Betsy Kelly's. Saul and Ethyl first took me there, and I became a regular. Saul was inexhaustible at the piano and a peerless accompanist. Everyone got up and performed just for the joy of it: Judy Garland, Phil Silvers, Lena Horne, Frank Sinatra, Betty Garrett, Johnny Mercer, Harold Arlen . . . whoever happened to be there on any given Saturday evening. Everyone participated in The Game and in improvised musical skits. Gene's competitiveness in any game was so fierce that it belied the charming grin that was his trademark. Most of the time people managed to laugh it off, but sometimes his aggressiveness got a bit off-putting, particularly at the Sunday volleyball matches. Regardless, he and Betsy were generous and gregarious hosts. Performing was a part of relaxing on these Saturday nights, and everyone took part willingly and enthusiastically. This was not necessarily true at all Hollywood gatherings.

The first time I was invited to Sunday lunch at Lee and Ira Gershwin's, I went upstairs to the bathroom at one point, and as I headed back downstairs, I overheard Judy and Lena talking in one of the bedrooms nearby. They were discussing what songs to do when "she" asked them to sing for their supper, or lunch, as was the case on this afternoon. I don't think you could find anyone in Hollywood who did not think that Ira was as sweet as he was talented, and his wife, Lee, was considered to be one of Hollywood's premier hostesses, but performing when requested is very different from doing it spontaneously. I particularly loved going there because the house was filled with paintings by my teen idol, George. I thought he was a terrific painter, and there was one self-portrait I coveted.

Another regular in the Kelly household was his close longtime friend, Stanley Donen. Stanley's presence in their house was such a given, everyone thought he lived there. Along with Van Johnson, Stanley had been in the chorus of *Pal Joey,* the Rodgers and Hart Broadway musical that made Gene a star. Stanley had come to Hollywood as Gene's sidekick and assistant. He co-choreographed many of Gene's early movie musical successes, including *Cover Girl* with Rita Hayworth and *Take Me Out to the Ball Game* with Frank Sinatra. His first co-directorial credit with Gene was *On the Town;* his most successful was the movie musical milestone *Singin' in the Rain.* He then went on to direct some very good films on his own, including *Seven Brides for Seven Brothers, Funny Face, Charade,* and *Two for the Road.*

Recently at a restaurant in the theater district in New York, I felt a tap on my shoulder. It was Stanley Donen, whom I had not seen in over fifty years. He sat for a drink, and we started reminiscing about the old days, laughing and trading stories. He concluded with a comment that has stayed with me. "You know, Farley, we didn't realize it at the time, but we were there right in the middle of what really were the best of the last of the golden days."

Chomping at the Bit

In 1947, those golden days were looking a little tarnished for me at the Goldwyn Studio. I went in for my scheduled scene work with Cathy. From bits and pieces of information I picked up around the studio, I realized that Mr. Goldwyn had no prospects at all in the pipeline for me. I was certainly less naïve than I had been before the war, but it was never a part of my nature to be in touch with all the behind-the-scenes machinations in Hollywood. What I later realized with the wisdom of hindsight was that after his triumph with the superb *The Best Years of Our Lives,* Sam Goldwyn went into a creative slump from which he never recovered. It began with the departure of his best director, William Wyler, and was accelerated by the death of his superb cameraman, Gregg Toland, in 1948, the same year that, as Goldwyn's youngest contract player, I was ready and chomping at the bit to resume what many thought, and I hoped would be, a promising career.

With William Wyler off in the Army, the fact that the Goldwyn Studio flourished during the war years was an accomplishment for which a former borscht belt comedian, Danny Kaye, should be given most of the credit. His first film for Goldwyn, *Up in Arms,* was a mediocre remake of Eddie Cantor's 1930 hit *Whoopee!* The film was a big moneymaker for Goldwyn, and made an instant star of Danny Kaye. In 1948, Goldwyn was in danger of losing Danny, who was unhappy with the rehashed scripts he was being asked to do, particularly *A Song Is Born,* a dismal remake of *Ball of Fire,* a wonderful film Goldwyn had produced only seven years earlier starring Barbara Stanwyck and Gary Cooper. Goldwyn was smart enough to leave Danny alone, but he forced Virginia Mayo to watch Stanwyck's performance in the original over and over. Used correctly, as Wyler used her in *The Best Years of Our Lives,* Virginia could be very effective, but she could never replicate Barbara Stanwyck, who was one of the most unique talents in the history of film. *A Song Is Born* not only didn't work, but it brought Goldwyn the worst reviews of his career. Danny was unhappy. His contract was coming to an end, and he was being wooed by Warner Brothers. Goldwyn was scrambling to find suitable material for his biggest star of the moment. That, and other developments within the industry, namely a growing alliance between the newly formed Motion Picture Alliance for the Preservation of American Ideals and the House Committee on Un-American Activities, HUAC, kept Mr. Goldwyn too busy to attend to the development of his youngest contract player's career.

Nick Ray vs. Howard Hughes

One evening at the Chaplins', Ethyl said that she wanted me to meet a new arrival from New York, a director named Nick Ray. He had recently directed a musical in New York for John Houseman that was a critical success but had flopped. I knew Houseman's name from the Mercury Theater and also as the producer of *Citizen Kane*. When Ethyl told me that Nick Ray had worked as Elia Kazan's assistant on the movie *A Tree Grows in Brooklyn*, I was suitably impressed. He was currently preparing to direct his first movie for John Houseman at RKO.

When we were introduced, I tried to make conversation but failed miserably. Nick was either shy, or inhibited, or taciturn, or all of the above. After a while, I gave up trying to communicate with him and went to get a drink and enjoy the evening.

Years later, Ethyl broke me up by saying she always knew when it was Nick calling because when she answered the phone, there would be silence on the other end of the line.

That night, and the next few times I was there, Nick spent the whole evening sitting in a corner with his drink watching me. I finally went to Ethyl and said, "This guy is giving me the creeps. All he does is stare at me."

Ethyl said, "Farley, he's just observing you. He thinks you could be terrific as the lead in his movie, and I think he is going to offer you a test. Now, just act natural. Relax and enjoy yourself."

I think we both had a laugh at "Relax." She knew exactly how I would react to what she had just told me. I headed straight for the bar.

The next day my studio called and told me to go to RKO for a meeting with John Houseman and Nick Ray. Nick was completely articulate when he talked to me about the part and what he thought I could bring to it. John Houseman was charming and, as I was to learn, more than articulate about everything. *Thieves Like Us* was the story of a young fugitive, the getaway driver for a couple of small-time bank robbers, who falls in love with the niece of one of the robbers. The lovers break away from the rest of the gang and, after a hasty marriage, hide out in a mountain cabin hoping to escape the law and her family.

They wanted me for the part of Bowie, the young driver, and gave me the screenplay to take home to read.

John explained that despite the fact that they wanted me, the odds were against my getting the part. Dore Schary, the head of RKO, had his own young contract players like Rory Calhoun and Guy Madison. He would resist borrowing me from Goldwyn, who was a tough negotiator. When Nick asked me if there was an actress with whom I would feel comfortable for the test, I mentioned Cathy O'Donnell, and Nick said he would make the arrangements.

The test was set for Monday morning. Cathy and I spent Sunday afternoon going over the script together and working on the emotional arc of the relationship between Bowie and Keechie, from their first meeting to falling in love. That evening at home I worked out my own backstory for Bowie, starting as a small boy and ending with his going to prison.

On Monday morning we worked with Nick and did the screen test. Before I knew it, everything was all set. Not only had Nick and John fought Schary to get me, they had also liked Cathy so much that they fought to use her as well. It was a great confidence-builder to know they had liked my work enough to fight for me. We went into production the following week. John Houseman, a very canny man, probably let the final casting go until the eleventh hour in order to be able to put that extra bit of pressure on Dore Schary.

Cathy and I had a wonderful group of character actors to work with. Howard Da Silva, who specialized in mean, heavy roles both on Broadway and in films, played Keechie's uncle, the one-eyed half-breed Chicamaw. J. C. Flippen, a Broadway musical actor who switched to films after the war, played his tough partner, T-Dub. The first day of shooting involved a helicopter shot that Nick had planned. I'm certain it was the first time one had ever been used in a feature film. The film opens after our escape from prison, and the camera follows from the air the old convertible we are escaping in until it has a flat and pulls off the dirt road and into a field. Our big problem was that Howard's toupee kept getting blown off by the downdraft from the rotor blades. Reshooting that setup took an enormous amount of time because of the helicopter, but Nick persevered and so, finally, did the glue on the hairpiece.

The next setup was of the three of us running across fields to a small highway. On the last take, my foot caught in a gopher hole and down I went with a badly sprained ankle. Fortunately, it worked in the following scene, in which the guys leave me hiding behind a roadside billboard while they go off to get some money. By the time we finished for the day, my foot had swollen so badly that my shoe had to be cut off. Howard refused to let me try to walk. He insisted on carrying me. He threw me over his shoulder in a fireman's carry. It was a long way to the car.

We were almost through shooting the film when we learned that Howard Hughes was taking over RKO and Dore Schary was going to MGM. I don't know if Nick had any idea of what this would mean for us. None of us did. It turned out that it meant a lot, none of it good.

Howard Hughes had made his name in movies in the late 1920s. In 1930, as the producer-director of *Hell's Angels,* he spent an unheard-of $3.8 million of his personal fortune to perfect the aerial sequences. It was a smash hit. He then produced the hit *Scarface* in 1932. His subsequent claim to Hollywood fame was the number of beautiful Hollywood stars he squired around town. In 1932, he left Hollywood in order to pursue his passion for aviation. His return to filmmaking in 1941 was to produce and direct *The Outlaw,* starring Jane Russell and her cleavage. The film was bad enough to disappear quickly but in a rare moment of Hollywood self-censorship, it was condemned by the Hays Office and withdrawn by Hughes. That action and Hughes's subsequent reaction, a well-publicized, protracted fight to have it released in 1946 and then again in 1950, made a star of the entertainer Bob Hope once introduced as "the two and only Miss Jane Russell," and a moneymaker out of a dismal movie.

Nick was afraid that our film would not be appreciated by Hughes. The first sign that he might be right was when Hughes insisted on changing the title because he thought people would think it meant *Thieves Like Us.* The title came from a line in the film when Chicamaw refers to bank owners as being "thieves like us." The next thing we knew the film was being called *The Twisted Road,* and then it became *Your Red Wagon,* the title of a song sung in a roadhouse in one scene in the film. Neither of these changes made any of us feel secure about Howard Hughes's understanding of the kind of film Nick was making.

I don't think anyone was terribly surprised several months later to open *Daily Variety* one morning and read that Howard Hughes had shelved Nicholas Ray's film starring Cathy O'Donnell and Farley Granger.

The Bel Air Circuit

Every major producer in Hollywood had his own private screening room in his house where they viewed old films, new films, and particularly films that were being made by rival studios. As soon as our film was finished, it played the "Bel Air Circuit," as the moguls' home screening rooms were called. For this reason, none of the actors felt that the shelving of *Thieves Like Us* had done serious damage to our future prospects. Goldwyn, who had viewed *They Live by Night* (its eventual new title), was so taken by Cathy and me in the film that he declared us his new Romeo and Juliet in a major publicity campaign that promised great things for us.

Quality work was hard to come by. To have his first film put aside by a man whose most recent claim to filmmaking fame was as tacky as *The Outlaw* was a lousy break for Nick.

Two years or so later, English good taste saved our film from oblivion. It opened with little fanfare in a small London art house, and the English critics loved it. Soon after that RKO released it in the States, where it received excellent reviews for Nick, Cathy, and me.

By 1954, under Hughes's sporadic management, RKO had lost $40 million. Although hardly a drop in today's Hollywood bucket, it was a lot of money back then. Hughes then bought all the outstanding stock from the studio's shareholders at bargain-basement prices and sold the studio for a ten-million-dollar profit.

Nick Ray

Nick Ray was one of the best and most sensitive directors I've ever worked with. For a man who was socially inarticulate, he was the complete opposite when working. If he wanted something special from any of the actors in a scene, he would put his arm around your shoulder and walk you away to talk privately about the situation and the character, even if it was for something as simple as wanting me to react differently to the sound of a car approaching. He made each actor feel as if he or she were getting special treatment. It took me fifteen years to encounter another director who worked that intimately. It was Eva Le Gallienne who was directing me in Chekhov on the stage.

I always wished I'd had the chance to work with Nick again. He did some cleanup work for Goldwyn on *Roseanna McCoy,* a film I was in a few years later, but the principal photography had already been finished, and there was very little he could do to improve the film. Beyond our initial warm hello, I couldn't get him to have a conversation with me. It was almost as if he were ashamed to be working as a cleanup director on a lost cause for Goldwyn. I still wonder about what might have been if Nick had been on the film from the beginning, with the original script.

Years later, he talked to me about playing Jesus in *King of Kings.* I did not feel that his heart was in it, and I knew that it was not a good idea for me. I tried to laugh it off by saying, "Nick, if I do that, I'll never work again."

He ended up using Jeff Hunter, a good-looking young man with bright blue eyes, and I think it did end his career. Now it seems as if that particular curse has been broken. Willem Dafoe's career survived playing the title role in Martin Scorsese's *The Last Temptation of Christ.* It also seems as if Jim Caviezel's career, though hardly taking off, was not been completely stalled by being flayed for twenty minutes as Jesus in Mel Gibson's *The Passion of the Christ.*

Much has been written about Nick's tendency to become emotionally and physically involved with his young leading actors, particularly James Dean, Natalie Wood, and Sal Mineo, the three stars of *Rebel Without a Cause,* but I never had any sense that he wanted our relationship to be anything other than professional. Certainly Nick's life was not exactly conventional. His second wife was Gloria Grahame, film noir's quintessential bad girl. Years later his son Tony by his first marriage, married Gloria. Nick was also plagued by substance abuse, both liquor and drugs, throughout his life, which partially accounts for the fact that such a talented director only sporadically lived up to his promise.

I did not see Nick again until 1979, when I returned to New York from Los Angeles after spending almost five years in Italy. I picked up *The New York Times* one morning and read that he was gravely ill and hospitalized. I tracked him down and went to see him. He was in a small ward with maybe half a dozen other terminal patients. He could not have been more surprised or more delighted to see me. I was surprised how happy I was to see him, even under these circumstances. Always taciturn, Nick now had an excuse not to say much. He was dying of smoking-related cancer, and it was difficult for him to talk. We reminisced a bit, and then I had to leave because he tired so easily. Before I could return for another visit, he died at age sixty-seven.

Nick is still considered one of America's film visionaries by students of the cinema all over the world. His reputation is based on three films: *They Live by Night, Rebel Without a Cause,* and *Johnny Guitar.* His other work in the 1940s, 1950s, and 1960s was not good. His personal life, the booze, the drugs, and the complicated relationships obviously kept this artist from realizing his great potential. I mourned him.

The Big Apple

Since Mr. Goldwyn had raised my salary to $250 a week when I started work on *Thieves Like Us,* I began to think about looking for a place of my own. This was still a relatively paltry salary at the time, but I had been away from the screen for almost four years while in the Navy, and I was insecure about having to prove myself again.

During this period, my love life was pretty barren. Just after I began the film, I met a young actress from New York named Patricia Neal. She had done wonderful work on the New York stage and was not a typical Hollywood ingenue, but she radiated star appeal. Pat was tall, with a throaty, cultured voice, a hearty laugh, and a quick wide smile. I really fell for her. We spent as much time together as we could, which was not nearly as much as I would have liked, since we were both busy working. Pat was filming *The Fountainhead* with Gary Cooper. Unfortunately for me and eventually even more so for Pat, she and Coop fell madly in love while making that film. In the end, he could not leave his wife, and the affair ended painfully for all concerned. Coop had a difficult time trying to paste the pieces of his marriage back together, and Pat suffered a much too well publicized nervous breakdown.

Harry Cohn, who ran Columbia, had the reputation of being a cheapskate, and it was a reputation that no one ever disputed. At the same time that I started working at RKO, Saul Chaplin left Columbia and went to MGM. It was a nice move upward for Saul, who had been overused and underpaid at Columbia. At Metro, for a very nice salary, he would be responsible for one film at a time. At Columbia he had been responsible for as many as five films at one time while having to deal with the crass and despotic Cohn. Saul and Ethyl celebrated by buying a new house on Doheny Drive in Beverly Hills. Their new living room could accommodate two baby grand pianos, and their new home continued to be a gathering place for the New York musical crowd.

About two weeks after I finished Nick's film, Ethyl called to tell me that Saul, Betty Comden, and Adolph Green had gotten the financing to put on their musical, *Bonanza Bound.* They had rented their new house and were leaving for New York immediately. She urged me to come to New York while they were there. While Saul was busy working, she and I could play together. Goldwyn had still not found "that great project" for me. I had never been to New York, and this was my chance to see it with good friends. Helen Craig, who had been in *They Live by Night* and went immediately into another movie, offered me her New York apartment at 55th Street and Sixth Avenue. She said it was a perfect location for going to the theater. I told my parents and the studio where to find me, packed a bag, and got on the first flight I could book for New York.

I treated myself to a first-class ticket on Pan Am. My seat was luxurious, comfortable enough to curl up and sleep in. The only problem was that I was much too excited to sleep. Flying may be a lot faster now, but it has gone downhill as far as comfort is concerned. In those days, when flying coast to coast, there was a stop in Chicago either to refuel or to change planes. When we landed in Chicago, I ran into the airport to call Ethyl with my latest brainstorm. Rather than go to a strange apartment on my first night in the big city, I asked her to get me a room in one of the best hotels in town. I must have sounded like an eight-year-old because she couldn't stop laughing, but she promised to take care of everything for me.

We got into La Guardia at about 8:30 P.M., and Ethyl and Saul were there at the gate. They were each holding up signs. Saul's said WELCOME TO NEW YORK, and Ethyl's said IT'S A HELLUVA TOWN! It was getting dark as we drove into the city. Los Angeles, which I had just come from, is a sprawling city with no one center. H. L. Mencken called it "six suburbs in search of a city." Manhattan seemed to be all in front of me in one magnificent vista. The setting sun backlit that glorious skyline in shades of crimson and copper. It so surpassed any expectations I had formed from movies and newsreels that the effect on me was visceral.

The evening was hot and humid. After we crossed the 59th Street Bridge into the city, I couldn't get over the fact that steam was coming up through manhole covers in the streets. With that, and the neon lights reflecting off parked cars and the pavement, I felt as if we were driving on top of Dante's Inferno. It was spooky and thrilling. I still feel that way whenever I return to the city at night.

We went straight to Betty Comden's apartment on East 55th Street, only two blocks from where I would be staying. Betty and Adolph were there, as well as Betty's husband, Steve Kyle. Adolph's wife, Allyn Ann McLerie, who was performing in *Where's Charley?* on Broadway, was joining us after the show. I was almost as impressed by Betty's apartment as I was with the steam coming up from the streets. It was all black, the walls, the furniture, everything but one bright green ottoman. I thought, This is it. This is bohemian. This is for me.

The champagne popped, and everyone was talking at once. I felt like an insider, hearing all the latest Broadway gossip as well as the plans for *Bonanza Bound.* We were high and happy and hungry by the time Allyn Ann got home from her show. Betty and Ethyl had set out a terrific spread from the nearby Carnegie Delicatessen that introduced me to some great New York tastes. There was chopped liver, pastrami, corned beef, noodle kugel, new pickles, and other deli delights. After supper, we gathered around the piano to hear the new numbers they had written for *Bonanza Bound.* After one number, the change in time zones and the energy I had expended in excitement caught up with me. I had to go to bed. We hugged good nights all around, and Ethyl took me to the Essex House, my hotel on Central Park South. I was so tired, I didn't take in the lobby or anything. I just went up to my room and passed out on the bed.

When I woke the next morning and pulled open the drapes, my breath was taken away once again. I was on the twenty-first floor, and all of Central Park stretched out before me. It was summer, and everything was in bloom and green, green, green. The phone rang. Adolph was downstairs in the lobby. He said, "Hurry down. I want to show you New York." I jumped in the shower and was in the lobby in no time. We went to a coffee shop where I had my first bagel with cream cheese—a schmear—and lox. Even breakfast was new and exotic. Adolph was as good as a professional guide. It seemed as if he knew everything there was to know about New York. We went from Radio City down Fifth Avenue to the Empire State Building and then to Broadway, where we had lunch at a wonderful place called Dinty Moore's. It was all brass and white tiles, with bentwood chairs and coatracks. Jerry Robbins, the great choreographer, came in, and Adolph hailed him over to join us. I had been a huge Robbins fan ever since seeing *Fancy Free* in San Francisco. Adolph and I had been talking about which Broadway show should be my first. After much good-natured bickering about what was worth seeing, the name Ethel Merman came up, and they said in unison, *Annie Get Your Gun.* Adolph had to go to work, so Jerry said he would walk me to the Imperial Theatre to make sure I got a good seat. He insisted that the only place to see a musical was from dead center in the first row of the mezzanine. I'm not sure directors or set designers agree with him, but lighting designers and choreographers all do.

Star Power

I had never seen a Broadway show, much less a Broadway musical. Even though I knew that Ethel Merman was a big star, I had never seen any of her films, so I didn't know what to expect. She was extraordinary! She was magnificent! I was transported! I was blown away! I was in love! Thank God I got to know her some years later to tell her how I felt. She was a knockout off the stage as well, with a vocabulary that could make the Army, Navy, and Marines blush.

There is a famous story, possibly apocryphal, about her first trip to Hollywood, and a visit to the set of a movie starring Loretta Young, a world-class Catholic who kept a "swear box" on the set into which everyone had to make a deposit for their naughty words. Merman saw it, turned to Loretta, and said, "What the hell is this?"

Loretta smiled sweetly and said, "Oh, Ethel, I'm afraid now you have to put twenty-five cents into the swear box."

Ethel gave her a look and grinned as she said, "How much will it cost me to tell you to go fuck yourself?"

That's my Merman.

I couldn't get enough of the theater. I saw *Brigadoon* with its marvelous dances by Agnes de Mille, featuring the superb dancer James Mitchell. A few years later James came to Hollywood under contract to Warner Brothers and became a very close friend. Many years later, he played Captain Wickham in *First Impressions,* my first Broadway show. I saw *Mister Roberts,* starring the great Henry Fonda, a wonderful comedy that I would do in stock years later. There was *Where's Charley?* with Ray Bolger and Adolph's wife, Allyn Ann McLerie. David Wayne was a captivating leprechaun in search of a pot of gold in *Finian's Rainbow.* I was lucky enough to see those peerless actors the Lunts in *O Mistress Mine.* Last, but in no way least, I saw Elia Kazan's ground-breaking production of *A Streetcar Named Desire* starring Marlon Brando and Jessica Tandy. Everyone in it was wonderful, but I couldn't take my eyes off Brando. He made me think about acting in a whole new way.

Now I knew what my destiny was. I was going to be up there on the stage someday. I had done three movies, all with good directors, but I had never experienced the feeling of electricity generated by the connection between audience and actor at a live performance. It was something I had to be a part of. I was going to come to New York.

On the Boardwalk

Adolph told me that Nancy Walker, a comic actress I had met in Hollywood, was doing *On the Town* in a theater at the end of the Steel Pier in Atlantic City. On Allyn Ann's day off, she and I decided to go see it. I thought Atlantic City was just somewhere across the Hudson river in nearby New Jersey, and Allyn Ann didn't have a clue where it was. We just hailed a cab and I asked the driver to take us to the Steel Pier in Atlantic City. He turned and gave me a funny look, then shrugged and said, "Anything you say, buddy," and we took off. A couple of hours later, and many dollars lighter, we finally arrived.

We were about twenty minutes late, but the show had still not started. The audience was clapping in unison and obviously getting restless. Allyn Ann protected our seats while I went back to Nancy's dressing room to find out if she was okay. It wasn't hard to find. As soon as I got backstage, I could hear Nancy raising hell with someone. I followed her voice to her dressing room. All five feet of Nancy had the theater manager backed into a corner, saying she would do the first act, but there would be no second act until she had the cash in her hands. As the manager backed out of her dressing room, she spotted me, blew me a kiss, and said with a big smile, "Come back after the show, Farfel, and we'll get something to eat." I made my way back to my seat thinking, This is all much more glamorous than working in movies.

Hitchcock

I had come to New York for two weeks, which had stretched to four. I was having such a great time that I completely forgot my commitments in Hollywood. The studio reminded me. They called to tell me that I had to come back immediately. Mr. Goldwyn had loaned me out to Warner Brothers to do Alfred Hitchcock's new film, *Rope.* Even though I never wanted to leave New York again, the idea of working with Hitchcock was intriguing. I loved his films, particularly *Rebecca* and *Shadow of a Doubt,* and I was sure I could learn a lot from a director as good as he was.

Ethyl and Saul felt this was a major opportunity for me. I made arrangements to leave the next day. Ethyl asked me to do her a favor. She had rented their house in Hollywood to a beautiful Broadway dancer named Sono Osato, who had played Miss Turnstiles in *On the Town.* She made me promise to stop by, introduce myself, and check on her cat. "Keedy" was an outdoor cat that lived in the alley behind her house. He was a little feral and a little crazy, but she loved him and fed him. She wanted me to make sure that Sono was remembering to feed him. I promised to check.

The next day I got an early-morning flight for L.A. that arrived early in the evening. I got a cab from the airport and went by Doheny Drive on my way home. I rang the bell and instead of a gorgeous dancer named Sono, a short, energetic man with a ready grin answered. When I asked for Sono Osato, he told me that she had to go back to New York and that he had arranged to take her place. We introduced ourselves. His name, Arthur Laurents, meant nothing to me. I told him why I was there, and we went into the kitchen and opened the door to the alley. Sure enough, Keedy came when called. He looked fine, just as ratty as ever. Sono had shown Arthur all about feeding the cat, and he wanted me to tell Ethyl not to worry. Then he said he was sure I must have some more questions. Was there anything I wanted to ask him? I had no idea what he meant, so I shrugged no, said goodbye, and left.

Rope

After an early breakfast, over which I regaled my parents with stories about New York, I called the studio to tell them I was back. I was told to go straight to Hitchcock's office at Warner Brothers to meet him and get a script of *Rope*. He was expecting me.

When I walked into Mr. Hitchcock's office, I was bowled over. Every wall was covered by eight-by-ten-inch drawings from ceiling to floor. I was completely absorbed in this visualization of the script when that famous voice spoke out behind me: "Won't you come in, Mr. Granger, and I will tell you all about *Rope*."

I was caught completely off guard and don't remember what I said, something clever like "This is terrific," or "You're terrific," or "Wow," and followed him into his office. He sat down with a mischievous smile and told me the story of *Rope* and how he planned to shoot it.

The movie was based on a play, *Rope's End*, by the British playwright Patrick Hamilton, which had been inspired by a famous murder case that took place in Chicago in 1924. Two college students, Leopold and Loeb, just for kicks, and because they believed that their intellectual superiority entitled them, brutally strangled a young boy just to prove they were smart enough to get away with it.

In the movie, they hide the body in a chest in their New York City apartment and serve hors d'oeuvres off this chest to the dead man's parents and fiancée, who come for cocktails a short while later. Their college housemaster, Rupert, played by Jimmy Stewart, is both the inspiration for this sociopathic behavior and the person responsible for their undoing.

Hitchcock said he had screened a rough cut of *They Live by Night* and liked the film and my performance in it. He wanted me to play Phillip in *Rope*. My partner in crime, Brandon, was to be played by a New York theater actor, John Dall, who had had a success in his first film as Bette Davis's young protégé in *The Corn Is Green*. Hitchcock explained that all of *Rope* takes place in New York between 7:00 and 8:40 on a specific evening.

He planned to shoot the film in ten or twelve camera setups, each lasting ten minutes. This was the amount of time you got from each reel of film on the color cameras. The setups would be continuous, with no cutting away from the action. The set, the furniture, and the lighting would all be on wheels so that everything could be pulled away for tracking shots as we walked through the rooms of the apartment, which consisted of the hallway and front door, the living room, the bathroom, and the kitchen. Outside the huge living room windows was a skyline of New York that would gradually change from day to night. Mr. Hitchcock loved telling stories. He could make the phone book sound intriguing. Imagine how great *Rope* sounded. We were to start shooting in two weeks.

I asked my parents not to disturb me and settled down in my room to read *Rope*. On the title page I saw "Screenplay by Arthur Laurents." The name was familiar, but it took me a minute to place it. "Oh, that's that little guy I met at Ethyl's! No wonder he wanted to know if I had any questions." I would call him after I finished the screenplay.

The next morning, Arthur's call woke me up. I apologized for not knowing who he was when we met. He said not to worry and asked if I would like to get together to talk about the character. When I said that I would love to, he invited me to dinner.

I arrived at Ethyl's house at the appointed time. Arthur and I had several vodka tonics. Since I had not eaten lunch, I was getting a little sloshed and suggested we go for dinner. Arthur said, "Oh, I'm a great cook, I've got some chops. Is it okay if we eat here?" I said sure and followed him into the kitchen, where we continued to talk about *Rope* as he fixed dinner.

Arthur was very smart, with a bitchy sense of humor that made him an amusing storyteller and gossip. He knew a lot about the theater, a world I wanted very much to become a part of someday. After dinner and some brandy, always a mistake, I got up to leave. He had made a few remarks in the course of the evening that made it no surprise when he suggested that I spend the night. I thanked him and politely declined.

He called to invite me for dinner again several days later, and again we spent the evening talking, mostly about *Rope* and the theater. That night I did not decline his invitation to stay. In fact, I stayed with him every night until we went into rehearsal the following week. We discussed the text and subtext, the unspoken homoerotic bond between Phillip and Brandon, and Rupert's influence on them both. Arthur was attractive, fun, and great company. Being this close to the writer of the script I was going to work on was an extremely valuable learning experience.

Bonanza Bound, Saul's musical, never made it to Broadway. It closed out of town in Philadelphia. Ethyl and Saul were coming home sooner than they had hoped and Arthur had to find another place. He saw a house he liked on Lookout Mountain off Laurel Canyon and wanted me to come by to check it out.

We went over to the house on Sunday afternoon. He had already signed a lease and planned to move in as soon as he could. He made an obvious allusion as to what a great space it was for two people and how convenient it was to Warner's, where *Rope* was being shot, but I didn't bite.

When I went home, my parents lit into me. They were angry that I had stayed away from home for the last several nights without discussing it with them. The fact that I had called, that I was over twenty-one and was already looking to find my own place, did not slow them down a bit. I finally shouted that unless they wanted me to move out of their lives that minute, they had better lay off. I was going into rehearsal the next morning, and I needed to be rested and prepared. I knew I had not heard the end of it and that I needed to do something, and soon.

Rehearsals began the next morning, and went on for fifteen days. The filming was completed in twenty-one days. Everyone on the soundstage, from Jimmy Stewart to the prop men, called Mr. Hitchcock "Hitch." He liked it, and smiled when I did likewise. The rehearsals were grueling. Since there were no cuts, as one walked through the apartment, walls had to be pulled out of the way, lights had to follow and/or precede you, and furniture had to be removed and replaced, and this activity had to be silent because of the sound recording. The Technicolor cameras were almost as big as modern refrigerators. There were many opportunities for technical problems, and they all happened. We had to shoot a number of the ten-minute reels over. Even after all went well on the set, when Hitch watched the rushes the next morning, he would see that the color didn't match because of lighting differences from one take to another. At the end of each take or reel, Hitch would end with the camera on someone's back or an inanimate object that he could match with the first shot on the next take. After a couple of days of what felt like total chaos, throughout which Hitch was imperturbable, things settled down a bit, and the mistakes became fewer. At the end of the first week, everyone was exhausted with the exception of Constance Collier and Sir Cedric Hardwicke, the old theater pros. They were having a ball. The constant swirl of activity was so different from the stage that they went along with it like kids on a roller coaster. Fortunately, I was once close enough to catch Connie when she trustingly started to sit on a chair that the prop man had not yet managed to get in place.

To this day, reporters and film aficionados still ask about the actors' discussions with Hitchcock about the implied homosexual relationship between the two young men in *Rope*, and how Jimmy Stewart fit into those discussions. My answer is always disappointing to them: "What discussions? It was 1948."

Arthur made sure that I was aware of what he felt was going on between the characters, and, of course, John Dall and I discussed the subtext of our scenes together. We knew that Hitch knew what he was doing and had built sexual ambiguity into his presentation of the material. Jimmy Stewart must have known that the film was based on Leopold and Loeb, but I'm sure he felt that as far as his character was concerned, any implied sexual relationship between his students was strictly their business.

Jimmy was a gentleman, the real thing, and one of the nicest actors I've ever worked with. I have wondered quite often if this quality interfered with his realizing the darker side of Rupert. After all, the character is partially responsible for what happened, and is the person who pushes those buttons in the boys. It might have been interesting to see what an actor like James Mason, with his quirky, dark quality, would have brought to the part.

After the first week's work, I was too beat to go to any parties on Saturday, or to get into a deep discussion with Arthur about his script, so I headed home. That was a mistake. My father had been drinking. As soon as I walked in the door, he started in on me. I went straight to my room, packed a bag, and left. I hugged my mother, who was crying, and said, "It will be better this way, Mom, you'll see. I'll get the rest of my stuff as soon as I can." I got in my car, headed for Arthur's, and never looked back.

Arthur didn't seem surprised to see me when he answered the door. To this day, I'm not sure if this was what he was hoping would happen. In any case, he did not object, which I assumed to mean that we were taking the next step in our relationship. This next step lasted for about a year. It turned out to be a very busy year, with Arthur going back to New York to have his new play produced on Broadway and my doing two films almost back to back.

We had a constant stream of visitors on the set of *Rope*. Hitch loved showing off. Whether it was the press, old friends, or other celebrities, he obviously relished having them there. He loved publicity. If you think about it, in the 1940s and 1950s the average filmgoer neither knew nor cared who directed the film they were seeing. One went to the new Clark Gable movie, the latest Judy Garland movie, or Dean Martin and Jerry Lewis's new comedy. The few exceptions like Cecil B. De Mille and Hitchcock had mastered the art of self-promotion. Hitch made a cameo appearance in each of his films. It became a game for the public. They loved spotting him. His friends, who visited the set, were always interesting people to meet. One day it would be Cary Grant, the next Ingrid Bergman. A high point was when Noël Coward dropped by for lunch. He knew Sir Cedric and Connie from their years in the English theater. Hitch invited John and me to join them. Noël Coward was charming, amusing, and a great raconteur. His clipped, flat delivery made his stories seem even funnier. One only has to listen to the recording of Sir Noël and his frequent stage partner and lifelong friend, Gertrude Lawrence, doing a scene from his play *Private Lives* to understand what I mean. Hitch asked him how Gertrude Lawrence was. Coward responded that he had just seen her on the stage in London. "She was wonderful." Then he took a slight pause and with a twinkle confided, "One has to be terribly careful onstage with Gertie, you know . . . give her a phone or a box of chocolates . . . you're in serious trouble . . . and a scarf . . . *disaster!*" He mimed her actions as he spoke and you could see Gertie upstaging him. Even Hitch laughed.

As time passed, even though they never completely disappeared, the problems with the filming of *Rope* had settled down. There were so many difficult technical demands that uninterrupted or good takes were the exception rather than the rule. For actors it was always rewarding to have that much rehearsal before each setup, but the focus of these rehearsals had to be on things like hitting your marks on time and not getting run over while doing it. The novelty had worn off. It began to get frustrating. Hitch was incredibly patient. Though it was obvious that he loved the various challenges, I'd bet that he, too, was getting weary of the restrictions within which he had to work. The storytelling limitations imposed by not being able to be honest about the real relationship between Phillip, Brandon, and Rupert only made it feel more constricted. *Rope* was an interesting technical experiment that I was lucky and happy to be a part of, but I don't think it was one of Hitchcock's better films. It's interesting to speculate on what the film would have been like had he shot it normally. It's equally interesting to think about what kind of film he would have made if he had not had to worry about censorship.

The Most Beautiful Woman in the World

Since Arthur had never met Ethyl and Saul, we decided to throw a homecoming/housewarming party for them at their house on Doheny. They were due back on a Wednesday, and we decided that by Saturday they would be rested up and ready. Our plan was to take Ethyl and Saul to their favorite restaurant for an early dinner while Judy was greeting the arriving guests. I thought it might be fun to have a few new faces among the regulars. We invited some musician friends of Saul's from MGM; Betty Garrett, whom Metro was grooming for musical stardom, and her husband, Larry Parks, who had played Al Jolson at Columbia; Anita Ellis, a wonderful singer from New York, who had such bad stage fright that she could not sing in public, but had dubbed Rita Hayworth's sexy singing voice in *Gilda, Down to Earth,* and a number of other films; Gary

Merrill, who was making *All About Eve* with Bette Davis; and Nick Ray and his wife, Gloria Grahame, who later won an Oscar as the bad girl in *The Bad and the Beautiful.* I invited everyone to arrive after 7:30, which was when Arthur had booked a table at The Players. The surprise party would be in full swing when we got back after dinner.

By the time we got to the Chaplins' home, everyone was having a swell time, and the boisterous chorus of "SURPRISE!" was heartfelt. Saul immediately sat down at the piano, and what was already a good party just got better. A musician friend of Saul's arrived with Hedy Lamarr, whom none of us had ever met. MGM had built Miss Lamarr up as "The Most Beautiful Woman in the World," and she was that. She was also so shy and withdrawn that when she sat on the floor against one wall, it seemed as if she wanted to disappear . . . she almost did.

Some time later Ethyl joined Saul at the second piano to play and sing Kurt Weill's *Threepenny Opera.* Hedy came immediately to life. She jumped up and hurried to the piano to sing with them. The transformation was amazing. She joined in with complete animated abandon. If she had only been able to bring some of that joy to her screen roles, there would have been no stopping her.

I went to the bar, and Gary Merrill came over to confide in me. I later learned that he confided in everyone that night. He was madly in love. He was sorry, he could not say with whom, but he had never been so crazy about anyone. She was a fantastic lady, brilliantly talented, beautiful and smart, with a great sense of humor. He couldn't wait for me to meet her. Of course, we all knew who he was talking about. The affair he was having with Bette Davis was not the best-kept secret in town. I just wished that he had brought her to the party. Bette, a two-time Academy Award winner, was always in trouble or on suspension at Warner Brothers. Whenever she felt that a film was not right for her or was junk, she had no hesitation about refusing to do it and marching unannounced into Jack Warner's office to tell him exactly how she felt. She was my hero. When I did meet her at Jack Warner's house, I told her that and how much I loved her singing "They're Either Too Young or Too Old" in *Hollywood Canteen.* The next morning a messenger rang my doorbell and delivered a recording of Bette singing the song. I realized that she was everything Gary had said and more. Later, when I got to know her better, I realized that she was as down-to-earth as they come, and couldn't bear pretentiousness in anyone.

Ethyl and Saul had finished playing Kurt Weill, and Saul was now accompanying Betty Garrett as she sang some of the songs from a new film she was working on at MGM with Gene Kelly and Frank Sinatra, *Take Me Out to the Ball Game.* I spotted Hedy making her way to the bar and went over to introduce myself. Obviously relaxed now, she was open and completely at ease. She said that she had seen *They Live by Night* at a screening at Louis B. Mayer's house, and had thought it was very good. She also thought Cathy and I were wonderful together. I asked her what it had been like making films in Austria before the war. We found a seat, and she explained that she had only been a bit player until that stupid Czech film *Ecstasy* came along and made such a commotion. She had appeared nude in that film in 1933, and it became a worldwide sensation. By today's standards, her chaste little nude swim would most likely not even get a PG-13, but back then it caused an international furor.

She told me that after that film, she had turned down a Hollywood offer in order to marry a wealthy Austrian industrialist and had retired from acting. Her husband then spent the next five years trying in vain to buy up all the existing copies of *Ecstasy*. She gave me a wicked smile. "He had no more luck with that than he did turning me into the contented mistress of his fancy country mansion."

He had ensconced her on his estate in the beautiful Austrian countryside while he was off wheeling and dealing all over Europe. For a while she enjoyed playing house, but then boredom began to creep into her new world. One day she decided to entertain herself by taking all sixteen toilet seats from the house out on the lawn that swept down to the lake to paint them in the sun. As she was beginning the last one, she spotted a long line of black Mercedes limos in the distance coming up the long drive to the house. Her husband had not bothered to call to warn her that he was bringing important guests for the weekend. Hedy laughed. "I took one look at his thundercloud of a face when he got out of the lead car and knew that I was going to revive that Hollywood offer." It is just too bad that Metro never learned how to use her, because "The Most Beautiful Woman in the World" was a lot more than an unforgettable face, she was a delightful dame.

The Little Tramp and Big Bill

One morning Arthur asked me if I liked to play tennis. I told him I loved to, especially when I could get the ball over the net. He laughed and said, "I've got a perfect solution. Charlie Chaplin called me yesterday. Bill Tilden is going to be giving lessons up at Charlie's house. He's down on his luck, and Charlie is helping him out by letting him use his courts to give lessons. Charlie's also calling a lot of his friends to encourage them to take advantage of this opportunity. What do you think?" I said I thought it was a great idea. Who wouldn't want to take lessons from the greatest tennis player in the world?

Bill Tilden, also known as "Big Bill," began playing tennis at the late age of twenty-seven. Before long, he began winning championships, eventually leading the United States team to seven consecutive Davis Cup victories, a record that has never been equaled. He was known for his cannonball serve, which enabled him to serve aces at will. From 1920 to 1925 he was considered the greatest player who ever lived. During the Roaring Twenties, he, boxer Jack Dempsey, baseball player Babe Ruth, footballer Red Grange, and golfer Bobby Jones dominated American sports. In need of money, Tilden turned professional in 1931. Ten years later, at the age of forty-eight, he was still playing professionally against players like Don Budge, the twenty-five-year-old world champion . . . and still occasionally winning.

His downfall started in 1946 when he was arrested for soliciting an underage male prostitute. Three years later, after a second arrest for a similar offense, he was being banned from teaching at tennis clubs and public courts. He was quickly down and out. Charlie Chaplin had been Tilden's friend before these problems and remained his friend after them. By making his courts available to Tilden and encouraging friends and acquaintances in the movie colony to avail themselves of the opportunity to improve their game by taking lessons from a champion, he helped Tilden during a very rough patch for the tennis champ.

I loved taking lessons from him, and it proved tremendously helpful when I played a tennis champion in *Strangers on a Train*, but I never really got to know him. Everything was strictly business on the tennis court, and after a lesson was over, Bill always left immediately.

Charlie's house was a lovely Spanish-style home in Beverly Hills above Sunset Boulevard. It was large, light, and airy, and beautifully furnished in a comfortable lived-in way. When you drove through the gates the first structure you arrived at was the tennis court. The house was above that. I do not remember a pool. Charlie was warm and open, and not only a world-class clown, but also a world-class intellect, which was quite an achievement in light of his growing up with his brother as hungry urchins in the streets of London. Charlie was married to his fourth wife, Oona, the daughter of America's greatest playwright, Eugene O'Neill. They had married in 1943 when she was eighteen and he was fifty-four, despite her father's objections. I have never met a happier couple. Oona was warm, gracious, and a perfect hostess. She made me feel completely at home and at ease. I liked her immediately.

Several years after this, I got a call from Jerry Robbins, who was coming to Los Angeles the following week to discuss re-creating his brilliant ballet, *The Small House of Uncle Thomas*, for 20th Century-Fox's film version of *The King and I.* The ballet was the highlight of the stage show and would be in the film as well. In it Jerry used traditional Siamese dance to portray an incident from

Harriet Beecher Stowe's ground-breaking novel, *Uncle Tom's Cabin*: Eliza's escape from Simon Legree over a partially frozen river.

I invited Jerry to stay, but he said he was getting the first-class treatment with a suite at the Hotel Bel-Air. I couldn't beat that, so I invited him to dinner and asked if there was anyone he would like to meet. Without a beat he said, "Yes. Charlie Chaplin. Do you know him?" I admitted that I'd gotten to know him slightly playing tennis at his house. Jerry jumped in before I could tell him about Big Bill and told me he could only be here for three days. He said he would call back later to check on which night I'd made the arrangements . . . and hung up. Not being the most experienced host in town, I needed a couple of minutes to screw up my courage to call the Chaplins. Oona answered. After beating around the bush for a couple of minutes I finally blurted out, "I'm having a small dinner party next Thursday and I was wondering if by any chance you and Charlie might happen to be free because a friend of mine . . ."

She interrupted me, "Farley, how nice, we'd love to come." Then she called out, "Charlie. . . . It's Farley Granger on the phone . . . He's inviting us for dinner next Thursday. . . . Good, that's what I said. . . . Farley, what time would you like us?"

It was that easy. Maybe it was too easy. I started to worry again. I called to invite Ethyl and Buddy, Arthur, and Millard and Lorry Kaufman. Millard was a screenwriter who was to write the classic *Bad Day at Black Rock*. His wife, Lorry, on whom I'd had a crush from the first moment I saw her, was a brilliant anthropologist. The group was set. Now I just had to plan everything. After probably my sixth call to Ethyl, she said, "Farfel, get a caterer and a bartender and stop driving us both crazy. OK?" I did. It worked.

Everyone was on time and, judging from the amount of chatter and laughter and cross-talk over drinks, getting along famously. Dinner was cold watercress soup, a superb rack of lamb with flageolets, and a Bibb lettuce with camembert salad, all served with a nice California red wine, and this was when everyone thought California wine came from someone's backyard in earthenware jugs. Dessert was a Grand Marnier soufflé. Everyone was impressed by "my" dinner, especially me.

After dinner, we went back to the living room for coffee, drinks, and games. Still working at being a good host, I suggested that we play The Game. Everyone got right into it, expecting wonderful things from Charlie. It took a while for it to dawn on all of us that ironically, for one of cinema's great silent film stars, he was really terrible at charades. Ethyl whispered, "Put on some music fast, this is getting really uncomfortable."

I interrupted to take coffee and after-dinner drink orders and put on a record. Everyone relaxed as the conversation got lively again. At one point late in the evening Charlie asked Jerry about a specific dance step. Jerry stood up to demonstrate and suddenly Chaplin was up and dancing with him. They danced together doing a variety of routines for a blissfully long time. Charlie was as quick and light on his feet as any professional. Being there was a rare treat for us all.

Disenchantment

Not too long after we finished *Rope,* the studio called to tell me that Cathy and I were going to be in Mr. Goldwyn's new film, *Enchantment,* along with Teresa Wright and David Niven. At last, I thought, the big project! We were all to report to the studio on the following Monday morning for a read-through of the script with the director, Irving Reis. The studio messengered a copy of the script to me to read over the weekend. It was not only bad, but my part was insignificant. By the time I got in my car to go to the studio on Monday, I had convinced myself that it would all work out. After all, the cast was terrific, and sometimes an inventive director could work wonders with inferior material. When I got to the rehearsal hall, no one was there except a production assistant, who told me that the rehearsal had been cancelled. When I asked him why, he said he didn't know. The studio would call me later.

Then Cathy ran in. Her face was ashen, and she had obviously been crying. She said, "Please, Farley, I've got to talk to you." I took her in my arms and said, "Sure, come on, let's go to my dressing room." As soon as the door was closed, Cathy started sobbing as if her heart would break. When she finally calmed down a bit, the story came out between great shuddering intakes of breath. Soon after *The Best Years of Our Lives,* William Wyler, who had directed the film, and most of the other movies responsible for the studio's classy reputation, promoted as "the Goldwyn Touch," left to form his own production company. Goldwyn, who wanted everyone who worked for him to treat him like a benevolent patriarch instead of the wily dictator he really was, took his departure as a personal betrayal and never forgave him. Wyler and Goldwyn went on to fight for years over Wyler's share of the profits from *The Best Years of Our Lives.*

The week before we were to begin work on *Enchantment,* Cathy had very privately and quietly married Wyler's brother, a man much older than she. Goldwyn did not hear about it until Monday morning just before we were to begin the rehearsal for *Enchantment.* He went ballistic. He called Cathy into his office and screamed at her that William Wyler had put his brother up to marrying her to get even with him. Cathy either would get the marriage annulled or she was fired, and he would see to it that she never worked in Hollywood again. She tried to reason with him, but he never stopped yelling, and finally told her to get out! She was "fired and finished in movies."

The next thing I knew, Evelyn Keyes, who had played Scarlett O'Hara's younger sister, was playing Cathy's part. Evelyn, who was about ten years older than Cathy, was a good actress and could not have been easier to work with, but she was in the middle of a stormy divorce from John Huston and was obviously not getting a lot of sleep at the time. She was not looking her best. They put a skinny mustache on me to make me look older. Instead, it made me look like a kid with a fake mustache.

Irving Reis was a far cry from the inventive director I'd imagined before rehearsal. He was no help at all. Even the considerable charms and talents of Teresa Wright and David Niven could not help. Nothing was going to make this turkey fly. "Just About the Most Wonderful Love Story Ever Made," as our ridiculous ad campaign trumpeted in all the publicity for *Enchantment,* was just about the year's biggest flop . . . so much for my first postwar movie at the Goldwyn Studio. Almost immediately after we completed filming, our cameraman, Gregg Toland, died. He had done most of Wyler's great films for Goldwyn as well as *Citizen Kane* for Orson Welles. He had worked for Goldwyn for many years and had perfected the technique of deep focus, which allowed the director to keep an actor in the background as well as the actor in the foreground in sharp focus. If Wyler's departure signaled the beginning of the end of "the Goldwyn touch," Toland's death was certainly another nail in its coffin.

Shelley

I can't even remember when or where we first met, but as long as I'd known her, Shelley Winters was important to me. She has been the love of my life and the bane of my existence. We have laughed and cried together and fallen into each other's arms. We have fought and not spoken for years. We have been friends, there for each other through the worst of all possible disasters and the best of all possible triumphs. You name it, we've been it . . . sometimes exhilarating, sometimes depressing, always surprising . . . I wouldn't have had it any other way.

Preston Sturges, the brilliant director of screwball comedies like *The Lady Eve* and *The Palm Beach Story,* owned a restaurant on the Sunset Strip called The Players. It served the best Caesar salad I have ever had. I liked his restaurant so much that I went whenever possible. Sturges was there every evening. One night with Ethyl, Saul, and Arthur, I spotted Shelley Winters, alone and crying, in a booth nearby. I had met Shelley several times and thought she was smart, sweet, and a little zany. I went over to ask her what was wrong. She told me that she hated the movie that they were making her do at Universal. She was having awful problems with the producer. And it was her birthday, and she was all alone, and nobody loved her. It only took a minute to talk her into joining us. After introductions all around, we sat down and she launched into her litany of woes again for the whole table.

I excused myself, found Preston Sturges, and asked him if he could have a lit candle in a cupcake brought to our table by a couple of waiters who could sing "Happy Birthday" to Shelley. He was delighted to help and said, "Just give me a few minutes; I'll take care of everything." I thanked him and headed back to our table, where things were looking up. Shelley had stopped crying and was the center of attention. Soon the waiters arrived, not only with the cupcake and the song, but also with a bottle of fine Champagne, "Compliments of Mr. Sturges."

Shelley blew out her candle as we all sang "Happy Birthday." As they were pouring the champagne, she burst into tears all over again and began wailing that nobody loved her. Ethyl took her hand and said, "Cheer up, Shelley. We all love you." The real Shelley surfaced and replied, "Yes, I know, but you're not producers."

My dating Shelley did not make Mr. Goldwyn happy. He wanted me to be seen in public with someone squeaky-clean like Ann Blyth, who in real life was the exact opposite of the bad girl she played in *Mildred Pierce*. Ann was quiet and serious, a very nice girl . . . with no sense of humor. She was lovely and proper and no fun. Shelley was totally unpredictable, a wise-cracking blonde who loved the spotlight. I was uncomfortable being a celebrity, but she loved being one. Faced with screaming fans at premieres, Shelley blossomed, while I turned to stone. She always had a crack or a quip ready for the press. I always mumbled incoherently. In a way, her public persona made it very hard for her to be taken seriously as an actress. I constantly tried to get her to calm down but soon realized that was impossible. Her pizzazz was one of the things that made her so attractive, and she did have a sense of humor, and we did have fun. What a paradox she was, though. She didn't smoke, she kept her drinks to a minimum, she never swore, and she didn't like it when I did. A blond bombshell in public, she was Miss Priss in private. She could be hell on wheels when she was being serious about acting. We never stopped talking and arguing about acting, or bitching about what we had to deal with as contract players.

Shelley had been involved in politics since she worked at a five-and-dime as a teen and became a union organizer. She was much more politically aware than I was, and she never stopped working to enlighten me. As everyone stood around the piano singing Rodgers and Hart or Cole Porter at the Kellys' she would be under it waiting for her chance to belt out a few old union songs. She was an original. We were a classic example of opposites who definitely attract. Shortly after I met Shelley, I ended the relationship with Arthur. I tried to make it amicable since we had so many good friends in common. Shelley knew all about him. We had no secrets from each other.

Shooting *Roseanna*

Through a writer friend who knew John Collier, I got a copy of an early draft of a screenplay that Collier was working on for Mr. Goldwyn. The script, as yet untitled, was based on a novel by Alberta Hannum about two feuding mountain clans, the Hatfields and the McCoys. Goldwyn had originally commissioned it as a vehicle for Cathy and me. It was Romeo and Juliet as southern hill folk, and it was flat-out wonderful. Collier, best known as a writer of fantasy fiction, was an inspired choice. He had enriched the tale with undercurrents of superstition and witchcraft. He set most of the tale at night, with coyotes howling in the hills and owls capturing helpless creatures by shadowy moonlight. I loved it and could not wait for work to begin. I was hurt by what Goldwyn had done to Cathy, and deeply disappointed that I'd be doing the movie without her. She would have made an enchanting Juliet.

The studio called to tell me not to leave town. A new film that I was to star in was about to go into production very soon. I innocently asked what it was, and was told the title, *Roseanna McCoy*. That is all anyone would tell me about the film. I asked who was playing Roseanna; no one knew. I asked who the director was; no one knew. They did tell me that the rest of the cast was terrific and included Richard Basehart, Charles Bickford, Raymond Massey, Aline MacMahon, and Hope Emerson. That was an impressive group of actors. With Collier's script and the right girl, I felt this could be a very special movie. Under threat of death if she blabbed to anyone, Shelley had wormed the information about *Roseanna McCoy* out of me. She was really happy for me even though her way of showing it consisted of constant moaning that she was destined to be cast in *Frenchie* parts, hookers with gumption and a heart of gold parts, for the rest of her life. As soon as I got the official call to report to the studio for work, I took her to Chasen's, the best restaurant in town, to celebrate.

The reality that hit like a sledgehammer on the following Monday is still hard to talk about. I walked into the studio where we all were to meet. The first person to greet me was Irving Reis, the highly neurotic and lackluster director of *Enchantment.* He introduced me to a kid named Joan Evans. She was the girl Goldwyn had picked as his new ingénue after a national talent search. Her first effort was to be replacing Cathy. She was a sweet, pretty fifteen-year-old who still had some baby fat, but no meaningful acting experience. I think her parents were Hollywood writers, and she was Joan Crawford's goddaughter. When I met her again, many years later, she admitted that she was really only fourteen when she started on the film. Perhaps that has something to do with the complete lack of sexual tension between our Romeo and Juliet. Her parents had added two years to her age in order to be able to say she was sixteen when the film was released. Unfortunately, a star was not born.

I was busy introducing myself to the other actors when the assistant director started rounding us up. The bus was there to take us to a train to the small town up in the Sierra Madre where we were to begin shooting the next day. The seasoned pros soon started to ask questions about the script, like where was it? We were told that the director was going to take care of that on the train. Irving, who had been driven to the station by one of Goldwyn's vice presidents, was the last one to hop onboard just as the train was pulling out. Once we were smoothly under way, the actors, who by now sensed that something was up, pinned him down and demanded some answers. He told us that Mr. Goldwyn had not been happy with the script and had thrown the whole thing out. He assured us that rewrites were already under way, and we could expect the first of them tomorrow after he had done some establishing shots. Irving's ability to lie convincingly was pretty much on a par with his ability to direct imaginatively. No one believed him. The empty feeling in the pit of my stomach spread. I could not tell anyone that I had read a bootlegged copy of the script, that it was wonderful, and that it had probably been thrown out because Goldwyn didn't understand it. I wondered if anyone else had seen it, but no one said a word.

The mountains were very beautiful. The town consisted of a hotel glued onto a small movie house, a post office, a bar, and a drugstore/general store/gas station. There were some wonderful ramshackle houses, and two sets built on opposite mountain ridges outside of town as the homes of the Hatfields and the McCoys, We all stayed in that one hotel. The rooms were clean and claustrophobic. We all ate at that one hotel. The food was all fried all the time. Everyone kept very much to him or herself. No friendships were forged, no sense of camaraderie surfaced at any time during the lengthy shoot of a film that should have been wonderful.

The entire first day was spent by the director and crew shooting establishing shots of the clan's two homes and the surrounding countryside. No pages arrived from the studio. The next day was a repeat of the first. For the next two weeks, we still had no script. Irving did all he could. He shot people standing outside the houses, entering the houses, and exiting the houses—the interiors were back at the studio. He shot me on a horse going from camera left to camera right, from camera right to camera left, up the hill, down the hill, on the ridge in the distance, on the ridge nearby, mounting the horse, dismounting the horse, with Joan on the horse with me, at a walk, at a canter, at a gallop, and just about anything you could imagine doing with a horse. Then he shot me walking with Joan, holding hands with Joan, chasing Joan through a field, and so on. This went on for two weeks and still no pages arrived from the studio. We were all beginning to feel a little crazed. Even the poor director was looking crazed. Suddenly we packed everything up and went back to Hollywood, where we were laid off for a week.

After our week of R&R, we reported to the studio anxious to get this impending disaster over with. Goldwyn had hired a writer named Phil Yordan to fix the script. Phil, who would not be miscast on *The Sopranos,* was a very funny man who had written some good screenplays. He had a reputation as the speediest script doctor in Hollywood. The rumor was that he had rotating platoons of writing students from UCLA chained to typewriters in his basement.

As the pages dribbled in, we went to work on the soundstage. The art department had built, along with the interiors, woods, creeks, and bridges to replicate the High Sierras. On some days we got a whole scene to shoot, on others we just got a page or two. Other times we would get different pages of the same scene. It was all very confusing. It's a testimonial to the professionalism of the cast that everyone worked hard and stayed cool. Joan and I had a scene riding together on a horse through the woods in which I was to sing a lovely song to her that Frank Loesser had written called "More I Cannot Wish You." This melody was intended to underscore all our scenes. Goldwyn hated it. He threw it out as soon as he heard it and had Loesser write a banal title song, "Roseanna."

Goldwyn took to appearing on the set every day. Someone always called down to warn the crew that he was coming. By the time he arrived, everyone would be extremely busy. When he was angry, which was often, his voice got even higher. This anger was usually directed at the director, whose tics just got worse. It took almost two chaotic months to finish this section of the filming. Then we were all laid off again.

It was several weeks before everyone was called and told that we were going back to the location in order to shoot some new scenes. Irving Reis was gone. When we got to the location, the first person I saw was Nick Ray. No one was ever told the why or wherefore of Irving's departure. When I saw Nick, I had a momentary surge of hope, but then I realized that it was too late for him to make any significant improvement. Nick must have realized it, too, because after a warm hello, he refused to talk about *Roseanna.* That night it started raining, and it did not stop for two weeks. Every morning at 4:00 A.M. we got up, got into makeup and costume, and drove up to the location. There we sat in our cars all day, waiting for the rain to stop. Then, every afternoon at 5:00 P.M., the cars would turn around and take us back to the hotel for a fried dinner.

Doris Day, one of the outstanding band singers of the war years, became a movie star in 1948. Her first film, *Romance on the High Seas,* was the beginning of a film career that flourished into the mid-1960s when she went on to become an equally big TV star. Miss Day has never had a bigger fan than me. I love her singing, her acting, her looks, her animal rights activism, and just about everything about her. For those two weeks in the mountains Doris Day drove me crazy. The little hotel we were in was attached to the movie theater in town, and my room had to be adjacent to the part of the movie house where the speakers were placed. Miss Day's first movie was playing. If I never hear the words "It's Magic" sung again, it will be way too soon. Believe me, it quickly ceased being magic to me. By the end of the first week, the crew and a few of the actors—to this day I don't know why, as I wasn't one of them—succumbed to cabin fever and began drinking, gambling, and fighting the nights away. Finally, we were called back to Hollywood to wait for the rain to stop. In a week it did, and we were hustled back up into the mountains. We began work the next morning.

The first setup we had to do was Roseanna and I walking along a mountain path on a steep slope. Suddenly her brother, my sworn enemy, played by Richard Basehart, appears on a ridge across from and slightly above us and takes a shot at me. For protection, I pull her down behind some bushes along the path. While he is reloading, I stand up to shoot back at him. Nick had us rehearse the scene with no blanks in the guns and was very happy with the way it went. So we loaded the guns and got ready to do the take. When Nick called "Action!" Richard fired at me, and I pulled Roseanna down behind the bushes. As I stood to shoot at Richard, the ground, which had absorbed weeks of rain, gave way under my feet. I slid downhill, falling flat on my face. At the same instant, there was an ear-splitting bang in my right ear. After a second or so, when I was able to look up, I was horrified. Joan was squirming in the grass like a snake, covered in blood, her hands over her face. She must have been screaming, but I couldn't hear anything. It was a terrible slow-motion moment during which I thought, "Oh my God, I've shot Roseanna!"

I'm sure it was only minutes, but it seemed like hours before we sorted out what had happened. The blank charge had only hit Joan in the wrist, thank God. The range was not close enough for any permanent damage, but it was close enough to penetrate her skin and cause a lot of bleeding. She was justifiably hysterical and needed to be taken to a hospital. We wrapped in the mountains and went back to Hollywood.

On the train back, one wag accused me of doing it on purpose to get us all out of the mountains. Another one said, "We don't know how we'll ever be able to repay you." Nick did his best to improve the quality of what was left of *Roseanna McCoy,* but too much damage had already been done. At least John Collier, Frank Loesser, and I knew what might have been. I wish Mr. Goldwyn did.

Solo

During one of the endless days waiting for the rain to stop layoffs that I had while making *Roseanna,* I got home unexpectedly early one afternoon and walked in on Arthur being a little bit too friendly with a delivery boy. I turned around, walked out, and found my first apartment. I was twenty-four and more than ready. It was in a small complex owned by the actor/designer/director Mitch Leisen. If I remember correctly, there were three separate buildings in a beautifully landscaped compound. Each building had four apartments. I lived over Mitch Leisen, and a nice middle-aged couple lived next door to me. We shared a terrace that was separated by a wrought-iron fence. Mitch directed a number of reliably good films in the 1930s and 1940s: *To Each His Own, Hold Back the Dawn,* and *Frenchman's Creek* are just three of many. He had begun his career as a costume designer and art director for Cecil B. De Mille. Needless to say, he had superb taste. All the apartments were decorated with antiques, gorgeous carpeting, and great paintings. I rented mine when I was still traveling back and forth to the High Sierra location, so I did not spend much time there. As soon as we finished the film, I got a dog, a great poodle mutt whom I named Gaby after the sailor in *Fancy Free,* and settled in.

Evelyn Keyes and Paulette Goddard shared an apartment identical to the one I had in one of the other buildings. They had me over for a welcome dinner soon after I arrived. Evelyn was over the trauma of her divorce from John Huston and looking terrific. Paulette was an irrepressibly delightful dame who as a young starlet had become Charlie Chaplin's third wife and starred in his films *Modern Times* and *The Great Dictator.* I had a great time with them at dinner and for the short time we were neighbors.

My tenure as a tenant was not destined to last. Neither, for that matter, was Evelyn's or Paulette's. In fact, they were the first to go. John Huston, in an effort to remain on good terms with Evelyn, returned from a safari in Africa with a present for her. It was an adorable adolescent chimpanzee. She loved it . . . for about forty-eight hours. Then the chimp had a tantrum, and it does not take too much imagination to guess what literally hit the fan. He wrecked their apartment and its antiques. I could hear the shouts and screams and chimpanzee sounds all the way over at my place. Mitch threw them all out the next morning.

It took another couple of weeks before he got to me. I really loved my dog, Gaby. I thought he was the smartest and best dog in the world. I was surprised every day by what great bowel and bladder control he had. After a long day at the studio or an afternoon of tennis lessons up at Charlie Chaplin's house, I would get home afraid of what I'd find because his morning walk had been so long ago. He never had an accident in the apartment. I was so proud. Then Mitch informed me that my neighbors had complained about me. They had been away in Mexico for a month and had returned late the previous night. When they opened the doors to their terrace they were greeted by mountains of dog doo, and plants that were yellowed and dead from dog pee. Gaby, in order not to soil his own nest, had obviously wriggled his way through the wrought-iron balcony divider and taken care of his needs next door. I think it was the fact that I was so proud of Gaby's smarts that upset Mitch the most. At least he gave me to the end of the week to clear out. Actually, I was not too upset. Mitch and his boyfriend, who lived directly below me, had all-too-frequent fights. The screaming, accompanied by smashing plates and slamming doors, was as loud as Evelyn's chimp. Also, I had never been completely comfortable in these chic surroundings.

The next day I found an apartment below the Sunset Strip in a complex that surrounded a swimming pool and was reassuringly ordinary. While I was packing the following evening, my doorbell rang. It was Arthur. He had heard what had happened from Ethyl, and had come to ask me to move back in with him. It wasn't until that moment that I fully realized how happy I was to be solo, completely on my own. I told him that and said that although I always would care for him, I had no desire to attempt to recapture something that was over.

Lenny

No sooner had I settled into my new digs when the studio called to say that Goldwyn had loaned me out to MGM for a film called *Side Street.* When I learned the particulars of the film, I was not unhappy to do it even though the script was ordinary and predictable. A big plus was that Cathy O'Donnell was to be my co-star. Louis B. Mayer, most likely in a move calculated to annoy

Goldwyn, had put her under contract shortly after Goldwyn fired her. The director, Anthony Mann, whose other films include *Winchester '73, Bend of the River,* and *The Far Country,* all with Jimmy Stewart, planned to shoot much of the film on location in New York. Location shooting was becoming more common even if it was more expensive. The post–World War II audience no longer accepted painted backdrops and studio streets as reality. Shortly before I heard about being loaned out, I'd found out that Shelley was having an affair with the very married Burt Lancaster while we were still together. The blowup that followed that discovery made New York seem even more attractive. I boarded Gaby with my parents, and left for New York ten days before we were scheduled to begin shooting there.

The Essex House was booked, but they arranged accommodations for me at the Plaza. I had a beautiful corner room that looked out on the park and east across Fifth Avenue into the sunrise. I felt as if I'd come home and slept better than I had since the last time I was in the city. After breakfast and a shower the next morning, I called Adolph Green to tell him I would be in town for almost a month doing a film for Metro. He said not to make any plans for that evening, because he had tickets to see Lenny Bernstein conduct the New York Philharmonic in an all-Stravinsky program. He had an extra ticket and was sure Lenny would love to see me.

I had gotten to know Leonard Bernstein at Ethyl and Saul's house in Hollywood. He was as attractive as he was articulate and passionate about music. He had expanded my favorite ballet, *Fancy Free,* into one of my favorite Broadway musicals, *On the Town.* At MGM, Arthur Freed had adapted the Broadway show into a hit movie musical of the same name, starring Gene Kelly, Frank Sinatra, Betty Garrett, Vera-Ellen, and Ann Miller, but he had inexplicably thrown out almost all of Bernstein's songs. The opening number, "New York, New York" survived Freed's error in judgment and is probably the one song that everyone remembers from the movie. Frank Sinatra was angry when he discovered that the lovely ballad "Lonely Town" had been cut, and Gene was equally upset to lose "Some Other Time." The experience had made Lenny wary of Hollywood. He protected himself much more successfully when they made the TV movie of *Wonderful Town* a few years later.

Lenny had recently been appointed assistant conductor for the New York Philharmonic. It was obvious from the way the musicians reacted to his conducting during the concert that they loved him almost as much as the audience did. When it was over, we went back to his dressing room, which was crowded with fans and well-wishers. Lenny spent time with each and every one of them, clearly enjoying himself. It seemed like hours before he was able to close the door on the last of his fans and get ready to go out with us.

Still high on the energy of the concert, we went to a tavern around the corner to eat, drink, and catch up on one another's lives for the next two hours. Adolph was the first to fade. He had to get home in time to see Allyn Ann, who was in previews with Irving Berlin's new musical, *Miss Liberty*. I was the next one to lose steam. I wasn't on New York time yet. Lenny, I'm sure, could have partied all night, but he took sympathy on me. We got a cab, and he dropped me off at the Plaza with a promise to call soon.

I got another perfect night of dreamless sleep and woke up early to a beautiful sunny day. The phone rang at 9:00 A.M. It was Lenny. He was driving up along the Hudson River to meet a young violinist. It was a beautiful day. Would I like to join him? It sounded like a great idea. We agreed that he would pick me up at 10:30.

As we crossed the George Washington Bridge, I was impressed by the beauty and size of the Hudson River. I had the same reaction to the lush greenery along the Palisades Parkway. Sure, Hawaii had plenty of lush, verdant vistas, but that was the tropics. This was only thirty minutes from Broadway. After another thirty minutes or so, we passed a sign that said Sneden's Landing and turned off the highway. We were on a road that ran along the top of a ridge that looked down to the river. We turned into a tree-lined driveway that went halfway down the hill to a big old shingled house in a grove of trees, surrounded by a green lawn that sloped past the house down to the river. We walked up to the front door. Lenny rang the doorbell. When the door opened, there stood Aaron Copland. I hadn't seen Aaron since our dinner at Jimmy Wong Howe's restaurant in Los Angeles just after I got out of the Navy two years earlier. He was grinning from ear to ear. Lenny had set the whole lunch up as a surprise for me.

Lunch on a flagstone patio overlooking the river was wonderful. I remember cold gazpacho, cold chicken, hot new potato salad, gorgonzola, and pears, all washed down with cool white Bordeaux. It was superb. After some great conversation and strong espresso, we went in to the sunroom, where Aaron and Lenny sat down at twin grand pianos and played nonstop selections from Haydn to Prokofiev. They played and stopped to discuss and replay passages and made musical puns as they played and joked—it was exhilarating. Time flew. What I've never forgotten about watching them was how happy they were just to be playing together. I didn't have to understand what was happening musically, because their joy was contagious. Years later, I watched a late-night television show about Yo-Yo Ma teaching at Tanglewood. The same joy passed between him and his students when they communicated musically and between him and the wonderful classical pianist Emmanuel Ax during their duets. After I die, if I have the choice of what to be in my next reincarnation, it will be a musician of that caliber. Before any of us realized it, it was almost 5:00 P.M. Lenny had a concert that evening and we had to leave.

In the late 1950s, I had another musical experience with Lenny and Aaron. At Tanglewood, Lenny was conducting a performance of Aaron's *Appalachian Spring* with the New York Philharmonic. Aaron and I were sitting together in the back of the tent, and he whispered a running commentary on tempi and interpretation throughout the piece. His remarks were basic enough for me to understand and not *too* bitchy. It was the best time I've ever had at a concert.

Lenny knew I was going to the theater that evening. He asked if I would meet him later at his place for a midnight supper. I did, and it could not have seemed more right when he asked me to stay. I did. We had a couple of glorious days and nights together. He was as passionate and enthusiastic a lover as he was a conductor. Then real life intruded. I started work on *Side Street.* That meant that I was up at six A.M. and worked all day, and Leonard was rehearsing in the afternoons and conducting every evening. Carving out time to be together became more complicated, but we managed. It was very easy to be completely caught up with Leonard Bernstein. Charisma was not a word in vogue at that time, but it could have been coined for Lenny.

One night during my second week of filming, Lenny surprised me with a ticket to accompany him on his South American tour, which was to begin at the end of the month. He also told me that he had decided to put his engagement to Felicia Montealegre, the Chilean pianist and actress, on hold. Both pieces of information came as a complete surprise to me. Nothing about any engagement had ever been mentioned, nor had we ever discussed our relationship as lasting beyond the present while I was working in New York. We had never been clandestine about being together. I'd assumed that Lenny and I were living completely in the now without a worry about the future.

I tried to explain why I couldn't go with him to South America—my film, which was not finished, my contract to Goldwyn, which was far from finished. . . .

"Don't you want to come? It will be terribly exciting. Think of all the beautiful places we can visit together, all the new people we will meet. We'll be the toast of South America."

"But, Lenny, it's just not possible. I have a contract, and I'm in the middle of a film. It would be like you walking out on the New York Philharmonic in the middle of a concert."

A man of his talent and powers of persuasion didn't get where he was by ever accepting "It's just not possible" as an answer. He got there by refusing to accept the impossible, but he eventually agreed that he had been hoping to postpone the inevitable.

I returned to Hollywood to finish the film at MGM, and Lenny left for South America. Shortly after his tour ended, he and Felicia were married. Our paths continued to cross for a number of years, and those occasions were always warm and affectionate. Our moment in time is one that will always stay with me..

Shooting so much of *Side Street* on location in New York was a good experience. Tony Mann knew how to take full advantage of the city as part of the texture of the film. Hollywood was just beginning to break loose from the shackles of the soundstages, and there were not many directors who had mastered this new technique. For its time, *Side Street* was a good-looking, well-made film that was not able to rise above the banality of its story. Cathy, still affected by what Goldwyn had done to her, was very subdued. She and her husband spent all of her off-screen time keeping very much to themselves.

The movie introduced a young theater actress who had been Judy Holliday's understudy in *Born Yesterday,* Jean Hagen. Jean and I became pals. She went on to give a wickedly funny performance as Lina Lamont, the silent screen vamp, in *Singin' in the Rain.* Aside from that musical, and her performance in *The Asphalt Jungle,* Hollywood didn't really know how to take advantage of this unique comedienne's talent any more than they knew how to use the gifted Judy Holliday other than in the film versions of her Broadway shows. Ironically, both actresses died young after cancer had curtailed their promising careers.

MGM

We finished the interiors of *Side Street* at MGM. Louis B. Mayer always claimed to have "more stars than there are in the heavens," and damned if his claim didn't seem true at lunch in the commissary. Everyone was there, from Clark Gable and Greer Garson to Ginger Rogers and Fred Astaire. I had matured some during my four years in the Navy, but I was still able to feel starstruck. Metro was the biggest and most glamorous lot in Hollywood. I loved just wandering around the other soundstages whenever I wasn't being used on the set of *Side Street.*

One morning on a break, I headed over to the Arthur Freed musical unit, where I knew so many of the people from parties at Gene Kelly's house. They had recently started production on *Annie Get Your Gun* starring Judy Garland and Howard Keel, directed by Busby Berkeley. I'd heard that they had been having some problems with Judy, and I wanted to see how she was. There were a lot of people in costume hanging around, but nothing was happening. I spotted Keenan Wynn and went over to ask him if Judy was working that day. Keenan, the son of the famous vaudeville and Broadway comic headliner Ed Wynn, was one of Hollywood's most versatile character actors of the 1940s, 1950s, and 1960s. Things were not going well. Judy had not shown up on the set yet, which had been happening a lot lately. The whole company was just waiting around for her, and Busby Berkeley, not a patient man, was steaming. Trouble was brewing. I had to get back to my set, so I asked him to hug Judy for me. I'd come back later when I had another break.

As I was leaving, I ran into Judy on her way to the set. She looked beautiful, and slimmer than I had ever seen her. She was dressed in white buckskins. With her long ponytail, she reminded me of a high-strung young colt. We hugged, and I asked how everything was going. She grabbed my hand and looked at me with panic in those huge brown eyes: "Everything is wonderful, just wonderful! Why shouldn't it be? I'm on my own set with all my own people, and they all love me, Everything is wonderful."

As she was saying this, she gripped my hand so tightly that her nails dug into my palm. An assistant came over to say that they were ready to shoot and needed her at once on set. I promised to come back to see her after I finished my scene. It was almost three hours before I was able to get back. When I arrived, the lights were off and the set was deserted. I finally found a guard who told me that Miss Garland had had a complete breakdown. "They" had taken her away and the movie was closed down.

Louis B. Mayer's next move was to offer the part to Betty Garrett, who, after *Neptune's Daughter, Take Me Out to the Ball Game,* and *On the Town,* was a rising star in the musical unit at Metro. Betty's manager, obviously thinking he had Mayer in a corner, demanded more money for her to step into the part, a mistake that was as stupid as it was big. Louis B. fired her instead, and borrowed Betty Hutton from Paramount. The terrible irony of that manager's mistake was that not only would *Annie Get Your Gun* have made a big star of Betty Garrett, it might have saved her husband's career as well. Larry Parks of *The Jolson Story* fame was making a movie at Metro with Elizabeth Taylor at approximately the same time as *Annie Get Your Gun* was released. He was subpoenaed by HUAC. Even though he named names, his career was finished. If his wife had been in Metro's big musical of the year, the studio would have gone to any lengths to quash that subpoena, and two careers would most likely have been saved.

The tense and frightened young woman who made my hand bleed that morning was a different person from the Judy Garland I knew who loved to laugh. It was as if the inner fears we all have about life and work had overtaken the real person. The uppers and downers and diet pills the studio had kept her on for years didn't help. The job of maintaining or living up to her MGM star image must have become overwhelming. Walking back to the soundstage where *Side Street* was being shot, I grimly resolved never to let Goldwyn or the system do that to me.

Many years later, in the mid-1970s, while working on a totally forgettable TV movie at Metro, I wandered through the back lot one afternoon remembering the New York streets, Welsh mining towns, Western towns, and various rural areas that had been the backdrops for so many terrific films. It was now a wasteland. I headed for some treetops I saw in the distance and came upon a perfectly preserved block of Victorian houses. I stopped, enchanted, in front of a familiar one. The lawn was lush and verdant; the flowers and shrubs were in bloom and perfectly manicured. With a sudden pang I remembered it as the house from *Meet Me in St. Louis,* arguably Judy Garland's greatest film.

Changes

As soon as we finished *Side Street* at MGM I decided it was time to find a nice place to live. Everyone I cared about seemed to be going through difficult times. Ethyl had met someone who was devoted to her. George (Buddy) Tyne was a loveable bear of a man and a good character actor. He worshiped her, which was exactly what Ethyl needed, and eventually even Saul accepted that. But getting there was not easy. It was messy and painful for all concerned, particularly for their daughter, Judy, who although wise beyond her years was still an adolescent. This time must have been hell for her. Meanwhile Shelley, still depressed over Burt Lancaster and also upset at the choices Universal was offering her, was not exactly good company.

I found a terrific house to rent high above the Sunset Strip. It sat on a point of land from which I had a panoramic view from the ocean to downtown L.A. The pool extended out on the point, and the house sat behind the pool. I could jump into the pool from the deck outside my bedroom on the second floor. I reclaimed my dog Gaby from my parents and moved into my first house. Every morning I would whip open the drapes that covered the sliding doors to my bedroom and walk out on the deck to greet the day. It was a new feeling for me to be in charge of my own domain. I could play music as late and as loud as I wanted to and pick out my own sheets and furniture. I really loved the feeling of having my own domain.

One morning, standing on my deck, I couldn't help noticing that the TV antennas were proliferating. It was obvious that this new form of entertainment could no longer be shrugged off as a passing fancy. It was here to stay and needed to be recognized and dealt with as a major challenge to the film industry. Another thing that caught my attention was a line in the sky that looked almost painted in. It extended as far as the eye could see from the Pacific to downtown L.A. Above it the sky was its usual beautiful clear blue; below it everything was a little hazy. As the months went by, the line got higher and less distinct, and below it the haze got thicker and more impenetrable. Smog, never heard of in California, oozed its way into being a Los Angeles fact of life.

Two Turkeys

In 1949 I did two more films for Goldwyn, who along with the rest of Hollywood was finally waking up to realize that the growing threat called television should be taken seriously. Confusion over what to do about it was the problem. Goldwyn decided to make *Our Very Own,* a film that ironically would lead the way for television sitcoms of the future like *Father Knows Best* and *The Donna Reed Show.* It was an attempt to return to the simple family values portrayed by the Andy Hardy series at MGM ten years earlier. I was the boy next door to Ann Blyth's pretty, perky teenager. Unfortunately, nothing about our charmless effort lived up to the joyful innocence of the Hardy films. The script by F. Hugh Herbert was pointless and meandering. After reading it, I referred to him as F. U. Herbert, to the delight of all the other actors except Ann, who had a gaggle of nuns on the set almost daily. My part was amorphous and Ann was as sweet as an overdose of saccharine. The director, David Miller, a perfectly nice man, was no help to anybody. Struggling through *Our Very Own* and *Edge of Doom,* my next film for Goldwyn, made it apparent to me how little I knew about acting. With good material and a good director I could relax and just let the performance happen. With bad-to-ordinary material and inadequate-to-unimaginative direction, I hadn't yet developed the resources to solve those problems on my own.

Frances Takes a Turn

My next film was Mrs. Goldwyn's idea. I read in Louella Parsons's column one sunny morning that "Frances Goldwyn has purchased the rights to a new book, *Edge of Doom,* for the studio's rising young star, Farley Granger." I had always felt that as the only young man under contract to Goldwyn I suffered from his inability to develop the right kind of material to build a young man's career. That is why the only good films I made while under contract were done at other studios on loanout.

Once again excited, I raced out to the closest bookstore to buy the book. It was a slight book, and I got through it quickly. The story was about a young man who, when denied what he thinks is a proper funeral for his mother by a mean older parish priest, picks up a crucifix from the priest's desk and clubs him to death with it. A sympathetic younger priest, played in the film by Dana Andrews, manipulates me into admitting my crime . . . THE END. The book had a little more to it than that, but not much. Even taking her well-known Catholicism into consideration, I couldn't understand why Frances Goldwyn had been so eager to buy the book any more than I could understand how it could be translated into a film.

Obviously, neither could Phil Yordan, the same writer whom Goldwyn had hired to remove all the magic from the original script of *Roseanna McCoy*. The script was barely coherent. Yordan managed to reduce what little substance there was in the book to what Walter Winchell later described as "raw meat." Our director, Mark Robson, a talented man, had directed the movie *Champion* and made a star of Kirk Douglas. But as the saying goes, "You can't breathe life into a stiff."

At the sneak previews in California, the audiences responded as negatively as I had. Mark edited and reedited for months, to no avail. Goldwyn decided my character needed a love interest. Even though young Joan Evans was already in the film, he hired another ingénue of the moment, Mala Powers, to play my girlfriend. Several scenes were added for us, but they came across as what they were—unnecessary afterthoughts that had nothing to do with advancing the plot. After the film opened in New York, the critics gave it the same kind of beating that I had given the priest. In a practically unprecedented move, Goldwyn pulled the film out of distribution and hired Charles Brackett and Ben Hecht to come up with a way to save it. No matter what was done to it, it remained a stiff. It was another bad experience for me. Instead of it being the big project, I felt that with *Edge of Doom* I had exceeded the three-strike limit. It was time for a meaningful change.

Out of America by 1950

George Coulouris, who had played the lawyer in *Citizen Kane,* was a balding character actor of British/Greek parentage who generally played menacing characters, superbly. In life, he was the quintessential curmudgeon, and my hero. Whenever he railed about someone we both knew, whom I would unfailingly try to defend by saying, "Come on, George, he's not that bad. He's nice," George would look up to heaven, pull at his remaining hair, and rant, "Nice . . . nice . . . What is nice!?" Then he would fix me with a piercing gaze and say, "You have to hate to be really alive!"

Of course, this was all an act . . . which I fell for every time. Despite his ferocity, George was shy and actually kind. Whenever his dramatic moments got too over the top, such as erupting at dinner when one of his children, who were then one and three years old, interrupted him—"Will I ever be free from the tyranny of children!"—Louise, his ever-patient wife, would just shake her head, sigh, and murmur, "Oh George . . ."

Trained on the British stage, his movie career took off after *Citizen Kane* and *Watch on the Rhine.* We became friends when he was working in Saul Chaplin's Broadway musical, *Bonanza Bound.* George's rallying cry, which tickled all his friends, was "Out of America by 1950!" We all knew that George was eccentric. We never knew he was prescient.

1950

Hand in hand with the arrival of smog and the sprouting of TV aerials came the Internal Security Act of 1950. I will leave it up to you to draw any parallels you choose with the Patriot Act of 2003. I happen to agree with one of our country's founding fathers, Benjamin Franklin, who said, "They that can give up essential liberty to obtain temporary safety deserve neither liberty nor safety."

Hollywood was shaken to its core by the blacklist. It affected almost everyone I knew and cared about. While I had been struggling through my D-quality double-header for Goldwyn, many of my dearest friends had been engaged in a different and much more deadly struggle. Senator Joe McCarthy had successfully used the Cold War to make a name for himself by whipping up fear and hysteria across the country and in Congress. The activities of the House Committee on Un-American Activities, dubbed HUAC, spawned the blacklist in the entertainment industry. It was particularly virulent in Hollywood and killed the careers of many innocent people by branding any support for antifascist activities during the Spanish Civil War in the late 1930s or any exploration of a postrevolutionary Communist ideal as treason. Despite the fact that Stalin was a despot and a monster, Russia's importance to us as an ally in World War II, fighting Hitler, seemed to slip the minds of the ambitious senator from Wisconsin and his allies in the halls of Congress. Hollywood was in turmoil and split down the middle. Ten of the foremost writers, producers, and directors in the film industry were summoned to Washington to appear before HUAC. They became known as "The Hollywood Ten." Rather than name names of others who might have been involved in various left-of-center fringe groups in their youth, they went to jail. They were also called "The Unfriendly Ten." Probably the best known of them were Dalton Trumbo and Ring Lardner Jr.

Most of Hollywood's known names, predominantly actors, directors, and producers, were friendly witnesses, also known as volunteers of information. Samuel Goldwyn was one of more than forty influential people from Hollywood subpoenaed to appear before the committee. Fed up after waiting to be called for over a month, Goldwyn finally released his statement to the press. It included the sentence, "The most un-American activity which I have observed with the hearings has been the activity of the Committee itself." I was proud of him.

Shelley and I had become close again, despite or perhaps because of a traumatic evening during which Burt Lancaster and I both came to her rescue when she had too much to drink and inadvertently almost overdosed on her mounting supply of medications. Several weeks after that evening, we went to a major fundraiser for the Hollywood Ten. That same evening we had a dinner date with Janet Leigh and my friend Arthur Loew, son of Marcus Loew, owner of Loew's Inc., the parent company of MGM and the Goldwyn Company. We first went to the fundraiser, which was held at Gene Kelly's house. Everyone in Hollywood who was not an extreme conservative was there. One impassioned speaker was a skinny young writer whom we both knew and liked, Norman Mailer. Norman was politically savvier than we were. Unbeknownst to us, he probably saved Shelley and me from bringing our careers to an early end. The writer of *The Naked and the Dead* was hoping to have many of the most important people in Hollywood sign an *amicus curiae*—friend of the court—brief, which could be presented with an appeal to the Supreme Court before the Hollywood Ten were put in jail like common criminals by HUAC. His speech was wonderful, and everyone in the room was shoving money at him. Shelley and I each gave him a check for $100 and ran to get the car because we were late for dinner.

After an exhaustive campaign, Shelley finally succeeded in getting George Stevens to give her a screen test for *A Place in the Sun*. She called Norman the night before the test and asked if they could have dinner. She desperately needed to pick his brains because she had not done her homework. She had not read Dreiser's *An American Tragedy*, on which the movie was based. Her justification for this laziness was that an important American writer could give her insights that she might overlook on her own. She went to Norman's house, and they spent the evening discussing the story and her character. Whatever he told her must have helped, because she got the part. As she was leaving Norman's, he gave her back the checks we had written at the Kellys' and told her he had torn up the brief. He had wanted to get some blockbuster names that evening, but she and I were the only ones who signed it. He didn't deposit our checks, either. Everyone else had donated cash. The blacklist was mushrooming into such an ugly mess, he was afraid that our signed checks could have been used against us. Norman proved himself to be not only a terrific writer but also a good friend.

Ethyl Chaplin had barely had time to let the fallout from her breakup with Saul settle when a pamphlet called *Red Channels* appeared branding 151 entertainment industry professionals as "Red Fascist" sympathizers. This meant that Buddy Tyne, who at one time during his unemployed idealistic youth had been a member of some club that could have been affiliated with the Communist Party in sympathy with the antifascist forces in the Spanish Civil War, was in danger of having his passport restricted. He and Ethyl, with Saul's permission, decided to take Judy and leave immediately for Paris.

I was still licking my wounds from the last two films I had done for Goldwyn and determined not to do any more crap. When he tried to loan me out to Universal for a second-rate flying carpet opus, I flatly refused. Goldwyn called me in to tell me loudly and at length what a no-good, ungrateful, bad son I was, and then he put me on suspension for the first time. This meant that my salary was suspended for the entire time it took to make the film at Universal, and that time was automatically added onto my contract. The suspension was meant to teach me a lesson. I felt liberated! The next step was easy. I went to Europe.

I decided to lend my friends moral support, two helping hands, and a few laughs as they settled in. The irony of how we had all laughed and imitated George Coulouris's rallying cry, "Out of America by 1950!" was lost on none of us.

Ethyl, Buddy, and Judy went to New York to deal with family business and then planned to travel to France by ship. I would fly ahead to Paris, and be there to meet them at Le Havre. Ethyl called after they arrived in New York to say that

Arthur Laurents, who was having his own blacklist troubles, would be coming along. Did I mind? Undaunted, I said, "Not a problem." I was taking my first baby steps of independence from Goldwyn. I was up to and ready for anything.

Arthur had been very meaningful to me as a young actor starting again in Hollywood just after the war. I met wonderful people through him and with him. He was older than I and he was very knowledgeable about the theater and the arts in general. I learned a lot from him and we had some wonderful times together. He had a sharp sense of humor that was as funny as it was cutting. We have remained on-and-off friends through the years, and Arthur has always been generous with his advice. Age hasn't mellowed Arthur. It has concentrated his ego and sharpened his defenses. Perhaps it's because, despite Arthur's brilliant creative solution to the early problems with the book of *Gypsy,* Jerry Robbins, Jule Styne, and Stephen Sondheim are the ones most often remembered as the creative geniuses behind that show, just as Leonard Bernstein, Jerry, and Steve are the ones remembered for *West Side Story*. Perhaps it's because he has never been considered one of our best playwrights. Whatever the reason, remaining a friend to Arthur has never been easy, but this was an earlier time and he needed all his friends.

Paris

There are many beautiful cities in this world, quite a few of them here in the United States. Anyone who has ever been to Savannah or San Francisco, not to mention New York, can attest to that. In Italy you can't avoid beauty. But there are reasons why so many love songs have been written about Paris. It only took me one day to know why. Many places fail to live up to one's expectations. Paris exceeded all of mine.

In the taxi from the airport to the center of Paris, I was too excited to be upset by the churlish behavior of the driver, who had disdainfully not even tried to understand my attempts to tell him where I was going. I finally handed him a piece of paper on which I'd written the hotel's name. This was typical Parisian cabdriver behavior. They made an average New York cabbie at the time seem like St. Christopher. After checking in at L'Hôtel Mayfair and leaving my passport, which I was sure I'd never see again, at the tiny front desk, I took the even tinier lift up five flights and walked another half floor to my room. It was a two-room apartment on the top floor that looked out on the rooftops. When I opened my curtains, it was as if the music from *La Bohème* flooded in with the late-afternoon sunlight. I filled the bath, took a long soak, and tried to rest. I was too excited. I dressed and went down to the lobby to find out where I could go for dinner nearby.

I was at the desk when the elevator opened and out came two familiar Hollywood faces, Peter and Jigee Viertel. Peter, a would-be screenwriter, had written his first successful book at age eighteen. His mother, Salka Viertel, who had purportedly been Garbo's lover as well as her writer, held sway over an Old World–style intellectual salon at her home in Santa Monica. Jigee, sharp, witty, and mercurial, was a really smashing lady. I'd always thought that she could have been the model for Lady Brett in Hemingway's *The Sun Also Rises*. Her first husband, Budd Schulberg, wrote *What Makes Sammy Run?* They had been friends of Ernest Hemingway's for years. Jigee insisted I come along with them to a cellar on the Left Bank where they were meeting war photographer Bob Capa and his current girlfriend for dinner. Capa was world-famous for his photos of death, carnage, and devastation during the Civil War in Spain, as well as World War II. I joined them. The food and wine at my first meal in Paris, accompanied by blue-gray clouds of Gauloise cigarette smoke, was terrific, but my adrenaline high was wearing off and travel lag was taking over. A lot of the conversation was in French, but I even had a hard time keeping up with the English part. As the evening wore on, all talk turned to Poppa. I had to ask to find out that they were talking about Hemingway. After a half-hour or so of obsessive Poppa talk, I decided to walk home. Jigee gave me directions back to the hotel, and with hugs all around, I left to get some much needed air.

The night sky was clear and hung with a bright full moon. Walking along the Seine, with its lovely bridges and quiet nighttime river traffic, I became acutely aware of how much more the world had to offer than I had ever imagined. When I saw Notre Dame silhouetted against the night sky, it was almost overkill. I was a willing victim, completely, hopelessly in love. No Hollywood movie could have prepared me for the reality that was Paris. This was the moment in which my unquenchable thirst for travel was born.

Back at the hotel, I enjoyed twelve hours of the deepest, best sleep ever. When I woke I found a note that Jigee had slipped under my door. She and Peter had checked out and were off to Africa with Capa to meet Poppa. Since Ethyl, Buddy, Judy, and Arthur were not arriving until the following week, I was on my own. I spent the day in the Louvre. After seeing enough paintings to bring on an acute attack of Stendahl's Syndrome, I ended up lost in the maze of sarcophagi and pieces of ancient Egypt that seemed to go on for miles in the lower reaches of the museum.

That evening I chose a perfect change of pace by seeing *Annie du Far West*. It seemed ideal symmetry that my first Broadway musical was also my first theater experience in Paris. What a difference there was. This production not only had horses onstage, it also had camels and elephants. Annie sang "You Can't Get a

Man with a Gun" as a tragic love ballad à la Edith Piaf. The production was so wildly off the mark and so uniquely French that it was impossible not to be enchanted by it.

The next day while wandering through Les Halles, the incredible marketplace that once fed the bellies of Paris, I bumped into Uta Hagen. I had met Uta in New York and of course knew her by reputation, but we were merely acquaintances. She was alone in Paris, I was alone, it was a beautiful summer day, and we had a wonderful lunch at a little bistro on the Île St. Louis in the middle of the Seine near Notre Dame. After our lunch, which included many carafes of *vin ordinaire,* we browsed through the bookstalls along the Seine. I spent two memorable days and nights seeing the city with this terrific lady, who went on to become one of the great acting teachers of our time as well as one of our greatest actresses.

We went to the ballet to see Zizi Jeanmaire dance an incredibly sensual *Carmen* that her husband, Roland Petit, had choreographed for her. After the performance, we went backstage to introduce ourselves and they invited us to have a late supper with them. I was completely captivated by Zizi, a feeling that was obviously mutual. We communicated like old friends even though she did not speak any more English than I did French. Two years later Zizi was, for me, the only good thing about *Hans Christian Andersen,* a film we did for Goldwyn together with Danny Kaye.

Uta and I walked home that night along the bank of the Seine, stopping to sit under all the bridges we passed, where we tried to outproject each other with lines from plays and movies. We wanted to find out which bridge had the best echo in Paris.

In the late 1990s, I went backstage to see Uta after a performance of *Mrs. Klein,* one of the last plays she did in New York. As we said good night, she smiled and said, "Remember how good our projection was in Paris?" She also asked if I had seen Arthur recently. When I said, "Not for some time, I'm angry with him," she laughed and commented, "Who isn't?"

At one of Gene and Betsy Kelly's open houses, I had met François and Patrice Pleven, a pair of French brothers who were hoping to become film producers. I had promised to call them when I came to Paris. Since I still had a couple of days before Ethyl and the others arrived, I kept my promise and was invited to go with Patrice, the younger brother, that very evening to a dinner party at a château on the outskirts of Paris. The château was magnificent, with formal gardens that seemed to go on forever in the early-evening light. The dinner party numbered about a dozen people, most of whom spoke charming English when we were introduced and not another word for the rest of the evening, with one face-saving exception. I wandered off into a galleria, and there on the walls was an amazing collection of French Impressionist paintings dominated by Cézanne. I had recently seen several of his paintings in the Louvre and had been very taken with them. Now here were a half-dozen of them on a wall in front of me in someone's home. I would have happily spent the rest of the evening right there if a butler tinkling a bell hadn't come through calling the French equivalent of "Soup's on." At the table our hostess seated everyone as skillfully as a world-class conductor, but my friend Patrice was at the other end. I was on my own. Soup was served and I was staring helplessly at the array of silverware choices when my dinner companion on my right, a lovely older woman, leaned in and whispered in flawless English, "Just start from the outside and work your way in." After a "soup to nuts" dinner during which I used every utensil, we had moved to the living room for coffee and brandy when Richard Rodgers and Oscar Hammerstein arrived from London, where *Carousel* had recently opened to triumphant reviews. R & H were both obviously very high on their London success. Without hesitation, everyone trotted out his English.

Mr. Hammerstein was a big, friendly bear of a man. Mr. Rodgers was compact, quick, and didn't miss a trick. At one point, after we were introduced, I asked him about a song called "Fair" that he had written with Lorenz Hart. I told him I'd forgotten what show it was from. He thought for a moment and with obvious surprise said, "Damned if I can remember, either." It was almost ten years to the day before I saw R & H again. Barbara Cook and I were appearing in the first revival of *The King and I* at City Center in New York. R & H attended the dress rehearsal and came backstage immediately afterward. Hammerstein grabbed me in a giant hug to say how much he had loved what we had done with the parts. Rodgers walked purposefully over to me, pointed a finger, and said, "*Babes in Arms,* but it was cut."

Waiting on the platform at the station when the boat train from Le Havre arrived, I heard Judy Chaplin yelling my name. She jumped into my arms. I was so happy to see her and Ethyl and Buddy, I didn't even mind that Arthur had tagged along. In fact, I was even glad to see him.

We got all the baggage and went back to get everyone settled at L'Hôtel Mayfair. Then we spent two weeks enjoying Paris as if none of us had a care in the world. Ethyl and Buddy looked for a place to live, but we also explored the city, its artistic treasures and the differences of its arrondissements. At the innumerable bistros, for a few francs we enjoyed food that was better than any we had ever had before, accompanied by inexpensive liters of *vin ordinaire.* We also set out to explore the nightlife.

Arthur ran into Jimmy Lipton, whom he had known in New York. Lipton, then an out-of-work actor picking up odd jobs in Paris, is now known as the TV host of *Inside the Actors Studio.* He convinced Arthur that we had to see an "exhibition"; "It's as much a part of Paris as the Eiffel Tower or the Louvre." If we gave him the money, he would take care of all the arrangements. Arthur was sure he was getting a commission. Ethyl was game, so several nights later we went to a tacky brothel in Montmartre, where we were taken upstairs to a bedroom with nothing in it other than a large bed and some chairs grouped nearby. A few minutes after we settled down, a rather ordinary-looking thirtyish nude couple in towels entered and took a very formal bow. When they whipped off their towels Ethyl looked at me in such a way that I knew I would lose it if I looked at her again. Our "actors" then proceeded to demonstrate lovemaking styles from around the world: very formal and stiff as the British; frisky and juvenile as the Americans; harsh and militaristic as the Germans; exaggeratedly passionate as the Italians. None of this was erotic. By the time they got to "and now the Russian way," the woman spread-eagled on the bed and the man launching himself at her from the far side of the room, Ethyl and I were laughing so hard that we had to help each other from the room. We went downstairs to a little bar where we sat drinking and talking with all the prostitutes who were not otherwise engaged. Buddy and Arthur soon joined us. It was the highlight of the evening.

Harold Clurman and his then ex (but still beloved) wife, Stella Adler, were also in Paris, and we saw as much of them as possible. One night Arthur and I took them to Le Grand Véfour, perhaps the finest restaurant in Paris at the time. As soon as we were seated, I excused myself. As I was coming back into the dining room I heard Harold's voice. He was explaining to the maitre d', "You see, in America she is one of our most famous stage actresses, so we would appreciate it if you could extend all possible courtesies to her." The sweet man was making sure that his ex-wife got special treatment. Stella later played an important part in my life when I moved to New York and studied for the theater. She was the best teacher I ever had.

London

Before leaving New York, Ethyl and Buddy had run into Jerry Robbins, who told them that he was coming to London for the first time with the New York City Ballet to present one of his works. Since he had no friends there, he invited them to come over from Paris for his opening. He was on the outs with Arthur, a familiar position for many of Arthur's friends through the years, but he asked Ethyl to try to talk me into coming over with them. I liked Jerry as much as I admired him, and Buddy needed to check out the opportunities for work in London. Arthur was delighted to be on his own in Paris. Off we went.

We were not prepared for the devastation from the war that was still evident in that great city. Most of the rubble had been cleared, but there were still vast areas that had been leveled by firebombing where only a few skeletons of buildings remained. Rationing was still in effect, and it was next to impossible to get a decent meal, but the Brits carried on cheerfully and efficiently, with no complaints. Hotel rooms were impossible to find, but Jerry got Ethyl and Buddy a room in the small shabby hotel where his company was staying, and I managed to talk the manager of the Savoy into giving me his "special room," the one held for last-minute emergencies. The room was big and gorgeous, and overlooked the Thames. Seeing the river through the fog in the morning light prepared me for my first Turner paintings. The room was not only large enough for two; it was very close to Jerry's theater near Covent Garden. Since our schedules conveniently dovetailed, I invited him to stay.

I didn't know Jerry well, but I had been a fan since that night in San Francisco when I had seen *Fancy Free* before shipping out for Hawaii. He had a fearsome reputation among dancers as one of the most demanding and difficult-to-please taskmasters in the business. He was of medium height, with a tight athletic build, quite nice-looking in a balding, ordinary way. His smile was infrequent but could light up a room. He was quick and smart and I really enjoyed his company. As friendly as he was, Jerry was hard to read. I sensed that in some part of himself that he kept carefully guarded, he was not happy. Maybe it was his work. Agnes de Mille wrote in *The Book of the Dance*, "There is no single work of Robbins' in which he has not felt soul-crushing disappointment and that it was a mistake to start. He longs to just get out and escape. That he does not is merely a matter of spiritual discipline. His doubts and disappointments are thunderous, his group testifies, and his disciplines are applied to others besides himself. Rehearsals are sometimes inspiring and sometimes hell." He also could have been feeling the growing pressure from HUAC, which led him to name names, or "rat on his friends," not too long after his London triumph.

Unfortunately, I hardly ever saw him because he almost never got back from rehearsal until I had already gone out for the evening.

We were all low on funds, so we did most of our drinking and eating at the Savoy, where I could sign for everything. I was still waiting for the money my new business manager was supposed to send me via American Express. I went every day, but nothing arrived. Meanwhile my tab grew alarmingly. Since no money had changed hands, management was beginning to look politely askance. Ethyl, Buddy, and I were getting nervous about the subterfuges our lack of cash drove us to, such as hiding in the bathroom like teenagers with the shower on to avoid tipping when room service arrived, shouting, "Just leave the check there, I'll sign it later!"

We spent an evening with George and Louise Coulouris over dinner in their little sixteenth-century thatched-roof cottage on the Vale of Health overlooking Hampstead Heath. George looked at me like I was out of my mind when I shouted, "Well, we did it, George! . . . out of America by 1950!" Maybe he wasn't aware of how many times we had all used his line.

The ever-resourceful studio managed to track me down. Both *Our Very Own* and *Edge of Doom* were opening on Broadway in the same week, one at the Astor Theater and the other a block away at the Victoria Theater. Goldwyn was desperate for me to come back in order to do appearances and publicity for the event. If I agreed, "All would be forgiven." Sure, right, I thought. Let's spell that out. I called my agent and agreed to do it if I was immediately taken off suspension and put back on salary. I suggested doing a *Times* of London interview before I left if the studio took care of my current bill at the Savoy. They agreed and set up the interview. We were off the hook.

On a roll, I checked American Express one last time. I discovered that I had been going to the wrong department to check for my money transfer. It had been there the whole time. To celebrate, on my last night I took us all to a Greek restaurant that I had heard about from the concierge at the Savoy. The White Tower somehow managed to serve delicious food at this time when rationing seemed to affect every other restaurant in London. The mention of "potted shrimp" still transports me back to that evening.

Farley Granger on Broadway . . . Twice!

Back in New York, I was put to work immediately. After what seemed like a lifetime of newspaper, radio, and television interviews as well as public appearances all over the greater New York area and as far away as Boston and Philadelphia, the movies were about to open back to back. I was starring in two films on Broadway simultaneously, and I was only twenty-five years old. An actor's dream come true? You would think so, but I was filled with foreboding. I knew both films were bad, and I felt as if I were about to be doubly exposed as a charlatan. The first to open was *Our Very Own*, which the critics merely dismissed as ineffective fluff. My favorite quote for this one was from Hedda Hopper: "The kind of picture America has been screaming for!!!" *Edge of Doom* was a different matter. Dana Andrews and I somehow emerged unscathed, but the critics unanimously hated the movie. Their reviews differed only as to how much. The defining quote for this turkey was Walter Winchell's "It's raw meat!" What salvaged that trip for me was seeing Ethel Merman in *Call Me Madam* while I was in Boston making publicity appearances. Also while in New York, I saw *Guys and Dolls,* which to this day I think elevated musical theater to an art form. The brilliant music and lyrics were by Frank Loesser and the superb direction was by Abe Burrows, who directed my Broadway musical debut in 1959 with much less auspicious results. They say composers never throw away a good song. Frank didn't. Imagine how I felt when I heard "More I Cannot Wish You," my song from *Roseanna McCoy* which Goldwyn had cut, being sung to Sarah Brown, the Salvation Army doll, by her father at the top of Act II.

Goldwyn contacted me to say that he was canceling the nationwide openings of *Edge of Doom* in order for Charlie Brackett and Ben Hecht to do a rewrite. The plan was for Dana to narrate a wraparound, a new scene to begin the movie and another to end it that would explain the story of my character and change the focus from the bad boy to the good priest. It was not a good idea, since the film was about the boy, not the young priest. Meanwhile, Goldwyn expected me to go on a nationwide PR tour for the film. I'll never understand why he flogged that dead horse for as long as he did, but I wanted nothing more to do with it. I refused to do any more promotional appearances. After yet another tirade on what an ingrate I was, back on suspension I went . . . and back to Europe to join my friends, who were now in Rome.

A. Scott Berg, in his definitive biography of Goldwyn, writes of *Edge of Doom*: "Goldwyn was chewing out his staff one day for not creating a successful advertising campaign for the film: 'I don't know what's the matter with you. This is a simple story about a boy who wants a fine funeral for his mother, so he kills a priest.' Upon hearing his own words, he suddenly grasped the fundamental problem with the movie. With his next breath he said, 'Let's not spend another dime.' "

Italy

I had been captivated by the romance and literary world of expats in Paris. I had been impressed by the bravery and humor of the Brits. Now I was about to be introduced to Italy. It was the start of a love affair that still burns brightly. No matter where you go, from every city to every town, from the Italian Alps to Sicily, it is beautiful. The people are gorgeous, funny, and totally cynical. Maybe centuries of being marched over and conquered by one country after the other has made them more resilient than most. On the surface, nothing seems to bother the Italians except paying taxes and losing at football (soccer). But I don't mean to imply that they are superficial. Nothing could be further from the truth. It could be that since they have had to adjust to so many different peoples wielding power over them through the centuries, they have developed a fine sense of welcoming wariness with strangers and an immediate distrust for anyone in authority. They trust only their own families. Once they come to know and like you, they are the warmest and most generous people I know. You become part of the family and are treated and protected as such. On a less sociological level, there is the food. You can eat pasta 365 days a year and it can be different and delicious every time, and that is only the first course! I still go back every chance I get.

When I checked in to the Hotel de la Ville in Rome, Arthur was waiting for me, but Ethyl and Buddy were gone. Arthur had gotten Buddy a job on *Decision Before Dawn,* a film that Anatole Litvak was about to begin shooting in Munich. Knowing the depth of Ethyl's feelings about what the Jews had suffered at German hands during the war, I knew how much they must have needed that job to agree to go to Germany. Arthur had bought a little Hillman Minx convertible and wanted to see Florence and Venice after we had finished exploring Rome. I agreed to travel with him. We often went our own ways in the cities, but the joy of being in Italy overcame any strain between us. By the time we left Florence to head toward Venice, I had seen so many beautiful things—paintings, churches, tombs, squares, and hillside towns—that my brain was on overload. We parked the car in a big garage near the train station in the Piazza Roma on the outskirts of Venice and took a water taxi into the city. When we rounded a curve into the Grand Canal, I felt I had passed through a portal into another world. The beauty of Venice made everything else I'd ever seen pale by comparison. It still has the same effect on me, but this first time was overwhelming. We got off at the stop for the Grand Hotel, where we were given two rooms overlooking the canal. The Venice Biennale was in full swing, and the first person we ran into was Stella Adler, who was staying at a hotel over on the Lido. When Arthur was otherwise engaged, Stella introduced me to two people who played an important role in my life a few years later when I was making *Senso* for Luchino Visconti. One was a British art dealer who owned a beautiful house in Venice, which I rented while working on the Venice portion of *Senso;* the other was Peggy Guggenheim, who became a good friend and whose companionship warmed my winter during that same period.

The Little Tramp

It was time to visit Ethyl and Buddy. *Decision Before Dawn,* which Buddy was working on, had begun shooting in Munich. It starred Richard Basehart, at whom I had been aiming my rifle in *Roseanna McCoy* when I slipped and shot Joan Evans, and a superb young German actor, Oskar Werner, who was nominated for an Academy Award for *Ship of Fools* and became an international star in 1961 in Truffaut's *Jules et Jim.*

Leaving Italy was not easy because I never wanted to leave. I had already decided I would be very happy to live there. Spending money in Rome, Florence, and Venice had been worth every lira, but I was on suspension again. I had to resolve something before I went broke.

Arthur and I got his car out of Venice's parking garage, and we headed over the Dolomites into Austria.

Salzburg was our first stop, a baroque gem of a small city. It had sustained appreciable bomb damage toward the end of the war, but the industrious Austrians had cleaned up the center of town and all around were signs of reconstruction.

Wilhelm Furtwängler was conducting Richard Strauss at the music festival the night we were there. After discussing whether or not to try for tickets, Arthur and I decided not to attend what could have been a memorable concert. Our decision was based on the fact that both the composer and the conductor were thought to have been Nazi sympathizers, and we felt that we had to draw a line somewhere, no matter how great the music might have been.

Vienna had been devastated by the war. While driving through the rubble of what had once been the musical capital of the world and one of its loveliest old cities, I felt the same mixture of anger and sadness that I had felt in London. Vienna at the time was occupied by the four powers: the United States, England, France, and Russia. It was uniquely exciting and chaotic. On our last night in Vienna, we went to a little restaurant where a pianist played popular American songs. I went over to him at one point to request that he play some Gershwin. He looked at me and said, "I was about to play some selections from *Porgy and Bess.*" Then he looked down at his piano and said softly, "That is, if you don't mind." Guessing what he was implying, I snapped, "What do you mean by that?" He looked up and, still softly, said, "Some Americans do, you know." I held his gaze until he looked down and I said, "Well, I'm not one of them," and stuffed some Austrian schillings into the glass on his piano. Back at the table, before I could tell Arthur what had happened, the pianist had launched into one of the most beautifully played medleys of *Porgy and Bess* I've ever heard. It took me right back to my adolescent worship of George Gershwin.

As I was paying the check, he came over to our table, introduced himself, and invited us to his flat for coffee with him and his wife. Arthur looked skeptical, but I was curious enough to accept immediately. We got into our car, which was parked nearby, and followed his motorbike, maneuvering our way with some difficulty through the rubble that had been Vienna until we arrived at a building that was only partially destroyed. Hugging the wall, we climbed a staircase that, like a fire escape, was completely exposed to the elements where the outside wall had been blown away. It was like a scene out of *The Third Man,* Carol Reed's brilliant postwar film with Orson Welles, Joseph Cotten, and Alida Valli. We entered his tiny fourth-floor flat and met his wife. They were a pale young Jewish couple whose family had managed to send them to Israel before the Nazi purge. They had recently returned to search for family survivors. There were none.

Over coffee, when we mentioned that we had come from Salzburg, he asked if we had seen Furtwängler conduct. I told him no, we had decided that we had to draw the line somewhere. He gave me a sad, penetrating look and said very softly, "Mr. Granger, if you have any lines to draw, you should never have come to Vienna."

The next morning we left for Munich. The drive was uneventful, but we could tell when we reached the city limits how much destruction there was ahead. I felt numb. I was getting used to rubble. What we had to do to win the war was absolutely necessary, but I couldn't help feeling how wonderful it would be when mankind evolved to the point where war and killing became unnecessary.

It wasn't easy finding our hotel because the façade had been destroyed, but once we found it and passed through the temporary entrance, the big and rather plain lobby was undamaged. We were on our way to the elevator after checking in when a familiar voice boomed out, "Farley!" It was Orson Welles, seated at a table nearby with the chanteuse Eartha Kitt. He had seen *They Live by Night* in London and wanted to tell me how much he thought I'd grown as an actor. What a great compliment from the man I had been too intimidated to meet in the commissary at Fox at seventeen. As soon as I got to my room and was able to get a telephone line, I called Ethyl. She invited us to dinner with Oskar Werner and his girlfriend. Oskar, who was no barrel of laughs, was as smart as he was talented. It was wonderful to see Ethyl and Buddy again.

Back at the hotel, I found that my ever-resourceful studio had tracked me down. Alfred Hitchcock wanted to see me about his upcoming film. Without hesitation, I left on the next plane available. On my way to the airport the next day, in a particularly leveled area of the city, I saw the outline of a familiar figure standing alone in the rubble. I asked the driver to stop, got out, and picked my way a block or so to the figure. As I got close, I realized that it was an undamaged life-size cutout of Charlie Chaplin as the Little Tramp, jauntily surveying the destruction around him. I'll never figure out how or why it got there, but I'll always treasure the image of one of cinema's most famous Jewish entertainers, the man who had lampooned Hitler so accurately in *The Great Dictator,* surveying the ruins of the city that had played such a major part in Hitler's rise to power.

Hitchcock Number II

Many connections later I was back in L.A. After a weekend of rest, the studio set up a meeting for me with Hitch at his home in Bel Air Monday afternoon. When I arrived, he seemed genuinely happy to see me. We went out on his terrace, which overlooked the vast green expanse of the Bel Air Country Club. Over tea he told me the story of *Strangers on a Train,* playing all the parts with great relish. Hearing a story told by Hitch was almost as good as seeing the film. I was enthralled. When he asked me if I liked it, I said, "I think it's great!" He said, "Good, because you're playing Guy." I almost jumped out of my skin. Then he asked who I thought should play Bruno. I hadn't a clue. He leaned in with one of his inimitable smiles and said, "What would you think about Robert Walker?"

Bob Walker, a fine actor, had been typecast at MGM as the boy next door in films like *See Here, Private Hargrove* and *The Clock* with Judy Garland. His wife, Jennifer Jones, was already romantically linked with David O. Selznick in 1944 when Bob co-starred with her in *Since You Went Away,* a Selznick production. She and Bob were divorced in 1945. The whole affair took a heavy toll on Walker. He began drinking heavily and suffered several nervous breakdowns, accompanied by some unfortunate tabloid publicity. After a six-week marriage to John Ford's daughter, Barbara, was annulled, Bob was arrested for drunken driving and institutionalized for almost a year. This would be his first major role following his release.

I remembered Hitch's *Shadow of a Doubt,* in which he cast Joseph Cotten, an actor who almost always played honest and trustworthy characters, as the murderous Uncle Charlie. It was masterful surprise casting, and so was this. I said to him, "What a terrific idea!" Then he leaned in with that same grin and said, "Wouldn't it be interesting if something happened on our film?" I knew he was trying to shock me, so I just said something stupid like, "Oh, Hitch . . ."

Next thing I knew, Bob and I were in Washington, D.C., preparing to shoot the opening of the movie in Union Station. We spent our first day there walking all around the city, visiting the tourist spots and getting to know each other. We hit it off well, and I was looking forward to working with him. That first night, after a well-fueled dinner with Hitch, he announced that we had been invited to the home of the *Washington Post*'s drama critic, Richard Coe, for after-dinner brandies and coffee. Off we went. After one drink, Hitch announced that it was past his bedtime. He was leaving, but he urged us to stay. We were both feeling no pain, and Coe was both knowledgeable and interesting, so we remained. An hour or so later, Bob was getting a little slurry, so I asked Richard to call us a cab. We went back to our hotel, where I helped him to his room. He flopped down on his bed. I got him out of his shoes and jacket. Then, as I turned to go, he grabbed my arm and, in a panic, said, "Please, please, don't leave me alone!"

He broke down about Jennifer and how she had betrayed him with that son of a bitch Selznick, who was twice her age, just because he promised to make her a big star, and about how deeply he had always loved her and depended upon her, and what a struggle it was trying to go on without her. I knew he had the first call next morning, so I sat down on the other bed and stayed to lend him some kind of support.

The next thing I knew, the phone was ringing. The driver of Bob's car was calling from the lobby. I stalled him for a half-hour and called the assistant director. I explained that Bob had had a rough night, and if they could switch the schedule to use me first, it would give Bob a few more hours' sleep. I could be ready in a half-hour. He said he was sure it would be no problem, since they were just doing walking shots of our feet at Union Station. I raced back to my room, showered, and got to the lobby in a half-hour. When I showed up at the station, Hitch did not say a word to me about the switch. When Bob showed up around noon, he didn't say a word to me, either. In fact, he never again mentioned that first evening.

Despite Hitch's morbidly mischievous speculation, after that first day, Bob was a consummate professional, always on time and always creatively prepared. We became good friends during the course of the film, and it ended with us both promising to keep in touch. Despite those good intentions, it was a month or so before I saw Bob again. He was busy filming *My Son John* at Paramount with Helen Hayes and Van Heflin. We were both excited about the advance word that was spreading around town regarding *Strangers,* and promised to get together for dinner as soon as he had some free time. Two days later, Bob was dead. He had suffered a severe panic attack at home after some heavy drinking, and his housekeeper had called his psychiatrist, Dr. Frederick Hacker. The good doctor administered a heavy sedative, which, interacting with the alcohol in his system, killed Bob. All of this happened just a short time before *Strangers* opened to unanimous raves, particularly for Bob. He got the kind of reviews that could have made him one of the most sought-after leading men in Hollywood, despite those bad years after Jennifer Jones left him. Flashing back to Hitch's now almost prescient remark on the day he read me the script—"Wouldn't it be interesting if something happened on our film?"—gave me a very strange feeling.

While making the film, I became friendly with Hitch's daughter, Pat, the generous and steady-handed bartender in the Hitchcock household. Pat, who was in her early twenties at most, was very good and quite funny as the younger sister of my love interest, Ruth Roman. Warner Brothers was producing *Strangers,* and Ruth was under contract to them. Hitch had wanted the then-little-known young actress Grace Kelly for the part, but Warners had refused. Since they had to pay MGM to use Bob and Goldwyn to use me, they insisted that he use Ruth, who was really not right for the part. Hitch did not like his artistic wishes thwarted. As a result, he was cold and sometimes cruel to Ruth, which was unfair because as a contract player she was just doing what her studio told her to do. But Hitch was right, she was wrong for the part.

All in all, working on *Strangers on a Train* was my happiest filmmaking experience. Often on many of the films I had done, the director would arrive on set without a clue as to how he planned to shoot the scene. He would go to the cameraman or cinematographer, explain what he wanted to shoot, then ask where should the camera be placed and what lens should be used and so on. The underrated and overworked cinematographer, who often did most of the visual creative work on a film, would then tell the director how to shoot the scene. That was never the case with Hitch. He knew exactly what he wanted and how to get it. He had an assistant art director seated on a high stool next to the camera who was in charge of a very thick binder that contained every setup and shot for the entire film. These were the drawings I had seen pinned to all the walls of his office. After he finished a setup, he would walk to the assistant, who would turn over a page. Hitch would look at it and say, The camera goes here, here, and there; the lenses are this, this, and that; the action takes place from here to there. Then he would relax while the crew got things ready. They respected and trusted him because he was able to be precise about what he wanted. He never had to peer through a lens finder to see how a shot looked. Since all his shots were so well planned, his film was practically pre-edited. One afternoon early in the shoot, I noticed Hitch slumped unhappily in his chair between takes. I approached him, and when he looked up, I asked if he was OK. He looked at me for a moment and then said, "Oh, I'm just bored." It took me a while to take that at face value. He *was* bored. He had already done all the creative work in his head and was now merely transferring it from paper to film. Today, in a world of instant playback, a video monitor monopolizes everyone's attention on a film set.

After the film, I began to receive dinner invitations to Hitch's home. They were always small dinner parties that included regulars like Ingrid Bergman and Cary Grant. His wife, Alma Reville, had already been established as one of England's foremost screenwriters and film editors when she met and married the upcoming young director after a two-year courtship in 1926. Hitch trusted her completely and depended on her opinion of his final cut. Alma also happened to be a natural hostess, and their daughter, Pat, poured those drinks that always guaranteed a smooth takeoff.

One memorable evening, the dinner party consisted of Ingrid Bergman, her then-husband, Dr. Peter Lindstrom, Pat, and me. After a typically English dinner of roast prime rib and Yorkshire pudding washed down by liters of very good burgundy, Hitch decided that we would all go out on the town to see the Katherine Dunham Dancers at Ciro's. This took everyone by surprise, because he usually wanted nothing to do with the Hollywood social scene, but we were all feeling no pain, and it sounded like a great idea.

When we got to Ciro's, the place was packed, but for the maestro two tables were placed next to each other front and center, almost abutting the stage. We were spread out side by side, kind of like a mini–Last Supper across the front of the stage. I was in between Hitch and Ingrid, and on the other side of Hitch, Peter sat between Pat and Alma. Drinks were ordered and brought to the table.

The lights began to dim, and the drums began to throb. As the lights came up, the dancers burst onto the stage gyrating wildly in their colorful costumes. Hitch promptly fell sound asleep. Head down, arms folded contentedly across his belly, he began to snore loudly. Ingrid and I had to suppress our giggles. Suddenly Ingrid began to cry, softly at first but then in a torrent. I tried to comfort her and find out what was wrong, but it took a while before she could talk about it. She was filming *Joan of Arc* for director Victor Fleming and was being burnt at the stake the following morning. She had not figured out how to do the scene and was upset about it. I said that I didn't think I could help her, and between sobs she got out, "Don't worry. I'll think of something . . . or they'll just have to burn me." I started to laugh again, and so did she. With Hitch's snoring, Ingrid's sobbing, and my laughing, it's a wonder we weren't all tossed out, or at least attacked by the Dunham Dancers, who had every right to throw their bongos at us.

A New Year's Eve to Remember

Goldwyn himself called me into his office. He said that he had found his next *Best Years of Our Lives.* It was called *I Want You* and would be for the Korean War what *Best Years* was for World War II. I wasn't sure what he meant by that, but his enthusiasm was contagious. He said the parts for Dana Andrews and me were the best he'd ever seen. He had borrowed Dorothy McGuire from Selznick, and he had a new, beautiful leading lady for me, Peggy Dow, "Not another puny girl." By that I assumed he meant pudgy and was referring to Joan Evans, with whom he knew I'd been unhappy. The writer was going to be the Pulitzer Prize–winning dramatist Robert Sherwood, who had won an Academy Award for the screenplay of *The Best Years of Our Lives.* Goldwyn wanted it to go into production soon after the first of the year, and he was almost ready to sign a first-class director for the film. He clapped me on the shoulder before I could ask any questions, and walked me to the door. "Everything is first-class, my boy, no more of that New York old-country business of yours!" I promised to stay in town. He told me he was very proud of my work in *Strangers on a Train* and said this was going to be my big year.

It was Christmas, 1950, time to forgive and forget and to party. I made peace with Shelley, and before long we were back having endless discussions about acting and our careers; many squabbles, mostly about her insatiable lust for publicity; and many laughs. She was still justifiably high about her work in *A Place in the Sun,* and I was high on *Strangers* and Goldwyn's promises. We were ready to enjoy life.

We went to Lewis Milestone's big annual Christmas party together. He and his wife always went all-out, and it was the most festive and traditional party in town. Their large entry hall was two stories high and accommodated an enormous Christmas tree, which was decorated in a traditional fashion. The part of the evening everyone loved the most came just after dark, when the children's choir from the local church arrived. Millie would dim the lights as they filed in holding candles and surrounded the tree to sing carols from around the world. With only the Christmas tree lights and the candlelight on the children's faces as they sang, the experience was very moving.

Later that evening, long after the children had gone and after much good cheer had been consumed, I met one of my screen idols, Humphrey Bogart. His young wife, Lauren Bacall, was a knockout. Tall and slender, she was a quintessential New Yorker whose presence was felt the minute she walked into a room. She was very much a man's woman: tough, completely direct, and without artifice. All of these qualities are still very much a part of my neighbor, Betty Bacall. Bogie, on the other hand, was nothing like his hard-boiled screen persona. Quiet, a little shy and soft-spoken, and something of an intellectual, he was every inch a gentleman. At one point we were standing at the bar deep in conversation when Bogart, his back to the wall, slowly began to slide down to the floor. He neither missed a beat of conversation nor spilled a drop of his drink. I decided the best thing to do was slowly sink down to the floor with him.

There was a French actor in the bar whose name I forget, but whose claim to fame I cannot. He ate glasses. When Bogart heard that, he was off the floor in a flash, urging the Frenchman to do it. He did, and Bogie was determined to learn how to do it. Before we realized what was happening, he had herded the rest of us out of the bar and locked the door. A few minutes later Betty came looking for her husband. When she heard what was going on in the bar, she started pounding on the door and yelling at Bogie to "get out here now!" The door finally opened, and out he came sporting a big, bloody grin.

A week later I went to pick Shelley up for the newly traditional New Year's Eve bash given by the international producer Sam Spiegel. She kept me waiting for almost two hours while she talked on the phone to her press agent in between changing dresses. Needless to say, we fought all the way to the party and went our separate ways as soon as we got there, a separation I've never regretted. That was the night I met Ava Gardner.

Ava

Ava and Burt Lancaster had been discovered by the public in 1946 in the screen adaptation of Hemingway's short story *The Killers.* She has always been considered one of the screen's great beauties, but film didn't really do her justice. She had an animal magnetism that heated any room she was in. She moved like a panther and laughed like a man. That night she had come with Howard Duff. They had arrived fighting like Shelley and me and also had gone their separate ways. I was standing alone near the piano next to the bar when she came over to get a drink. After trading a few glances across the Steinway, I smiled at her, put my drink down, went over, and introduced myself. She laughed and said, "I thought you'd never come over." We drank for a while and made small talk until she said, "Honey, do you want to get out of here?" I nodded enthusiastically and took her hand.

Off we went without a word to Howard or Shelley, whom we had determined deserved each other, to a club where Nat King Cole and his trio were appearing. We celebrated with Nat at midnight, and ended up at my place. It was a memorable New Year's Eve. We both loved Nat Cole and went back to that little club many times during our short-lived but long-remembered affair. Ava was smart, honest, unpretentious, and outspoken, with a bawdy sense of humor. Ava hated all the demeaning, pretentious games actors had to play while working to learn our craft and hoping for a good role in a decent film to apply that knowledge. She was practical about her looks without being remotely vain. She felt they were a mixed blessing, because even though they opened a lot of the right doors, they were also responsible for getting her into sticky situations with the wrong people. Good looks tended to get an actor typecast, playing the same kind of part again and again. People took you at face value with never a thought about what more you might have to offer as an actor. Ava loved her work when the material warranted it, but she wasn't remotely driven by ego or ambition. She was also ahead of her time in terms of equality for women. Ava felt that for a man to be admired when he played the field while a woman was called a slut for doing the same thing was "bullshit, honey!"

I knew what we had going was not a lasting thing, but it certainly was a good thing. Ava was involved in a well-publicized on-again, off-again marriage to Frank Sinatra. She had first been married to Mickey Rooney, and then to the "intellectual bandleader" Artie Shaw. In between them, she had a serious relationship with Howard Hughes. She was not at all bitter about her experiences with men. Her life force was too strong to waste that kind of time. I think she really loved Frank, but the tempestuousness of their marriage had worn her down. All she wanted to do was have some fun without any hassles. I had not figured out how I really felt about Shelley, but the opportunity to spend time with this terrific lady was too tempting to walk away from.

Ava came from a small town in North Carolina and had never gotten time to see the real beauty of California. We took long nighttime drives up the coast to explore Big Sur and climbed down steep paths to get to lonely beaches. We went to San Simeon on a foggy day when the place was deserted and loved that it was all ours. I showed her the small beach town of Capitola where I spent summers as a child. The press had not discovered that we were spending time together, and we went to some effort to keep it that way.

After about a month, our real world intruded and our time alone ended. Ava got the part of Julie, the beautiful black girl who was passing for white, in MGM's upcoming remake of Jerome Kern's ground-breaking Broadway musical *Show Boat*. The film had started with Judy Garland in the part, but Judy's mental and physical collapse had shut it down. Ava always felt that the part should have gone to her good friend Lena Horne, but it was 1951, and Louis B. Mayer was not exactly interested in righting racial injustice. He was interested in adding to the bottom line. It had been easy enough for Metro to plan their all-star musical extravaganzas so that the ravishingly black Lena's solo numbers could be excised in the South in order to maximize box office potential, but the part of Julie could not be messed about with in that way. It was as integral to the piece as the young lovers, Gaylord and Magnolia. Mayer took the easiest or smartest way out, depending on your point of view, and cast his most Southern white beauty in the part.

Ava talked to Lena, who told her not to be a fool, but grab the part. Ava did after Louis B. promised her that she could sing Julie's songs. Her life got very busy. She took intensive singing lessons and was swamped with period costume fittings and everything else involved in the preparation for a big Metro musical. Not surprisingly, Louis B. didn't live up to his promise, and her songs ended up being dubbed. Recordings that surfaced many years later proved that her husky voice was not only very appealing, it would have worked perfectly for the part.

Finding the Method

There was a slight delay before *I Want You* could begin production, and Goldwyn said I could go to New York if I promised to stay in touch and get myself back to Los Angeles the minute he needed me. Shelley heard that I was going. Even though she was still angry about Ava, I had been somewhat understanding about Burt Lancaster, and she wanted to go to New York, so she buried her hatchet elsewhere.

We were both aware of a new kind of acting that was having a major impact on movie audiences, particularly the younger members. It was exemplified by Montgomery Clift in *The Search, Red River,* and *The Heiress* and by Marlon Brando in *The Men* and *A Streetcar Named Desire.* We knew that we wanted and needed the kind of training they had experienced before they made any films. The only place to get that training was in New York and in the theater. Our problem was that we were both under contract in Hollywood, and nothing comparable existed on the West Coast. The teachers employed by the studios ranged from inept to incompetent.

Shelley and I went to New York to explore the acting scene, or more accurately, the teaching scene. Because of its growing reputation, the first place we observed at was the Actors Studio. What I remember most about that day is a young actor who came onstage to do a scene, stood for a long time in seemingly frustrated silence, then looked at Lee Strasberg and said, "I'm not ready yet. I need a little more time to prepare." Lee nodded. The actor left the stage. We waited . . . and waited . . . for more than twenty minutes. The actor returned, stood silently for a few minutes more, turned back to Lee, said, "I'm sorry I just can't get there," and walked offstage to Strasberg's assurances that they would try again.

When an audience is in their seats or a camera is ready to roll, an actor who just can't get there is going to be in big trouble. In the course of that day, other things were said that I could not grasp, for example, that inner truth was even more important than the text.

That evening Shelley and I had our first fight about "the method." She had loved everything she heard that day, particularly the idea of developing a way to get at the inner truth in her acting. I agreed that inner truth was necessary, but felt that an actor had to be able to get to it through the text, not through his personal experiences. Chekhov, Shaw, and Shakespeare used words to lead an actor to the truth. One had to be faithful to the text, not adapt it to some personal sense memory in order to play a character truthfully. I knew that the actor I admired most, Monty Clift, had been involved with the Actors Studio, but he also had been a member of Alfred Lunt and Lynn Fontanne's company. They along with Eva Le Gallienne were considered America's finest stage actors of the 1920s, 1930s, and 1940s, and they did the classics as well as contemporary plays. I'm sure none of them ever said that a personal truth was more important than the truth of the text. And I know from my own experience that they would never put up with actors who just couldn't get there.

Marlon had come to fame with Elia Kazan, one of the founders of the Actors Studio, as his director in *A Streetcar Named Desire*. Kazan also directed two of Brando's other most successful films, *Viva Zapata!* and *On the Waterfront*. Even though Marlon's name has always been linked with "The Studio," he never studied there. His only teacher, and the one to whom he always gave complete credit, was Stella Adler. Stella was not a fan of the Actors Studio or the Method. She had gone to Paris in 1934 to meet with and study with Stanislavsky for five intense weeks. When she arrived back in New York, it was to explain to Lee Strasberg that he had gotten "it" all wrong. He paid no attention to her, and she went on to become one of our greatest acting teachers.

I went to the Neighborhood Playhouse to observe and met Sandy Meisner, another teacher with an excellent reputation. After his class, which made great sense to me, I went to his office to meet him. I was babbling on about acting when he interrupted with a simple question. "What do you want to study with me for? You're already a movie star."

"I want to learn how to act," I replied.

After a beat he shook my hand and said, "You're on. I teach a class for professionals. As soon as you settle in New York, I'll fit you in."

Many years later, in the early 1980s, I went back to the Actors Studio one day because Shelley was teaching there. Lee's class on comedy was in progress when we arrived, so we sat in to listen for a bit. He was still talking the same old nonsense about truth being more important than text when a pretty young girl asked him how that applied when doing Noël Coward. After a long pause he said, "Well . . . with Noël Coward you have to do the words as written or it just won't work."

Now that Shelley and I had figured out where we wanted to study, figuring how to do it was the big problem. That was temporarily postponed when reality in the form of Hollywood interrupted our New York odyssey.

Universal had a project for Shelley called *Frenchie* and needed her back yesterday. The film turned out to be a mediocre remake of *Destry Rides Again* with Shelley as the Western saloon owner memorably created by Marlene Dietrich in the original. Goldwyn also wanted me back immediately. He was ready to go with *I Want You.* He seemed genuinely excited about it. His previous six films had been failures, and he needed this one to be a success. It was based on an idea that had come to him when his only son, Sammy, had been called up from inactive duty in the Army Reserves during the "police action" in Korea. Goldwyn wanted to tell a story about how an average American family was affected by America's involvement in another war just as the country was getting back on its feet after World War II. His first choice to write it had been Robert Sherwood. Sherwood liked the idea and told Goldwyn so but had to turn him down because of other commitments. Goldwyn then got Irwin Shaw, who had been writing undistinguished screenplays since 1936, but was now hot from the success of his first novel, *The Young Lions,* to do the screenplay. He then hired Mark Robson, the competent director whom he had saddled with *Edge of Doom.*

I felt that the screenplay was not only dull, but felt dated. Even though the part wasn't bad, I wasn't looking forward to playing a character who was self-involved to the point of indifference about his country. On the positive side, I was going to work with good actors. Dana was once again playing my older brother. Dorothy McGuire, always a particular favorite of mine, was playing my sister-in-law. My love interest was a talented newcomer, Peggy Dow. Peggy was a tall, leggy blonde with a husky voice who never took Hollywood seriously. This was to be her fourth and last film. She fell in love with a tall, handsome Oklahoma oil man and left the business without a backward glance. They had three tall, handsome sons who married three tall, gorgeous blondes. I met them all many years later when I was appearing in a play in Kansas City in the late 1970s. They all came backstage after the curtain, and Peggy could not have been more radiantly happy.

On the first day of rehearsal, I showed up on the soundstage where we were supposed to rehearse, and no one was there. Memories of *Roseanna McCoy* flooded back, and I thought, Oh Lord, not again. I don't think I can make it through another one.

Then Dorothy walked in, looking like a million bucks in a simple white dress. We introduced ourselves and sat down, and I asked her about her time in New York acting in the theater. We were deep in conversation when a secretary from Mark Robson's office came to apologize that they had not reached us at home before we left for the studio. There was no problem, just a slight change in the rehearsal schedule. The company call had been pushed ahead to 2:00 P.M. that afternoon. We were free until then. It was not quite 11:00 A.M., so Dottie and I decided to go for a relaxed early lunch.

The only reasonably decent restaurant near the Goldwyn Studio was a dingy Chinese place, the Formosa Café. They were not open yet, so Dottie suggested we go back to her place, where she would fix us "a little something." We did, but the cupboard was bare, and the only little something in the fridge was a bottle of very good champagne. She gave me a mischievous look and said, "Do we dare?" We did and before we knew it, it was time to get back to the studio. We arrived on time; slightly giddy and light-headed, and thankful for the ubiquitous coffee and Danish. The reading went smoothly, except that Dorothy and I got the giggles during a confrontation scene around the dinner table. We could never get through that scene again without losing it. Neither of us wanted to; in fact, we were ashamed of ourselves and tried desperately not to let it happen, but the harder we tried, the harder we laughed.

The day we filmed it was hell. Remote, taciturn Dana finally blew his top, turned to Dottie, and yelled, "For god's sake, Dorothy, pull yourself together! Farley is just a Hollywood kid, but you're from the theater! You should know better!!"

She looked at me and up we went again . . . helpless. Somehow we finally got that scene in the can and the rest of the film went smoothly.

I Want You, which turned out to be as tepid and old-fashioned as I had feared, had the additional misfortune to open just as the cease-fire negotiations with Korea began, so it was no longer even topical. Goldwyn pulled out all the promotional stops for his latest release, but it had neither the style nor the impact of *Best Years.* His losing streak remained unbroken.

The film that won the Academy Award that year was MGM's lavish musical

An American in Paris, a movie as different from Goldwyn's *Saturday Evening Post* cover take on American life as Toulouse-Lautrec's art was from Norman Rockwell's. Goldwyn then tried again to loan me out again to Universal for a piece of junk like *Son of Ali Baba.* I refused and was put on suspension.

The Dog Stole the Movie

The title of my next film, also starring Shelley Winters, embodied the one thing that she never learned how to do, *Behave Yourself*. I was on suspension, and she had finished something she knew was terrible for Universal. We were planning to go back to New York to work on our growth as actors when my agent, Charlie Feldman, called me to say that he had a good script that he wanted me to read. It was a screwball comedy owned by RKO, still run by Howard Hughes. It had great parts for Shelley and me and a wonderful cast of supporting actors. My agent was right. It was funny, well-written, and very different from anything either of us had ever done. Shelley and I played happy-go-lucky young marrieds who, along with our beloved dog, get involved with the mob in a series of smuggling misadventures. We both thought it would be great for our careers as a change of pace as well a lot of fun to do. Our agents arranged loan deals for us. A director had not been set, and we were hoping for someone with comedy experience. Timing is all-important in this kind of near-farce, not just in the performances, but also in the cutting room. When we got word that Hughes, whose involvement with production at the time was half-hearted at best, had given in to the writer's demand to direct his own script, Shelley and I were devastated. There have been a few genius comedy writers who can direct their own material. Preston Sturges and Billy Wilder spring to mind. Our writer/director, George Beck, was not only way out of their class, he was an untried novice . . . with bad instincts. He was clueless with actors. Faced with Shelley's horrendously bad behavior during the entire shoot, he was also helpless.

Shelley's short time observing at the Actors Studio on our New York trip had a deeper effect than I realized. She proved to be a superlative example of the cliché "A little knowledge can be a dangerous thing." Before she would shoot any close-ups, she would vanish into her dressing room and listen to *Madama Butterfly* to get in character. I could never figure out which sense memory she was trying to get to, or how Puccini could help prepare her for a screwball comedy about a couple who were a ripoff of Nick and Nora Charles of the *Thin Man* comedies. One day, when she was holding things up even longer than usual, the director asked me to help get her on the set. When she wouldn't answer the door to her dressing room, I charged in, and there she sat, *Butterfly* blasting, stuffing herself with jelly donuts . . . and it was many years before *The Poseidon Adventure.*

On another occasion, the first setup of the day was a walking two-shot. Shelley accused our cameraman, Jimmy Wong Howe, of favoring me because we had worked together before. Nothing would convince her otherwise, and she walked off the set, refusing to come back until the next day when she could see the rushes. Of course, they proved her wrong, and without so much as a "sorry," we went back to work. She may have been angry because RKO insisted on my getting top billing. We eventually flailed our way to the finish. When I saw the edited version, all of my fears proved to be well founded. The only funny thing about the film was that the dog stole the movie. That my affection for Shelley managed to survive this first time working together is miraculous.

Fortunately for me, *Strangers on a Train* had recently opened and was a triumph. It revived Hitch's then-flagging career. It demonstrated Bob Walker's amazing versatility, and it moved me to Hollywood's A-list of young leading men.

The Grand Tour

Shelley obviously decided that there were fences to mend, because after enough time for me to cool down had passed, she invited me to dinner at Chasen's, then one of the top restaurants in Hollywood. After a long evening of inarticulate efforts to apologize, she finally said, "Will you forgive me if I get us a free trip to Europe and Israel?"

I asked how she intended to do that. She arched her brows. Gesturing grandly, she had a phone brought to our table. Then she rummaged through the yard sale interior of her purse and came up with a scrap of paper that had a phone number on it. She dialed the number and after a short pause said, "Howard . . . hi, it's me, Shelley."

I knew at once what she had done. She had gotten Howard Hughes on the phone . . . in Chasens! . . . and proceeded to convince him to give us a free first-class trip on TWA around the world.

Hughes had entered that time in his life when he was becoming a recluse, and none of us had seen him during the film. Given his reputation as a womanizer, I wasn't too surprised that she had his number, but that she got him on the phone so easily and accomplished what she did so quickly astonished me. I was too taken with her chutzpah to stay mad at her, even though the trip was not without strings. She promised him that we would do "a little" publicity for *Behave Yourself*.

Ten days later, the night before we were to leave, I gave her a friendship ring, which she proceeded to tell the press that mobbed our departure was an engagement ring. I realized at the airport that "a little" publicity was probably going to be a lot more than I had bargained for. I forget which of the two gorgons, Hedda or Louella, outraged by the fact that Shelley and I were publicly traveling together and not married, headlined her column: "First to disgrace Hollywood worldwide, there was Ingrid Bergman and Roberto Rossellini, then Rita Hayworth and Aly Khan, now it's Shelley and Farley!" That was meant as a major slap on our wrists, but we were delighted to be in such glamorous company.

Unfortunately, just before we boarded the plane, a friend of Shelley's, probably Doris Dowling, an actress known mostly for her excellent performance with Ray Milland in *The Lost Weekend,* told her that she should have a tiny freckle on her upper lip looked at, because it might be "serious." After going through an endless photo session that began at the TWA desk, moved to the TWA limo that took us to the plane, then to the top of the gangway that was next to the TWA logo on the plane, then to an interior shot of us being greeted by the TWA captain, and finally to us being seated and served champagne by two comely TWA stewardesses, the press was herded off the plane, and we strapped ourselves in for takeoff. As soon as we were airborne, Shelley started to cry. After a minute or so, she told me that someone had told her that a freckle on her upper lip looked cancerous. No matter how I tried to comfort her, the drama played us to Chicago, where we stopped to refuel. By the time we were preparing to land at Idlewild, as New York's JFK Airport was then called, Shelley had cheered up and applied fresh full-glamour makeup, which made me realize the press was waiting for us. We were met on the runway by John Springer, a young publicist RKO had arranged to chaperone us through our press commitments in New York and London. In a roped-off area inside the terminal, the entire New York press corps was ready to spring. After that concluded, we were grateful for the police-escorted limousine that whisked us to the front entrance of the Plaza. Fans in front of the hotel and in the lobby screamed our names and tried to get at us for autographs. John and a couple of New York's finest got us through the mob and the lobby unscathed and up to our grand top-floor suite, with two bedrooms for propriety's sake. The enormous living room was filled with flowers, fruit, cheeses, liquor, and chilled champagne from Howard Hughes, Universal, RKO, the Theatre Guild, and the management of the Plaza. We could have thrown one helluva party, but we would have slept through anything, we were so tired. John handed us two single-spaced pages of a grueling publicity schedule for the rest of the week. I wanted to let Shelley have it about the price we were paying for our "free trip," but she was too tired, and so was I.

The next morning I had at John instead, and he eliminated some of the less important newspaper interviews and most of the personal appearances. John Springer was doing his job well, because he saw to it that there were featured items about us in the papers every day, topped off by several important television interviews.

I wanted to carve out some time to take Shelley to see the major museums and a couple of shows. I made her buy a pair of comfortable shoes, but after I had dragged her around the Metropolitan and the Museum of Modern Art, it was clear that she probably would have been happier doing interviews. The Broadway shows were another matter.

We saw and were completely captivated by Rodgers and Hammerstein's masterpiece *The King and I,* with Jerry Robbins's stunning ballet, *The Small House of Uncle Thomas.* We also saw a brand-new musical, *Flahooley,* which was a complete dog, except for a golden-voiced ingénue who lit up the stage. I believe it was Barbara Cook's first Broadway show. Nine years later, Barbara and I starred in the first revival of *The King and I* at New York's City Center to smashing reviews. During our hectic time in Manhattan, Shelley also managed to find two Park Avenue specialists who told her that her freckle was just that, nothing more, but she was not really convinced by their diagnoses.

As the time for us to leave for Europe got closer, Shell started acting up and out. She blamed me, rather than room service, for the fact that she had put on enough weight to need her girdle in public. When John told us that he had planned an official party in the Palm Court downstairs to announce our engagement to the press before we left for the airport, it came as a complete surprise. I did not know if I was ready to take such a public step. What I was ready for was a little acting up myself. John must have sensed that, because he headed me off at the pass by telling us that while he was off in London to set up a few press things for us to do there, he wanted us to go ahead to Paris where we could both relax and enjoy life, because he knew how tired we must be. Our TWA Clipper was to leave from Idlewild Sunday evening at nine, and after a stop for refueling in Ireland would arrive at Gatwick Airport outside of London. He would get off there, and we would continue on to Paris alone! We were so grateful at the thought of being on our own that we promised to be on our best behavior at the big party.

At 4:00 P.M. Sunday afternoon chaos reigned at the Plaza. John, as usual, had done his job well. It seemed as if every reporter and photographer in the greater New York area was crammed into the Palm Court. It was past our time to leave when John, with the help of two policemen, extricated us from the mob. They cleared a path for us. I took Shelley by the hand and ran for the waiting limo. As we started to pull out, Shelley screamed, "Stop! We forgot my girdle!" At one point during the melee, she had gone to the ladies' room and taken it off, because it was killing her. When she came back out, she had tried to get me to stick it under my coat. I dumped it into a potted palm. It seems that it was her favorite and "also very expensive," so she wouldn't leave it, even though we were in danger of being late for our plane. I had had enough for one day and flatly refused to go back into that mob to search for a girdle in some palm in a court full of potted palms. John went with her, and they finally emerged triumphant.

Though the stewardess found me an empty row to stretch out in, I just couldn't sleep. The whole situation, which had started out innocently enough with a friendship ring, had taken on a life of its own that I was not comfortable with. I really did love Shelley, but we were polar opposites who fought as much as we agreed, especially about life in our chosen profession. She adored being a star. I hated it. Now I felt as if we were somehow on a runaway train with no way off, and it scared me.

It was early afternoon when we arrived at Gatwick and said goodbye to John and responsibilities for a couple of weeks. We were both feeling strangely melancholy on the flight to Paris. When I asked Shell if she was okay, she said she was just worried about the possible cancer on her upper lip, but I thought it was more than that. By the time we got to Paris, she had sublimated all her other misgivings by focusing on that damn freckle again and convincing herself that she was at death's door. In the cab on the way to our hotel, I could not get her to look out the window at the beauty of the city. She said the Champs-Elysées looked just like the Grand Concourse in the Bronx. In fact, the entire time we were in Paris, all she really looked at was a little card that tabulated the conversion of dollars to francs. She did have two close brushes with death in Paris: at the hotel when she tried to get a better room by slowly and loudly explaining to a rather grand desk clerk, in her best pigeon French, "me no likee" about her current room; and at Le Grand Véfour, when she used the same tone with the maître d' to order a Coke. It took twenty-five minutes to arrive and was presented on a silver tray in a bottle that had not been dusted since before the Germans marched into Paris.

Ethyl and Buddy had a pretty walkup apartment, and we spent a couple of evenings with them. I bought a little Hillman Minx convertible that first week and proceeded to spend way too much time ferrying Shelley from doctor to doctor, none of whom she believed when they told her she did not have skin cancer. I finally refused to continue to be her chauffeur and told her to use taxis. After two days of dealing with Parisian cabdrivers and not finding a compliant doctor to remove her "tumor," she begged me to take her to London. I gave in, knowing that I would not have a minute of peace until she had exhausted all possibilities. We called John to tell him that we were coming to London sooner that expected and asked him to arrange a suite for us at the Savoy. Even though he had not arranged our press schedule yet, he managed to have as many photographers and reporters waiting for us at Gatwick as he had had in New York. London was still shaking off the ashes of World War II, and like the rest of Europe was not yet a PR destination for American film junkets. Since *A Place in the Sun* and *Strangers on a Train* had already been released in Great Britain, we got the real celebrity treatment.

In London Shelley finally found a sympathetic M.D. with an impressive Sir attached to his name who agreed to remove her worry and have it examined in his laboratory. Peggy Mailey, an old friend of Shelley's, showed up at the Savoy. When Shelley, caught up in the drama of her impending surgery, decided she was too weak to attend the Festival of Britain, to which we had been invited, I took Peggy. We went into one exhibition that was televised, and when we were introduced as Farley Granger and Shelley Winters, we just smiled and waved and played movie stars. When Shelley saw that on the TV news, she was ready for therapy as well as freckle removal. The next night, on "preop eve," I had to get out for a little quality time alone, so I convinced Shelley that she should stay in bed and prepare for the big event. I was going out to explore the city for the evening: "Don't wait up for me." Covent Garden was close to the hotel, so I wandered into the opera house and impulsively bought a ticket to see *Peter Grimes,* which was playing that evening. I knew nothing about it or Benjamin Britten. It was stirring, grand, and moving in a way I never expected. My knowledge of opera up to that point was mostly limited to the Puccini of Saul and Ethyl's four hands. Mr. Britten was a whole new world. At intermission, I was in the bar when a gorgeous couple came over to introduce themselves and to "pick me up," as they put it. I liked them at once. Peter and Mary Noble quickly became two of my most cherished friends. He was then a struggling young reporter, and she was a struggling young actress. They invited me to their adorable mews house for lunch the next day while Shelley was under the knife, having her freckle-ectomy. The other guests at lunch were Dolores Gray and her mother. Dolores was a Broadway musical star with a knockout voice and an equally knockout figure. Dolores, who did all of Ethel Merman's parts in London because Merman would not fly, was a bigger star here than she was in New York. They were dressed in identical blue-and-white gingham pinafores and, for a lady with a reputation as one extremely tough cookie, Dolores acted as demurely as she was dressed. She also never said a word, which was completely at odds with her reputation. Her mother, on the other hand, more than made up for both of them. She never shut up, and her conversation was punctuated with lots of, "Well, we told Cole that Dolores just had to have . . ." and, "We said to

Irving, that number is all right, but don't you think . . ." Lunch was an uninterrupted mama-logue. Promptly at 3:00 P.M. the two little girls in blue got up and daintily departed so Dolores could get her beauty nap for the evening performance of *Call Me Madam*. The door closed and the three of us fell about laughing at the incongruity of it all.

A few days later, when her Band-Aid was small enough for her to be seen in public, and after she had gotten the news that her freckle was benign, I took Shelley to meet Peter and Mary. It was love at first sight all around, just as it had been for me. We decided to drive to Stratford-on-Avon together to see a young actor named Richard Burton, who was being hailed as the new Olivier. I rented a car the following day, and off we went. On the drive to Stratford I was concentrating so hard on keeping to the left that I had not looked at the gas gauge. In the lush, verdant countryside of the Cotswolds, with no sign of civilization as far as the eye could see, we ran out of gas. We had no option except to sit and wait on the narrow road for a car to come our way that we could flag down for help. We were at the bottom of a long steep hill, and the road ahead curved gently to the right. Shelley was the first to spot eight or ten cyclists headed in our direction. She got out of the car, yelling for us not to worry, she would get help. She huffed energetically up the center of the road toward them waving her arms and screaming, "STOP!!! . . . STOP!!!" As they got closer to her, they peeled off, as neatly as a formation of dive bombers, into a ditch on their side of the road. We watched in stunned silence as they picked themselves up one by one. Fortunately none of them was seriously injured, and one of them was even gallant enough to go back to the nearest petrol stop to get us enough gas for us to make it to Stratford. Shelley fussed and doctored and charmed the rest of the cyclists until our man of the hour returned with the petrol. In no time we were back on the road.

We got rooms at the Stratford Arms, and purchased our tickets to see *Hamlet* that evening and *Henry V* the next afternoon. I have seen a lot of *Hamlet*s in my life, including the one that Burton later did on Broadway early on during his marriage to Elizabeth Taylor, but never one as good as I saw that evening. It fairly crackled with energy. I swore to Shelley that I could smell the fuse burning in this time bomb of a young Danish prince. And the way he sang the language swept us along with him. The scene where he rages at his mother for sleeping with his father's brother had such searing sexual energy that it was almost painful to watch. We all went backstage to see him after the performance. His first wife, Sybil, was there, and before we could get a word out about his performance, Richard said he was a big fan of our work in films. Peter and Mary jumped in with their compliments on his performance, thank heaven, because Shelley and I were like two stagestruck inarticulate kids mumbling ours. He grinned like a teenager when we praised him and accepted immediately when I invited him and Sybil to join us for supper. He and I sat up drinking Irish whiskey and talking about acting long after all the others had crept off to bed. He could not understand why I wanted to leave movies for the theater. He wanted the exact opposite. The next afternoon I could hardly drag my hung-over self out of bed for some sustenance before the matinee. I didn't envy Richard having to go on as *Henry V*. But he performed splendidly and looked terrific. His rallying speech to the troops before the battle of Agincourt was so rousing that I would have followed him anywhere.

That evening, two friends richer, we drove back to London with Peter and Mary, who remained friends for life. A short time later, the Nobles, with their daughter Katina, moved to a big house in St. John's Wood, where they had their second daughter, Kara. They had more space in their new home on Abbey Road, and were able to expand their famous dinner parties. I have met more fascinating people at their home than I can remember, from the Beatles, whose studio was just down the road, to Sean Connery to a prime minister. For a countless number of famous actors, directors, painters, opera singers, and their many lesser known but equally wonderful friends, 46 Abbey Road was an open door. Shelley, through the years, would stay with them whenever she was in London. That must have been a mixed blessing, since Shell could never have enough heat, and their beautiful Edwardian house had plenty of cool drafts.

Shelley's surgery and convalescence complete, we contacted John, did a few more interviews, and then got on with our world tour, next stop Rome. Shelley had the name of a lady who made inexpensive ripoffs of couture dresses. No sooner had we checked into the Excelsior than, without even unpacking, she took off to get herself a bunch. I thought, Who knows how long that shopping spree will last? and, breathing freely, set out to walk around Rome. Half a block down the Via Veneto, I ran into Humphrey Bogart and Betty Bacall. We went to a Tuscan restaurant nearby for a great lunch, one of the world's best grilled veal chops, with liters of good wine. They told about their experience making *The African Queen* deep in the Congo with Kate Hepburn and John Huston. Hepburn, who was there all on her own with no friend or companion, was a consummate trooper who adapted to everything and anything cheerfully. John Huston segued from director to great white hunter effortlessly. In fact, it had often seemed as if he preferred the hunter to the director. Betty, who was trying to keep all of them in balance, said Huston took off to hunt whenever it rained. This infuriated Bogie, who hated the experience of roughing it and wanted Huston to get them all back to civilization quickly, if not yesterday. This meant that these two old pals had more than one memorable shout-up.

Bogie mentioned that Errol Flynn was living in Rome and said that we should look him up because life at his villa was a nonstop party. He gave me the number and, as Shelley knew and adored him, we did call a few days later and were invited over the next evening. I had never met him but had always been a fan, so we were both looking forward to it. We arrived at around 9:00 P.M., cocktail time in Rome. There was plenty to drink, but no sign of any dinner to come. Flynn, a little drunk and a lot out of focus, was dressed in a white and gold Tunisian robe. He could not have been more welcoming, and he was very flattering about our work in a vague sort of way. In truth, I had a feeling that he was just being nice and had never seen anything either of us had done. After a few glasses of champagne, we were not feeling comfortable with the fawning bevy of young female and male beauties that were very much in evidence. We left after a respectful couple of drinks and went to a restaurant in Rome's ghetto where we had my first *carciofi alla giudea,* Jewish-style baby artichokes deep fried until they open into a crispy dark gold flower. They tasted even better than they looked.

Shelley, having finished the fittings for her new wardrobe, was anxious to go to Israel. No attempt to persuade her to see the wonders of Rome worked. I should have realized in Paris when she told me that the Champs-Elysées reminded her of the Grand Concourse in the Bronx that she was no world-class traveler.

On the flight to Tel Aviv she said to me gleefully, "Now you'll see how it feels to be in the minority." I had to laugh. "Shelley, you know that almost everyone I love is Jewish," but she just gave me a little self-satisfied smile and repeated, "You'll see." A delegation met us at the airport, and on the way into town we passed the main movie theater. *They Live by Night* was playing. When we got out at the hotel, everyone recognized and made a big fuss over me and no one paid any attention to her. She didn't speak to me for two blissful days.

That night I went to the theater alone to see a good production of *Death of a Salesman.* At intermission I met a young Israeli journalist named Yuval Elizur. After the show I joined him and his girlfriend for a drink. We spent hours talking politics and show business. It was very late when we reluctantly decided it was time to say good night. He said that if I would like to see the real Israel, he and his girl would be delighted to show it to me and Shelley when she emerged from her funk. He had roared with laughter when I told him why she was sulking. I jumped on his invitation.

Shelley called the next morning and sheepishly admitted that she had not been at her best the day before. I told her about Yuval and his offer, and she was thrilled. The next day the four of us went to Jerusalem in a little car Yuval had rented. We stayed at a small, luxurious hotel that was partially bombed out and was located opposite the Wailing Wall. To touch that wall, which was all that remained of the ancient temple that existed in the time of Christ, stirred feelings in me that I didn't know were there. In the true sense of the word, it was awesome. We traveled all around Israel, from Haifa to the Dead Sea, and spent the night in several kibbutzes, all of which were in varying stages of being carved out of the harsh, rocky terrain. The spirit, hospitality, and courage of the settlers was inspiring. Dotted all over the place were spindly saplings that were so loved and cared for that you absolutely accepted that they would one day be mighty trees.

On our last night back in Tel Aviv, Shelley and I went to a large restaurant with a courtyard where a wedding party was in progress. The people in the wedding party were dark-skinned and not dressed in modern clothes as most of the rest of the people in the restaurant were. I leaned over to ask a man at an adjacent table what that signified, and he said with a smile, in a heavily accented stage whisper, "Oh, they are Yemenites . . . they are our niggers."

The blood drained from Shelley's face. I thought she was going to be sick. She ran out of the restaurant while I paid the bill. I found her outside shaking and just held her. She had been so excited and moved by the spirit of the people we had met that she wasn't ready to deal with the awful truth that the evil of prejudice could exist here in this land of promise, just as it has through the ages in the rest of the world.

It was time to go. Shelley booked a plane to Rome in order to pick up her dresses, and I went ahead to Paris to spend time with Ethyl and Buddy. Shell planned to join me as soon as possible to return to L.A.

Jerry Robbins was in Paris when I arrived. That night we all went to the Lido, a chic nightclub on the Champs-Elysées, because Jerry wanted to introduce us to two American dancers, Forrest Bonshire and Joe Milan, who were in the show there along with the famous "Bluebell Girls." These showgirls, all English, were known for their beauty, their stature, at least five feet eleven inches, and for the fact that they were all required to have classical ballet training. After the show, Jerry took us backstage and introduced us to Forrest and Joe. After the last show, sometime after 3:00 A.M., we all ended up in Les Halles having café au lait and fresh-baked croissants. None of us kept track of the time because Forrest kept us laughing constantly. He was one of the funniest guys I've ever met and reminded me of Freddy Ney, Betty Grable's favorite chorus boy. I went back to the Lido several times, and Forrest and Joe, along with as many girls as could pile into my little Hillman Minx, would party into the wee small hours. Shelley called several times postponing her arrival—"dress problems," she said. Jerry also introduced me to Ned Rorem, the young American composer who was living in Paris. Ned, knowing how taken I was by modern French painting, took me to lunch at the home of a countess who had a marvelous collection of contemporary art. Her apartment was a triplex on Boulevard Montparnasse that included a 1,500-square-meter garden. It was a bit like having your own park. The whole place was Art Deco and if it had been in black-and-white, I would have known that I'd stumbled into a Fred Astaire and Ginger

Rogers movie. The countess was a chic beauty of indeterminate middle age who spoke flawless English. Her collection included several American artists, including one Whistler that I coveted and a Milton Avery that I could have happily spent the rest of my life looking at. She offered to introduce me to the best small galleries in Paris, and I could not pass up the opportunity. At one of the galleries, I fell in love with two paintings. One was a small modern still life and the other was of Les Halles. I couldn't afford them both, so I chose one and bought it on the spot . . . my first real painting. The gallery owner promised to wrap it carefully so that I could carry it on the plane with me back to L.A. When I went back to pick it up, there were two paintings wrapped and waiting for me. I protested that there must be some mistake. I had only purchased one. The owner assured me that there was no mistake; the second one was a gift from the countess. Completely flustered, I stammered that I could not possibly accept it and made him redo the package. I was not able to reach her before I left Paris, so after much deliberation I wrote what I hoped was a graceful note of thanks for her extravagant gesture.

It was forty-five years before I saw Ned again. Patricia Highsmith, the author of the book on which Hitch had based *Strangers on a Train,* had died, leaving her estate to Yaddo, a well-known retreat for artists and writers. The event was celebrated by cocktails, dinner, and a showing of the film at the Museum of Modern Art. I was talking to some people before the dinner when I spotted a vaguely familiar face across the room smiling at me. As he started over, I realized it was Ned. We hugged, and before he could speak, I said, "I know what you're going to say." He laughed and said, "It's probably still there waiting for you."

Nick Ray contacted Buddy to ask him to work on a costume epic that Nick was preparing in Spain, so Buddy and Ethyl were getting ready to leave Paris. Jerry Robbins had already left, and I decided it was time for me to get home and deal with my life. Shelley finally called from Rome to give me the number of the flight she would be on when connecting to L.A. through Paris. I told her I would get a ticket and meet her on the plane. She was very subdued and a little vague about why she had stayed in Rome so long. Sitting on a secret was not something she was ever successful at, and soon it all came out. Somewhere over the Atlantic she dropped an ultimatum: "Are you going to marry me? . . . Because either you marry me or I am going to marry this Italian actor I met in Rome." I was shocked, since we had been apart for such a short time. I said, "Shelley, what actor? What the hell are you talking about? We've only been apart for three weeks. You just met this guy. You just want to get married, and you don't care who it is." "He's very nice," she said. "He's a very talented actor, and he's half Jewish."

I realized then that however much we enjoyed being with each other, we weren't really in love. We had gotten caught up acting out our publicity. I wanted nothing but happiness for Shelley, but I worried that this precipitous leap into what she considered respectability was a very tricky maneuver. Her Italian actor was Vittorio Gassman, who turned out to be extremely talented, extremely nice, and a good match for Shelley in the self-absorption category. He was tall and handsome with classic aquiline features and was a big star in Italy, both onstage and in films. Best known in the U.S. for his films *Big Deal on Madonna Street* and *The Easy Life,* he, along with Marcello Mastroianni, was a regular in the group of actors used in stage productions by Luchino Visconti. He eventually formed his own theater company in his native Genoa.

Vittorio came back to Hollywood with Shelley, where she managed to get him a contract at MGM. They settled down in Beverly Hills and had a beautiful little girl named Vittoria, or Tori for short.

Life on the A-List

I had let my rented house go before Shelley and I left on our grand tour. I was living at the Hotel Bel-Air until I found a new place to rent. Word had gotten around town that Shelley and I were no longer a couple, and the success of *Strangers* apparently opened a new set of social doors to me.

Gary Cooper called to invite me to a dinner party he was giving for Clark Gable at his house. When I accepted and he asked if I would mind picking up Barbara Stanwyck, I was delighted. I had always thought she was one of the greatest. *The Lady Eve* and *Double Indemnity* are two of my favorite films and feature two of the many terrific performances she gave through the years.

I arrived at her door promptly at 6:30 P.M., a huge bouquet of pink peonies in hand. The maid said she would be right down, took the flowers, and offered me a glass of champagne. Barbara came down a few minutes later, looking terrific in something silver and slinky. She carried on about the flowers as the maid brought them in and joined me for some champagne. I was anxious to get things off to a good start with the right kind of small talk, but unfortunately I was out of touch with the latest gossip. I asked how and where her husband was. An expletive told me how she felt about her husband: "That son of a bitch ran off with some kraut starlet."

As I struggled to pull my foot out of my mouth, she started to laugh and said, "Don't worry about it, baby, he's not worth sweating over," and the rest of the evening went like gangbusters.

We arrived at 7:30 on the dot and were met at the door by Rocky, Mrs. Gary

Cooper, who hugged Barbara and said, "He's going to be so glad to see you." Cooper and Stanwyck had made a couple of great films together, *Meet John Doe* and *Ball of Fire,* the latter for Sam Goldwyn, whom she liked even though she referred to him as "that tough old bastard." Rocky sent Barbara out to the garden to see Coop, took my arm, and showed me around their lovely home. As we walked into the garden, I spotted him laughing with Barbara. Rocky took me over to meet him. He was tall, lean, warm, and friendly. The thing I remember most about him is the twinkle in his deep blue eyes, which were framed by thick dark lashes. He was a movie star.

The group that evening turned out to be almost a who's who of Hollywood royalty, many of whom were Brits and all of whom could not have been kinder to this new kid on the block. Some of the people I remember meeting were: Greer Garson; Ronald Colman; David Niven, who had also been under contract to Goldwyn, and who was the best raconteur I have ever met; Myrna Loy; Ray Milland, with whom I later worked in *The Girl in the Red Velvet Swing*; and James Mason, who never seemed to be in the moment. It was as if he was off in his own secret places. Meeting him confirmed what I'd always suspected: he would have been terrific as Rupert in *Rope.*

Barbara and I had arrived early, so I got to admire everyone's entrance. We were seated at tables around a dance floor that had been set up on the lawn behind the house. Barbara and I shared a table with Deborah Kerr and her husband. Deborah, a lovely English redhead, had been brought to Hollywood to play opposite Clark Gable in *The Hucksters.* Louis B. Mayer needed a cool, refined beauty to replace the enormously popular redhead, Greer Garson, who had married a wealthy oil magnate and retired from the screen in the midfifties. Deborah, like her predecessor, had an ultra-ladylike air about her that was misleading. In fact, she was quick, sharp, and very funny. She and Barbara got along like old school chums.

Jimmy Stewart was also there with his wife. It was the first time I'd seen him since we'd worked for Hitchcock. It was a treat talking to him, and I felt closer to him than I ever did on the set of *Rope.* He was so genuinely happy for my success in *Strangers on a Train* that I was quite moved.

Clark Gable arrived late, and it was a star entrance to remember. He stopped for a moment at the top of the steps that led down to the garden. He was alone, tanned, and wearing a white suit. He radiated charisma. He really was the King.

The party was elegant. Hot Polynesian hors d'oeuvres were passed around during drinks. Dinner was very French, with consommé madrilène as a first course followed by cold poached salmon and asparagus hollandaise. During dessert, a lemon soufflé, and coffee, the cocktail pianist by the pool, who had been playing through dinner, was discreetly augmented by a rhythm section, and they became a small combo for dancing. The dance floor was set up on the lawn near an open bar, and the whole garden glowed with colored paper lanterns.

Later in the evening, I managed a subdued jitterbug with Deborah Kerr, who was much livelier than her cool on-screen image. She had not yet done *From Here to Eternity,* in which she and Burt Lancaster steamed up the screen with their love scene in the surf.

I was, of course, extremely impressed to be there with Hollywood royalty that evening, but as far as parties go, I realized that I had a lot more fun at Gene Kelly's open houses.

I took Miss Stanwyck home and had a great time listening to her dish the party and everyone there. We went in for a nightcap, and I ended up spending the night. We enjoyed each other's company to the fullest.

The next day I resolved not to fall into the trap of becoming the new, available young stud about town for the unattached A-list ladies. Other young actors I knew, like Peter Lawford, had been there and done that, and never ended up any better for the wear.

"The Gift of the Magi"

Goldwyn loaned me out to 20th again, and I took the opportunity to make another pitch to have my contract split with Fox, but Goldwyn refused to listen. The movie was *O. Henry's Full House,* a film version of five of O. Henry's short stories with an all-star cast that included Charles Laughton, Marilyn Monroe, Richard Widmark, Anne Baxter, Jean Peters, Fred Allen, Oscar Levant, Jeanne Crain, and me. Jeanne and I were appearing in "The Gift of the Magi," perhaps O. Henry's most beloved short story. Our director was Henry King, an old-timer with a solid reputation. It was a delightful change of pace for me. I had always enjoyed working at 20th, and Jeanne was not only beautiful, she was a delight to work with. It was a particularly good experience.

In the commissary on my first day there, Tyrone Power joined me for lunch. In person he was even more handsome than he was on screen. He was also devoid of pretension, easygoing, and friendly. I felt at ease with him right away. When he heard that I was living at the Hotel Bel-Air, he insisted that I stay with him and his wife, Linda Christian. They had a big hacienda-style home in Bel

Air with a large guest apartment over their garage, where I could stay until I found a place of my own. He was so genuinely welcoming that I accepted without hesitation.

When I got to their house the next day, Linda was there to greet me and help me settle in. Linda, who was born in Mexico, the daughter of a rich Dutch oilman, had grown up all over the world. She was gorgeous and charming, but I sensed something a bit calculating behind that lovely exterior. Their living room was dominated by a large portrait of her painted by Diego Rivera. In it she was naked from the waist up and surrounded by calla lilies, which were very much "in bloom again." She was justifiably proud of the portrait. It was very beautiful. A studio car came for Ty and me each morning. Since 20th was so close, my staying there was pleasant and convenient . . . until Linda stopped by one evening to be sure I had everything I wanted. Over a glass of wine, she smiled and asked whom I preferred, her or Ty? I managed to stammer out something intelligible about what an ideal couple they were and how much I liked them both while resolving to light a fire under my real estate agent. She let it slide and asked if I would come to a big party that she and Ty were giving next weekend. "Everyone is going to be here, and we will be disappointed if you don't come." I, of course, accepted. As Linda was leaving, she turned to add sweetly, "Shelley and Vittorio are coming. I hope that won't be a problem for you." I said, "Not at all, it sounds like fun."

I wasn't sure about the fun part, but actually I was looking forward to seeing how Shelley would behave. The day of the party, Ty asked me if I would do him a favor and pick up Hildegard Knef, a German actress whom David O. Selznick had just put under contract. I said that I would. A stunning German blonde with turquoise eyes set off by luxuriant dark lashes, Hildegard had a deep throaty voice, and a fascinating past. She was wearing a dark green strapless satin gown that showed off the most beautiful back I can ever remember seeing. She was already fighting with Selznick, who wanted to change her name to Gilda Christian and her nationality to Austrian. I liked her at once. She never made it in Hollywood, but in the mid-fifties she was a big success as the leading lady of *Silk Stockings,* a Broadway musical version of the classic Greta Garbo film *Ninotchka.* She wrote a refreshingly blunt and forthright bestselling autobiography in 1971 titled *The Gift Horse.* It detailed her growing up in wartime Germany under Hitler.

It rained heavily the evening of the party and the tent leaked, so everyone crowded into the living room. Hedda and Louella were there gathering scraps for their columns, and salivating for trouble between Shelley and me. When the Gassmans arrived, I went up to them. Shelley was obviously a nervous wreck, but Vittorio just clapped an arm around my shoulder and said, "*Ciao, Farley, an-*

diamo al bar per un po' di vino. Let's go to the bar for a little wine." And we walked off, leaving Shelley dumbstruck for the first and probably only time in her life. Vittorio and I talked about how much he already missed Italy. He couldn't get over the fact that there was no street life in Los Angeles. He compared his life here to "being in a cocoon with four wheels all the time," and this was before there were any traffic problems.

A couple of weeks later, I received an invitation to a party at Jack Warner's home. I took Hildegard, knowing that it would be a good thing for her to meet the Warner Brothers crowd. She was excited, and I was happy to have a chance to see her again. It was also when I saw the last of my top three favorite Hollywood portraits. The first had been George Gershwin's self-portrait, which I still coveted. The second was Diego Rivera's painting of Linda Christian with the calla lilies in bloom. This third one was priceless. As we walked into Jack Warner's large entry hall with its three-story atrium ceiling, two well-lit portraits dominated the area from alcoves on either side of the hall. Ann Warner's was fairly straightforward, as I recall, but Dalí had portrayed Jack Warner as a particularly venal-looking tycoon standing in a great pile of golden coins. Hildegard and I were at a loss for words standing in front of it when a familiar raspy voice behind us said, "It's perfect, isn't it . . . and he loves it." Then he winked at us and, with that famous emphysemic laugh, walked off. It was Sydney Greenstreet, the great (both in terms of girth and talent) character actor from *The Maltese Falcon.* Bette Davis was also there that evening. As soon as I spotted her, I went over to say hello. This was the evening when we had the conversation about how much I loved her singing "They're Either Too Young or Too Old" in the film *Hollywood Canteen.*

It has always confounded me that a man as tightfisted with money and as reactionary as Jack Warner, who, when he was introduced to Mme. Chiang Kai-shek, supposedly said, "I forgot my laundry," had not only a superb roster of actors, but perhaps the most politically liberal group of actors in Hollywood. The list included Edward G. Robinson, Humphrey Bogart, Lauren Bacall, Bette Davis, Errol Flynn, Peter Lorre, Sydney Greenstreet, and Olivia de Havilland, to name just a few. In the early 1940s Miss de H. took Warner Brothers to court and won the suit that set the limit of contract players at seven years, including suspensions. It was the beginning of fair and equitable treatment of contract players in Hollywood. The next step was residuals for actors. Unfortunately, I didn't benefit from that one.

Not too long after the party at Jack Warner's, I found a small, very private house above the Sunset Strip and bought it on the spot. I can't remember why I chose to buy at this time in my life, since I was thinking all the time about New

York and how I could spend time there studying acting. I must have been deluding myself by thinking I could straddle both worlds, film and theater, in the kind of bicoastal way that really didn't become practical until the 1970s with improved air travel.

Hans Christian Andersen

The emperor has no clothes, and this movie has no plot, was my reaction to the script for *Hans Christian Andersen.* Not only was it a shapeless mess, the story boiled down to boy meets girl, boy loses girl, boy gets boy. My character did not even appear until about halfway into the film, and then I had very little to do other than yell at my wife. Unwilling to play ball after my last three disasters for Goldwyn, I told him I wanted no part of it. He went ballistic and threatened me with suspension for the rest of my life.

Danny Kaye had made five pictures under contract to Goldwyn, who let him go after his last one flopped. The flop was not Danny's fault, it was Goldwyn's. The movie was *A Song Is Born,* a lugubrious remake of a superb movie that Goldwyn had made only seven years earlier. The original, *Ball of Fire,* written by Billy Wilder and Charlie Brackett, was directed by Howard Hawks. It starred Barbara Stanwyck and Gary Cooper at the top of their form and had been a huge hit. The remake with Danny and Virginia Mayo was a paste imitation of a real gem. It deserved to fail. Danny landed on his feet with a five-picture deal at Warner Brothers. Now, at great expense to Goldwyn, he was coming back to his old studio to play the Danish storyteller Hans Christian Andersen. My part was the ballet master of the Copenhagen Ballet. Moira Shearer, the red-headed Scottish dancer who had a huge artistic success in Michael Powell's ballet film *The Red Shoes,* was to play my wife, the prima ballerina of the company. Erik Bruhn, the famous Danish dancer, was to be her partner. The great George Balanchine was choreographing the ballet sequences, and Frank Loesser had come back from New York to write the score. Moss Hart, author of *Lady in the Dark,* the Broadway musical that made Danny a star, was writing the screenplay. Goldwyn already owned some thirty-odd treatments of the story. It took Hart and Loesser close to five months to cobble together a treatment that was heavily indebted to the original 1938 version, which told the story using Andersen's fairy tales rather than his actual life. He was not a happy man and is said to have been a closeted homosexual. He was also not a very nice man. Some wags about town called this typecasting. I had great admiration for Moss, but even though this film remains popular, with a defining role for Danny, it is a mess. The best thing about it is the enchanting score by Frank Loesser.

At the last minute, Miss Shearer said she was pregnant and pulled out of the film, and was replaced by Zizi Jeanmaire. When I heard that, I agreed to do the part, much to Goldwyn's surprise. I had felt such chemistry with Zizi when we met in Paris that I knew we would have fun working together, and it would keep me off suspension. Zizi had become an international sensation when she danced Carmen in Paris in the ballet of the same name choreographed by her husband, Roland Petit. It was the first time that carnality had been so openly expressed in the world of ballet, where love was most often poetic. *Life* magazine had done a big story on her, and Goldwyn obviously hoped that this would help the box office. Unfortunately, with his schedule now in conflict, Balanchine, a true genius, pulled out of the film. He was replaced by Zizi's husband.

Zizi's English had not gotten any better since I last saw her, so Goldwyn sent me to New York for two weeks to work with her and Moss on our scenes. Roland went ahead to Hollywood to work out some details of Zizi's contract. We were both as happy as naughty kids to be on our own. It gave us time for me to show Zizi my New York. At the end of two weeks of Moss's coaching, not only was she wonderful in the part, her English had improved dramatically, although you would never know it by the way Danny behaved on set when we got to Hollywood.

I had originally met Danny on the set of his first film for Goldwyn, *Up in Arms*. He was very nervous about his lack of experience in front of a camera. I respected what I knew about his reputation as a performer and told him that I would be delighted to show him the ins and outs of the studio if he wanted. He seemed extremely grateful and promised to call if he needed any advice. I stayed on the set to watch Dinah Shore do a number. Danny never called, but I never really expected him to. After that, I ran into him at the studio a few times, always with his wife, Sylvia, and he was always friendly.

I saw him onstage once at a Hollywood benefit at Ciro's. A number of well-known performers were appearing that evening, including the inimitable Kay Thompson. Kay was the vocal arranger for the Arthur Freed unit at MGM. She, along with the musical director Roger Edens, was responsible for all the great Judy Garland production numbers like "The Trolley Song" in *Meet Me in St. Louis* and "On the Atchison, Topeka, and the Santa Fe" in *The Harvey Girls*. In 1957 she appeared in Stanley Donen's film *Funny Face* and effortlessly stole the movie from its two stars, Fred Astaire and Audrey Hepburn. In it she played a Diana Vreeland–like editor of a famous fashion magazine. Her opening number, "Think Pink" is a classic. She was not pretty, but she was the epitome of chic. She also had her own nightclub act with the Williams Brothers before

Andy Williams became a solo singing star. The benefit was sold out. When the house lights dimmed and the curtain came up, Kay was onstage alone in a skin-tight white gown, with the four Williams Brothers behind her in silhouette. She began singing Cole Porter's "It Was Just One of Those Things," accompanied only by bongo drums. She must have been almost halfway through the song when the lights changed. At that moment I realized that is wasn't the Williams Brothers. It was Van Johnson, George Burns, and two other comedians whose names I can't remember. At that same moment I realized that it wasn't Kay Thompson, it was Danny Kaye. He was fabulous.

On our film, I was never able to figure him out. It was as if he were two different people. Sometimes he was unnervingly cozy with me, and other times he cut me dead. He treated Zizi either with insufferable rudeness or as if she didn't exist, which made me begin to dislike him. When he demanded that the duet Frank Loesser had written for Zizi and me, "No Two People," be given to him, I was flabbergasted. Who was he going to sing it with? The young boy who was always with him in the film, although his presence was never explained? When Goldwyn gave in to this demand, I was beyond angry. It gave Danny every song in the picture. My determination to get out of my contract at any cost was fired up with a vengeance. When Danny walked off the set with a caustic crack to the director that he would come back when and if anyone could understand Zizi, I don't know who I wanted to punch most, Danny or Charlie Vidor, our impotent director, who just shrugged hopelessly and let him get away with it. As a matter of fact, Zizi's English had improved so much since we began the film that Vidor reshot most of our scenes to take advantage of this improvement. A day or so later Danny sidled up to me, caressed my shirt, and whined, "How come you get to wear all these beautiful clothes and I have to wear rags?" I came dangerously close to telling him what I and a lot of other people on the film really thought of him.

When the film wrapped, at my insistence, my agent, Charles Feldman, and I met with Goldwyn to discuss my increasing unhappiness with my contract and how much I wanted to be released in order to move east to study and work in the theater. After a long pause that indicated he was thinking it over, Goldwyn made me an offer. After my twelve-city personal appearance tour to promote *Hans Christian Andersen,* he would give me two years off to do whatever I wanted: go to New York and study, work in the theater, whatever I wanted to do except movies. After that, I would come back to him for two additional years at the old terms. He smiled benevolently and sat back. I stood up calmly, said, "Thanks a lot, but no thanks!" and walked out.

Suspended Again

Shortly after that, I was told to report for another B picture at Universal. Some B pictures were the best things being made in Hollywood. In this case B merely stood for bad. When I said, "Not a chance," I was once again put on suspension. I went to see Charlie and told him that if Goldwyn continued to refuse to split my contract with 20th the way he had with Dana's, Charlie had to find a way to get me out of it. If he couldn't, I would just walk out and move to New York. He made me promise to be patient for a little while longer, because he had two good projects in the works for me at MGM. If they came through, it would buy him a little more time to work on Goldwyn. I told him that I'd do my best to hang in a bit longer, but I wouldn't make any promises. One morning the following week I got a call from Columbia. I had an appointment that afternoon with Harry Cohn, the head of Columbia Pictures.

Cohn, a short, dark, balding, barrel-chested specimen, had a reputation as the most vulgar, most despotic, most feared producer in Hollywood. The writer Ben Hecht dubbed him "White Fang," a name that fit perfectly. A well-known anecdote about Cohn tells how most actors, writers, directors, and producers in town felt about him. Almost every name in Hollywood attended Cohn's funeral. It was a huge turnout. As the service was about to begin, Red Skelton, the beloved comedian, turned to the person next to him and was overheard saying; "Well, it only proves what they always say . . . Give the public something they want to see, and they'll show up every time." Even Hedda Hopper had something to contribute. Her comment was, "You had to stand in line to hate him."

I called Goldwyn to find out why I was going to Columbia, but could not get through to him, and his secretary knew nothing about my appointment. Then I called Charlie, but he was not in his office. At the appointed time I went to Columbia and was ushered into Cohn's presence. Jerry Wald, who had produced *Behave Yourself* at RKO, was now head of production at Columbia, He was waiting for me in Cohn's outer office and greeted me warmly. When we entered the office, Harry Cohn stayed seated behind his desk. After an uncomfortable pause during which he gave me the once-over, Cohn finally spoke: "Sit down, kid." I did, and after another pause he said; "Okay, kid, what am I gonna do with you?"

This took me completely by surprise. So it was a minute before I said, "I don't know what you're talking about."

"I won you from Sam in a poker game last night," he said. "Now what kind of movies do you wanna do?"

I felt as if someone had hit me in the chest with a shovel.

Jerry jumped in with the title of something they had in development, and Cohn snarled at him, "Not that, you asshole. He's all wrong for that. What the fuck do I pay you for, anyway?"

He then had Jerry give him other ideas and with each suggestion continued to belittle him. I finally got up and without a word walked out.

I went straight to my agent's office to raise hell. When I stopped for breath, he jumped in to tell me to relax, no court in the land would accept the poker game as a legal transfer of contract, it was probably Goldwyn's idea of a joke to teach me to behave. When I started in with "Well, that bastard can shove . . ." Charlie cut me off by saying that he had just gotten word that Vincente Minnelli wanted me for his upcoming film at Metro. That shut me up. Minnelli was a wonderful director. I still think his film *Meet Me in St. Louis* is the best musical film ever made. Vincente wanted me to be in "Mademoiselle," one of three short films that made up *The Story of Three Loves.* The other actors in our segment were Leslie Caron, Ethel Barrymore, and a newcomer, Zsa Zsa Gabor. The story was a champagne bubble. It concerned a boy, played by Ricky Nelson before he became a teen idol, who hates his French lessons, and his tutor, played by Leslie Caron. One evening, in a secluded glade on the grounds of the hotel they are staying in, he meets a mysterious old lady in a wheelchair, Ethel Barrymore. The boy is fascinated by her and has a long conversation with her about his troubles. She wisely counsels him not to be so impatient, because things are not always as they seem to be. Later that evening, while dressing for dinner, Ricky looks in the mirror to tie his tie and reflected back at him is me. He has magically transformed into a young man. Now grown up, I walk into the bar to sit down and to order a drink. In comes a ravishing blonde in a scarlet dress that emphasizes her milky white cleavage. She has a captivating smile and a killer Hungarian accent. It is, of course, Zsa Zsa, in one of her first movie appearances. She comes on to me with charming but alarming speed. I manage an escape to the garden, where, wandering in the moonlight, I suddenly bump into my tutor, Leslie, whom I, of course, see in a whole new way. As we get to know each other, she confides her unhappiness at what she feels is her failure to be a good tutor to her young charge, who she thinks hates her. We fall deeply in love on this enchanted night. The script was mysterious and magical. Many years later, in a much less subtle version, the same idea was recycled as the award-winning *Big.* Tom Hanks, an actor who can do no wrong in my opinion, was wonderful in it, as was Elizabeth Perkins, but the film was beer, not champagne.

Unfortunately, the producer of *The Story of Three Loves,* Gottfried Reinhardt, also directed the other two segments. Reinhardt cut "Mademoiselle" mercilessly to make more time for his two episodes. Aside from the joy of working with Miss Barrymore, Leslie, and Vincente, despite the fact that he stood next to the camera mouthing and miming every word of every take, my most vivid memory of this film was Zsa Zsa's first day on the set. The part she played of the woman who flirted with me at the bar may have been small, but when Zsa Zsa was called to the set, she arrived with the entire hair, makeup, and wardrobe departments in tow, fussing over her as if she was royalty. She made a very big entrance.

Some time after this, Oliver Smith, who was then Broadway's leading set designer and one of the formative forces behind American Ballet Theatre, and I were invited to Vincente's home for dinner. His latest film, *Brigadoon,* was opening that same evening on Broadway. During drinks an adorable seven-year-old Liza Minnelli kept appearing in different, perfectly executed costumes with wigs and makeup to match. She would enter and curtsy as Marie Antoinette, then a while later as Little Bo Peep, then as the Wicked Witch of the West. While this was happening, Vincente kept getting called to the phone to hear the New York reviews of the film, which were not good. Needless to say, everyone's focus was fractured. Oliver and I were trying to appreciate Liza; eavesdrop on Vincente's calls, to one of which we heard him say: "It was that bad!?"; and keep sober. We accomplished the first two efforts, but the third wasn't easy.

Liza was dear that evening, doing something that could have been obnoxious. I loved both Judy Garland and Vincente, and I know that they both worshiped Liza, but childhood and growing up cannot have been easy for her. The last time I had a chance to sit and talk with her was after a performance in *Best Foot Forward,* her first New York show. She was such a combination of talent, intelligence, and humor, all fueled by a fierce desire to please, that it made my heart hurt.

Shelley

Out of sheer chutzpah, Shelley had gotten a contract for Vittorio at MGM, where he made several films that he did not think were any good. He was right. He came home from the studio one afternoon and announced to his wife that she should pack up, they were going home. She said, "But darling, we are home." He replied, "Italy is home. Pack!" By this time in her career *A Place in the Sun* had given Shelley recognition as a serious actress. That and the birth of her daughter had given her the respectability she had always wanted. She was not about to walk away from Hollywood to become Signora Gassman in Italy any more than

Vittorio was about to remain in Hollywood as Mr. Winters. The result was that he went home, and she stayed home. They tried to put a good face on things for several years. Their daughter, Tori, who bore the brunt of the separation, was secondary to their work schedules and was shuttled between them whenever it could work out. The final blowup took place in Italy in a much too public way, when I just happened to be making a film there.

Much to the confusion of the Hollywood gossips, Shelley and I started seeing each other again. She was unhappy and needed a friend. As her friend, I wanted to be there for her. I think we made much better friends than lovers, and we both felt, "To hell with people who don't understand our relationship, it is what it is, and it works for us."

Charlie Feldman had been busy. He had gotten me the lead in a musical, *Small Town Girl,* for the Joe Pasternak unit at Metro. The most prestigious musical unit at the studio was headed by Arthur Freed, but Pasternak had done his share of good and successful films. This was a remake of an old Janet Gaynor/Robert Taylor movie about a rich playboy and a small-town girl. I was the playboy who, while having an affair with a jazzy showgirl played by Ann Miller, gets a speeding ticket driving through a small town and is put in jail, where I meet and fall for an all-American girl played by Jane Powell. My mother was played by Billie Burke. S. Z. (Cuddles) Sakall and a terrific young dancer, Bobby Van, were also in the film. Pasternak had assigned his brother-in-law, whose name was Lazlo Kardos, Americanized to Leslie Kardos, as the director. The cameraman was Joe Ruttenberg, one of the most highly esteemed cinematographers in town. The famous, or infamous, choreographer Busby Berkeley did Ann's dance numbers. I adored Billie Burke and could listen to her stories about her husband, "Mr. Ziegfeld," as she always called him, and the Broadway stage for hours on end. Annie Miller and I got along like two kindred souls. She wore a fake nose, the result of a bad nose job, and she would always say to me, "Don't make me laugh or I'll flip my nose!" At around 5:00 or 6:00 P.M. every afternoon, when the ravages of a long day began to show on everyone's makeup, Annie would touch her loosening nose and say; "Oh, oh . . . Shangri-la time." I could barely get through any scenes with S. Z. "Cuddles" Sakall. His endless repertoire of Viennese shtick never failed to bring me to the point of breaking up. I never felt that Jane Powell and I connected on the film. She was pregnant and having a difficult time. We could never lock in the shooting schedule since we never knew if she was going to show up.

Annie had two wonderful dance numbers, one of which, "I've Gotta Hear That Beat," became a classic, and Bobby also had two terrific numbers. In retrospect, they should have been the stars of the movie. One morning when we were almost finished, the director failed to show up. Nobody was ever told why. I think he had a nervous breakdown. He had been getting a little twitchy. Nobody knew what to do, and nobody from the front office knew what we were to do. Since the remaining scenes involved just Ann and me, and we had spent a lot of time working on them, I went to Joe and told him that Annie and I had them down cold. I suggested we just shoot them and finish the film so we could all go home. With no fanfare that's what we did and no member of management ever said a word.

An A-List Diva

I got a call one evening from Joan Crawford's press agent. Miss Crawford wanted to meet me and would be most pleased if I would agree to have dinner with her one evening next week. I was surprised and intrigued. She was a major star, up there with Garbo and Gable. What could she want with me? Maybe she was planning a movie with a good part in it for me. I said of course I would like to have dinner with Miss Crawford. We set it up for 7:00 P.M. the following Tuesday at Don the Beachcomber's, a Polynesian restaurant that was then Hollywood's answer to Trader Vic's. I was there on the dot, but Miss Crawford had not yet arrived. The maitre d' showed me into a private dining room, and I ordered a Navy Grog, a large drink with the least fruit, the most rum, and no umbrella. It was more than an hour and two more Navy Grogs later when she swept in with a PR man and a secretary in tow. She asked if I'd had anything yet, and I answered, "Just a couple of drinks." She said, "Then I'll order a drink and some appetizers," which she did. While issuing orders to her PR man and her secretary, she'd toss an occasional question my way, like, "Do you know so-and-so?" I'd say, "Yes," and she'd say, "Aren't they mahvelous?" or "Don't you just love him, her, or it?" and I'd say yes or no. This went on for a while before I realized she wasn't even listening. The result was that my answers got more contrary. Finally she turned to me and with a high-voltage smile said, "There. I'm done." I stood and smiled back and said, "So am I," and walked out. I hope to this day that I didn't stagger. In the cab on my way home, I wondered what project it was that she had in mind.

The next day, when I told Charlie Feldman the story, he roared with laughter and said that it was probably a very personal project that she had in mind. I then told him that I was going to New York to find a place to live and that he could tell Sam in his own misspoken words to please, please "include me out." I knew he would not appreciate me using one of his most well-known malapropisms against him; in fact, I was hoping it would make him angry enough to throw me off the lot. I repeated to Charlie what he already knew about how determined I was to get out, but for the first time I added the words "at any cost." He was neither happy about that choice nor optimistic about it happening.

It was 1953. I found an apartment on the Upper East Side in Manhattan that was just around the corner from Bloomingdale's, which to my Los Angeles eyes was the chicest store I had ever been in, and the Third Avenue El, an elevated subway line that is long gone. Riding on it made me feel as if I was in some film noir where when I looked into someone's apartment, I might discover some terrible secret that could change the course of my life forever. My old pal Roddy McDowall and also Monty Clift lived on the same block. That helped me to feel like I was in the right place at the right time in my life.

I went back to the coast ready to pick up and pack out, but Charlie did not have good news for me. Goldwyn would not budge. There was no way he was going to let "that boy" out of his contract. He then had gone on about how he had loved me more than his own son and what it had cost him to make a star of me and here I was turning on him like a viper, plunging a knife into his heart and on and on and on. He finally said that he wouldn't let me go even if I was to pay him every penny of the salary that would come to me in the remaining two years of my contract. Charlie said, "I knew the moment he said it that was the only way Goldwyn would let you go." I told him, "Do it. You know I don't care what it costs!" He did it, and it cost me every penny I had.

I went in to Charlie's office to sign all the papers and to say goodbye. He said to me. "Farley, you can't go to New York, you can't go anywhere. You just bought out your contract. You have no money!" I told him I had already rented an apartment, and I had to go. I think I was indulging in some romantic dream about being a starving artist in the big city who works and slaves to become a great actor.

Charlie repeated, with less patience, "Farley, listen to me! You have no money!!!" Before I could say anything else, he said, "But I think I have a solution. Marlon Brando has just turned down a film in Italy for a very interesting Italian director named Luchino Visconti. Although he is not yet known in this country, he has a terrific reputation as a genuine artist in Europe."

I said that I'd never heard of Luchino Visconti, and in any case I didn't want to go to Italy, I wanted to go to New York to begin studying and working in the theater. Before I could repeat my mantra, he said that I was their next choice and that he had negotiated a sweetheart deal for me. For a three-month commitment, I would be paid the equivalent of the top dollar Goldwyn had gotten for me on my last loanouts to Metro, a goodly sum. If the film went over schedule, that amount would double.

As I started to shake my head no, he jumped in with "And the English dialogue is being written by Tennessee Williams and Paul Bowles."

Tennessee's name stopped my objections. Here was a chance to work with one of the most talented theater writers of our time. How could I pass that up if I was going to be a theater actor?

Senso

Two weeks later, on a hot summer evening in late August, I arrived at Leonardo da Vinci Airport on the outskirts of Rome. I breezed through passport control, then barely a formality for anyone with an American passport, and could not even find a customs control checkpoint. I went outside to get a cab only to find a chauffeur holding a sign with my name on it. Lux Films, which was producing and distributing *Senso* for Visconti, had sent a car to meet me. My bags and I were gathered, and I was taken directly to an unpretentious trattoria in Trastevere (which means "across the Tiber"), where in my jet-lagged state I met what seemed like dozens of people.

Count Luchino Visconti was a striking presence, darkly handsome, with a leonine head, chiseled features, and piercing dark eyes. He spoke not one word of English. His assistant directors, Francesco Rosi and Franco Zeffirelli, were there along with his principal writer, Suso Cecchi D'Amico. Also present were the English dialogue writers, Tennessee Williams and Paul Bowles, as well as various other members of the film company and representatives from Lux Films. Only Tennessee, Paul, and Franco spoke English. Platters of wonderful food never stopped arriving, and wineglasses were magically always full. It was festive. It was a feast. It was overwhelming. The din of excited Italian drowned out the few English voices in the crowded little restaurant. I was never able to get into any kind of meaningful conversation with Tennessee. When I was about to collapse from exhaustion, after endless hugs and kisses and *ciao bellos*, I was taken to the Hotel de la Ville, at the top of the Spanish Steps. I crashed for twelve hours. The next morning I found out that everyone had left Rome. It was a month before I was able to see or speak to or even locate any of them again, including the representatives from Lux Films responsible for providing my per diem.

The next morning, I had a luxurious bath, fresh blood-red Sicilian orange juice, a double cappuccino, and a tray of flaky Italian breakfast pastries. It was that morning that I developed a lifelong love of the pastry that Italians call *ventaglios,* the French *palmiers,* and New Yorkers elephant ears. I called Lux Films to see about collecting some per diem. I reached a secretary who spoke no English and responded to each name I mentioned with a cheerful "*Scusi, signore, ma non l'ho capito.* Excuse me, sir, but I don't understand you." Fortunately, I'd brought along enough cash and traveler's checks to carry me for a while.

That afternoon, after lunch in the atrium of the hotel, I went to the front desk to check for messages. The clerk who spoke a little English told me no messages, *niente,* nothing. Of course, he knew who the count was. He even knew who Francesco Rosi was, but Lux Films drew a blank stare. He was very sorry but it was Ferragosto, the last two weeks in August. No one was in Rome. Everything was closed. Everyone was in the mountains or by the sea. He was very sorry, but there was nothing he could do to help me. I wandered around Rome for two days, certain that someone from the film company would be contacting me. The Eternal City was glorious but deserted and shut down aside from a few tourists and me. I was ill at ease at having been abandoned like this. I had to do something. Before leaving Hollywood, Shelley had called to say good-bye and had given me the phone number of a friend of hers in New York who she said spoke fluent Italian and would make a great secretary for me in Italy. I'd met Janet Wolf several times with Shelley and found her a bit flaky. Besides, I had no intention of hiring a secretary. Why on earth would I ever need a secretary?

Two days later Janet arrived. Helping her check in, I soon realized that her grasp of the Italian language was basic at best. After dinner and a lot of laughs, I also realized how good it was for me to have someone around who spoke English. The next day at the office of Lux Films, after many "*Non capisco*'s"—I don't understand—from the gorgeous young Italian woman who seemed to be the only person who worked there, I had my third realization: Janet's Italian was less than basic, it was *pochino,* very little. We walked over to the Via Veneto for some lunch and people-watching, but it was too hot to eat, and there were only a few tourists wandering by. As I was paying the check, Janet lit up: "I know what we can do!" "What?" I asked her. "Let's go to Capri!" said Janet. "Okay," said I. We went back to the hotel and asked the concierge to find us two rooms in Capri. He was not very hopeful at this late date in August with everyone at the resorts. We refused to bow to his pessimism and were in our rooms packing when he called me to say that my name had worked *"un miracolo."* A miracle. He had gotten us two rooms at the Hotel Quisiana e Grande, the best hotel on Capri. I called Janet, and, excited as two kids, we raced down to the lobby, left a message for Lux Films telling them where we would be, tipped our concierge handsomely, and left for the train station. We hopped a train for Naples and arrived several hours later. As we were entering the main station, I realized that I

My father, Captain Farley E. Granger, returns to his wife, Eva Mae, after World War I with a Silver Star and a Purple Heart.

Me in 1927, as a two-year-old gaucho, in front of my father's dealership in San Jose. I have no idea who the fellow on the high-wheeler is.

Me in 1926.

My parents and me in 1943, outside the studio the day I signed my exclusive seven-year contract for $100 a week with Samuel Goldwyn.

The North Star, the first movie I made for Mr. Goldwyn, 1943, put Anne Baxter and me on *Look* magazine's cover. *(Courtesy of the Academy of Motion Picture Arts and Sciences and the Samuel Goldwyn Foundation)*

The North Star. Escaping after I had been blinded by the German troops invading our small Russian town. *(Courtesy of the Samuel Goldwyn Foundation)*

The Purple Heart, 1944. As crew members of the first American bomber to crash in Japan in World War II, Sam Levene and Dana Andrews stand trial with me in Tokyo, after my tongue had been cut out by our captors.

Saying good-bye to my pal Roddy McDowell after I had enlisted in the U.S. Navy and was shipping out. I had turned eighteen in July 1943.

Boot camp in Farragut, Idaho.

My first film after being discharged from the Navy in 1947 was Nicholas Ray's *They Live by Night,* co-starring Cathy O'Donnell. Thanks to Howard Hughes, it almost didn't get released. It is one of three favorite films that I made.

Three of My Least Favorite Films

Riding back and forth and forth and back with young Joan Evans while awaiting script rewrites for *Roseanna McCoy*, 1949. *(Courtesy of the Samuel Goldwyn Foundation)*

Frances Goldwyn bought this property for me. It was a bad idea. *(Courtesy of the Samuel Goldwyn Foundation)*

Our Very Own, 1950, sizzled only in this frame. It was really a tepid little film. *(Courtesy of the Samuel Goldwyn Foundation)*

Rope, 1948, with John Dall and James Stewart. Working with Hitch was always fun, even when the film turned out to be just an interesting experiment in technique. *(Photofest)*

Strangers on a Train, 1951, was one of Hitch's great films. *(Photofest)*

Strangers on a Train has a great performance by Robert Walker, who died just before the film was released.

Hitch loved to make a surprise appearance in each of his films. *(©Sunset Boulevard/Corbis)*

My Favorite Leading Ladies

Cathy O'Donnell in *They Live by Night,* 1948; a unique talent whose career was badly damaged by Mr. Goldwyn.

Dorothy McGuire in *I Want You,* 1951; a classy lady with whom I shared a bottle of good Champagne before our first rehearsal. We giggled our way through our big scene from that day on. *(Courtesy of the Samuel Goldwyn Foundation)*

Jeanne Crain in "The Gift of the Magi" from *O. Henry's Full House,* 1952. She was as sweet as she was lovely and talented. *(Billy Rose Theatre Division, The New York Public Library for the Performing Arts, Astor, Lenox and Tilden Foundations)*

Zizi Jeanmaire in *Hans Christian Andersen,* 1952. This was the delicious French ballerina's first English-language movie, and my last movie for Goldwyn. *(Courtesy of the Samuel Goldwyn Foundation)*

Leslie Caron in "Mademoiselle" from *The Story of Three Loves,* 1953; two French knockouts in a row.

Ann Miller in *Small Town Girl,* 1953. Annie was a hoot. I laughed every minute we worked together. *(Photofest)*

Joan Collins in *The Girl in the Red Velvet Swing,* 1955. Joan was a raven-haired British stunner with a wonderfully bawdy sense of humor. *(Photofest)*

And Shelley

Shelley and me in an unguarded moment. *(Photofest)*

Behave Yourself, 1951. During the shoot Shelley didn't, and I wanted to kill her.

The real Shelley, whom I always loved, at my sixty-fifth birthday party. *(Photo by Valerie Brea Ross)*

The opening sequence in Luchino Visconti's *Senso*, 1954, at La Fenice, the beautiful little opera house in Venice, shows the Italians demonstrating against the Austrian occupation. *(© Paul Ronald/Archivio Storico del Cinema/AFE Roma)*

As Franz Mahler, the amoral Austrian officer in *Senso.*

Talking over a scene with Luchino. *(Photofest)*

With Alida Valli, as the obsessed Countess Serpieri in *Senso. (© Paul Ronald/Archivio Storico del Cinema/AFE Roma)*

With Anne Bancroft in *The Naked Street* (1955), my last Hollywood film before I moved permanently to New York. *(Photofest)*

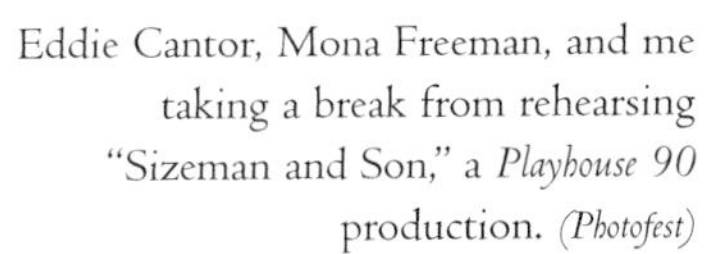

Eddie Cantor, Mona Freeman, and me taking a break from rehearsing "Sizeman and Son," a *Playhouse 90* production. *(Photofest)*

Ten-year-old Ricky Nelson went to bed as an unhappy boy and woke up as a very surprised me in Vincente Minnelli's *The Story of Three Loves*.

First Impressions, 1959. My first Broadway show was an adaptation of Jane Austen's *Pride and Prejudice,* with Polly Bergen and Hermione Gingold, who never spoke to each other off stage. *(© Bettmann/Corbis)*

With Julie Harris in a television adaptation of *The Heiress. (Photofest)*

"Shall We Dance?" from the 1960 City Center revival of *The King and I,* with Barbara Cook. Everything about this experience was glorious, especially Barbara. *(Billy Rose Theatre Division, The New York Public Library for the Performing Arts, Astor, Lenox and Tilden Foundations)*

First rehearsal of *The Warm Peninsula,* 1959, with Ruth White, Larry Hagman, June Havoc, and Julie Harris. *(Billy Rose Theatre Division, The New York Public Library for the Performing Arts, Astor, Lenox and Tilden Foundations)*

Frances Ann Dougherty; one of the National Repertory Theatre producers was a North Carolina beauty who had been JFK's first sweetheart. She was dynamic and passionate about her work.

My first NRT tour, 1962–63, brought Eva Le Gallienne, Denholm Elliot, Anne Meacham, and me to New York in Arthur Miller's *The Crucible* and Anton Chekhov's *The Seagull.*

My second NRT tour, 1963–64, starred Signe Hasso and me. The plays on the program cover, in descending order, are: Oliver Goldsmith's *She Stoops to Conquer,* Henrik Ibsen's *Hedda Gabler,* and Ferenc Molnár's *Liliom.*

With Eva Le Gallienne in Jean Anouilh's *Ring Round the Moon.* I got to play identical twins in this French farce. *(Photo by Van Williams; Billy Rose Theatre Division, The New York Public Library for the Performing Arts, Astor, Lenox and Tilden Foundations)*

As John Proctor in Arthur Miller's *The Crucible. (Photo by Van Williams; Billy Rose Theatre Division, The New York Public Library for the Performing Arts, Astor, Lenox and Tilden Foundations)*

With Eva Le Gallienne in Anton Chekhov's *The Seagull. (Photo by Van Williams)*

With Princess Lee Radziwill in a remake of *Laura* (1968), adapted especially for her by Truman Capote.
(© Bettmann/Corbis)

At our house in Malibu in 1968.

Molly, me, Luke, and Bob in Rome in 1972.

With Marian Seldes as my trusting wife and Steve Bassett as my scheming lover in *Deathtrap,* 1981. *(Billy Rose Theatre Division, The New York Public Library for the Performing Arts, Astor, Lenox and Tilden Foundations)*

Al Hirschfeld's drawing of me in *Talley & Son,* the play for which I won an Obie Award in 1986. Staged by Marshall Mason at the Circle Repertory, the Lanford Wilson play also featured Edward Seamon *(foreground)* and *(from left)* Julie Bargeron, Steve Decker, Laura Hughes, and Joyce Reehling Christopher. *(© Al Hirschfeld. Reproduced by arrangement with Hirschfeld's exclusive representative, The Margo Feiden Galleries, Ltd., New York. www.alhirschfeld.com)*

had left my passport on the train with a book. Janet turned, raced back to the train, and a few minutes later, as it began pulling out for Reggio Calabria, jumped off triumphantly waving my passport and book. She had more than earned her salary that day.

We fought our way through the chaos that was Naples and made it onto a late-afternoon ferry for Capri, where we spent two lazy weeks that carried us into early September. The crowds on Capri started thinning out, which was a sure sign that Italy was getting ready to go back to work. Even though no one from Lux Films had called, we decided it might be best to return to Rome.

Venice

Waiting for us at the Hotel de la Ville was a message from Lux Films. The Venice Film Festival was about to start, and they were expecting me to be there for interviews and other public relations work. A room had been booked for me at the Hotel Danieli on the Grand Canal just off the Piazza San Marco. Before we left for Venice, I had to go to an address in Rome for a costume fitting. Janet, still acting out her Italian translator fantasy, came along to help me communicate. Taking our bags with us, we went to the address and into a large building that looked like a big empty church. Splendid costumes that had been designed for *Senso* by the great Marcel Escoffier were everywhere, stored on rolling racks in lofts, hanging on double-tiered racks placed against the walls, draped over clothing dummies, and spread out on worktables, where seamstresses attended to minute details of buttons, jeweled bodices, and lace inserts. The fabrics were luminous silks and velvets, rich brocades, the finest linen, and transparent cotton. The colors ranged from deep-stained glass jewel tones to brilliant yellows, pinks, and lavenders, and everywhere the white capes, tunics, and trousers of the Austrian officers. I was overwhelmed by the beauty of it all.

I was soon to learn that Visconti was not only fanatical about historical accuracy, but that his attention to the detail of costumes, props, and set décor as well as to the sets themselves was scrupulous and never-ending. The man executing the costumes for Escoffier, a talented designer in his own right, was Piero Tosi. He spoke no English, which was not a problem because by using the clothes he was able to communicate perfectly. Aside from the dressing gown I wore in one scene near the end of the film, my only other costume was the white uniform of an Austrian lieutenant.

Janet was seated nearby and I was standing on a small platform surrounded by a three-sided mirror. As we were finishing, Piero asked me something that I couldn't understand. I looked to Janet, who just gave me her best Italian shrug. Piero gestured toward my crotch with his right hand and then his left hand and finally with both hands. I still didn't understand. Janet got it and burst into raucous laughter. She finally contained herself enough to explain, "He needs to know what side you dress on, dummy!" I didn't know what that meant.. By then everyone in the workshop was trying to hide or stifle giggles. When Janet blurted out what he needed to know in basic Anglo-Saxon, I turned crimson. Piero then lost it as well. I guess my secretary/linguist earned her salary again that day.

As soon as the fitting was completed, Piero called us a cab. We went to the train station, where I bought our tickets to Venice. There was a short wait, just time enough to get some coffee before they posted the next express train for Venice. After several hours, which we passed having a marvelous lunch, the train pulled into the ugly 1930s modern train station in Cannaregio, Venice. A porter helped us with the bags, and I splurged on a gondola to take us directly to our hotel, which was located on the Grand Canal just past the Piazza San Marco. I thought I would be prepared for Venice this time, but I don't think anyone who doesn't live there can ever be really prepared for that splendid city. It was a crystal-clear evening, and the setting sun turned the water to molten copper as the gondola slipped under the first bridge past the station. Every time I have been there, and I go to Venice whenever I can, it casts the same magical spell all over again.

The lobby of the Danieli was beautiful, with a stained-glass atrium several stories high, all very Art Nouveau. Our rooms were like two little cells in which we would have felt like prisoners had we stayed. Back at the front desk, the manager swore that he had nothing better to offer because of the Biennale and the upcoming Regatta. I asked him to get the Grand on the phone for my secretary and told Janet that I had stayed there the last time I was in Venice. "Make it work."

They remembered me! Within the hour, we were being escorted into the most luxurious suite that I had ever seen. The foyer was all white marble with a chandelier, and was as big as most hotel rooms. It opened into a sitting room of white marble with four big Venetian glass chandeliers over four sitting areas, each with a jewel-toned silk damask couch, four armchairs, and an appropriately sized coffee table artfully arranged on huge silk oriental rugs. There were also many well-placed, ornate, gilded-framed paintings and two huge mirrors. The manager opened the doors at the far end of the sitting room, and we entered a beautifully appointed antechamber off of which there were two large bedrooms, each with its own splendid bathroom. My bedroom was all deep red, with silk damask on the walls and a gilded fourposter bed on a dais. Janet had a slightly smaller but just as lavish pale green and gold bedroom at the other end of the antechamber. The manager said that if everything met with my approval, he would send for our bags. I murmured a *grazie.* He handed me the keys, bowed, and left the suite. Neither of us spoke or moved for a long minute. Then I moved silently around the room picking up things and looking at them. By the time I got back to Janet she said to me quietly, "What are you going to do?" I told her to call room service and order some champagne and caviar, and we would worry about how to pay for all this tomorrow.

In the morning, I was awakened by a phone call from a Lux Films press representative, who had tracked me down through the Danieli. They were expecting me to give an interview that afternoon at the Venice Film Festival, which was in progress out on the Lido, a smaller island that had a number of the city's best hotels as well as its famous beach. I was to meet him in the lobby of the Grand at 4:00 P.M., and he would take us there. Janet and I went for a light lunch to the Taverna Fenice, a restaurant next to Venice's exquisite little opera house, La Fenice, where months later Visconti shot the brilliant opening sequence of *Senso.* We met the press agent later that afternoon and were taken to the Lido. I made my dutiful appearance at the film festival, after which I informed him that I was not available for any more press until I received the per diem that was coming to me. He was sympathetic and understanding and promised to contact the producers about my problem. Feeling a little bit more hopeful, Janet and I went off to the Excelsior, the oldest luxury hotel on the Lido, to have a cool drink. As we walked into the lobby, I spotted Stella Adler and her daughter Ellen. Stella was staying there, and Ellen, who lived in Paris at the time, had come to Italy to visit her. I'm sure she really was there because Marlon Brando and Billy Redfield were cycling into Venice from Paris, and Ellen always had a thing for Stella's star pupil, Marlon. They joined us in the bar, and we were soon all laughing at my predicament of no per diem, little money, and lots of hotel suite.

Stella said, "Darling, there's only one thing to do . . . throw a party!"

I laughed along with the rest before realizing that she not only was serious, she was right. It's better to go out with a bang than a fizzle. "But I don't know anyone in Venice," I hesitated.

"Not to worry, cookie, I do. So all we have to do is pick a date," said Stella.

We decided on the afternoon before the last day of the film festival.

The next morning I received a phone call from a Countess Marina Cicognia. Visconti had called to tell her parents that I was in Venice and asked them if she would look after me. I met her for tea that afternoon. She was a young woman, around my age, who spoke excellent English and turned out to be a good friend for the remaining weeks I was there as well as later, in November and December, when we were shooting the rest of the Venice sequences. She told me that

Luchino was, as usual, behind schedule shooting the battle sequences in Custoza, and he wanted to be sure that I was enjoying myself while waiting for them to arrive in Venice for the opera house sequences. Since I had known nothing about the progress of the film, this at least was a welcome sign that I wasn't totally forgotten. Marina asked if I was planning to attend the Volpi Ball that was held at the end of the film festival. The press agent had given me an invitation, but since I didn't know what it was, I was not planning to attend. She insisted, "But you must, it marks the end of the Biennale, and is the beginning of the Venetian social season." She explained that Count Giuseppe Volpi di Misurata, who had founded the Venice Film Festival in 1932, planned the ball as an event to thank all his friends who had helped make the festival a success. It was also a prelude to the Regatta, which was coming up. Giovanni, the present Count Volpi, was still very involved and the ball was a must. The best families from all over Italy would be there. She asked if I would do her the honor of escorting her and I, of course, said that it would be my pleasure.

That evening I went with Stella to dinner at the home of a British art and antiques dealer whom she knew. It was a gem of a house on a side canal not too far from my hotel. There were only eight people there, and I was seated next to Peggy Guggenheim. Yes, that Peggy Guggenheim, whose father, Benjamin, went down with the *Titanic.* She inherited a small fortune when she turned twenty-one. It was small only in comparison with her father's siblings' riches, particularly her Uncle Solomon's. The Solomon R. Guggenheim Foundation owns and administrates some of the finest museums in the world. Before, during, and after World War II, Peggy Guggenheim acquired one of the most important collections of modern art in private hands in the world. It was and is housed in her home, the Palazzo Venier dei Leoni in Venice. Upon her death, she willed it to her Uncle Solomon's foundation with the stipulation that it always be kept in Venice, but maintained by the foundation. The Venetians venerate her.

Not only did she match me drink for drink before and during dinner, she introduced me to a fiery new one called Grappa after. At one point, I asked her how she got to know so much about modern art. She thought for a moment and said, "When I first realized how little I knew about early twentieth-century art, I decided the best way to learn was to buy a painting a week . . . and I did."

After dinner that evening, as I walked Stella back through the Piazza San Marco, I told her about Marina and the Volpi Ball. I could tell by her wistful tone of voice that she would love to go to the ball, but had not been invited. I determined to see if I could do something about that.

The next day Janet made arrangements with the hotel for our cocktail party. When they asked how many people we were expecting, she said expansively, "Oh, at least sixty or seventy." Then, when they asked how long we were planning to stay, she said grandly, "Oh, at least through the Regatta." That seemed to make them happy, and they did not ask about money, which made us happy.

I got a call from the press agent. He had talked to Lux Films, and they promised that there was no problem with my per diem. "The problem is, I don't have it!" I barked. Nonplussed, he went right on to ask if I would attend the early screening of *The Bad and the Beautiful.* Kirk Douglas and Lana Turner would be there along with the director, Vincente Minnelli. I liked the idea of surprising Vincente, so I agreed, as long as the press agent arranged for us to have a private motor launch for the evening. He did, and later, just as Janet and I were leaving for the Lido, Ellen Adler rushed in. Marlon had just called her from the Piazza Roma. He and Billy had parked in the public garage there near the station. They were on their way in to meet her at a cafe in the Piazza San Marco and needed a place to clean up before they tried to get a room. She wanted to know if they could use my suite at the Grand. Her room was so tiny and we had two huge bathrooms . . . I said of course and gave her my keys. We arranged to meet for dinner at 10:00 P.M. at La Columba, a restaurant that was then well off the beaten path and was full of paintings by local artists. It also had great food.

The press agent was there to meet us when we arrived, and he ushered us immediately into the grand salon at the Excelsior. Vincente was surprised and delighted that I was there. He said that he was very proud of this film. He had every right to be. It was not only very good, it was also a wickedly truthful look at the underbelly of the film industry. He got excellent performances out of everyone. Both Kirk Douglas and Lana Turner displayed more range than they ever had before, and Gloria Grahame won a Best Supporting Actress Oscar for her work.

We finally broke away from the festival and made it to the restaurant by around 10:30. Marlon and Billy were having a great time polishing off a liter of white wine. We ordered another and dove in. Marlon told us that as they were finishing their baths that evening, an assistant manager barged in on them. He said they were not guests in the hotel and told them to leave at once. Marlon got out of the tub and agreed to leave . . . as he was, dripping wet and stark naked. That had scared the overzealous young man off, so they had time to finish their clean up. I was mortified that I had forgotten to tell the front desk, but Marlon had enjoyed the whole situation. He had us all laughing by the time Ellen arrived. It took a while to get her to join in the general high spirits of the group. She was a bit miffed about her Marlon having been disrespected by my hotel.

Stella came over early the next afternoon to help me plan for the rapidly approaching party. The very thought of making the arrangements had been too daunting for me. She took care of everything with a few brief instructions to the manager: "Have the bar stocked with your best champagne and plenty of good liquor, and be ready for fifty or sixty people to begin arriving at five P.M. As for food, nothing too difficult, no dinner plates or silverware, plenty of Beluga, and make sure that your most attractive young men are serving." She gave him her best smile, turned to me, and said, "Now, where shall we have lunch, cookie?"

Over a couple of Bellinis and carpaccio of Chiana beef filet at Harry's Bar, Stella showed me an invitation that had been delivered to her hotel that morning. It was to the Volpi Ball. She was beaming. God bless Marina.

Two days later my party went off without a hitch . . . if you don't count the fact that I hadn't a clue as to how I would pay for it. As a matter of fact, until around 6:30 P.M. it looked as if it was going off without people as well. Then an assortment of fabulous Italians began to arrive. I recognized no one until Rex Harrison and his wife, Lilli Palmer, made an appearance. Sexy Rexy, as he had been dubbed by the entertainment press, had married the lovely German actress in 1943, and as a team they became stars of the English stage and film. In 1945 he came to Hollywood to do *Anna and the King of Siam,* which made him an international star. Even though he had a reputation for being demanding and difficult, I was always a big admirer. Ellen arrived looking lovely but lonely without Marlon and Billy, who had decided to take off for Rome that morning. Stella came late, entering with her usual flair and with a very attractive gentleman, Mike Todd. By that time, the place was packed. In the course of the evening Mike Todd pulled me aside to ask how long I would be in Venice. I said, "I'm not sure, but at least for several weeks." He said, "Good! I'll see you soon," and was off in the crowd before I could ask what he meant. This was four years before he and Elizabeth Taylor met and married.

At about 9:00 P.M., Marina stopped by with her parents, who were gracious in that way that seems unique to Italian aristocrats. I made sure that they met Stella, knowing that even though she was socially the most secure person I'd ever met, it would be nice if she knew some titled Italians at the Volpi Ball the next evening.

Janet finally rousted me out of bed around noon the next day. When I went out into the sitting room, it was perfectly restored and filled with flowers. It was as if last night's party never happened. I knew I was going to have to pay for it somehow, but at that moment I didn't care. I was so grateful it had all been taken care of so effortlessly that it was worth whatever price I was going to pay. After I rented dinner clothes for the evening, we went out to the Lido to find Stella, but she was having her hair done, so, avoiding the festival crowd as much as possible, we relaxed on the beach and got some sun.

That evening Stella and I went with Marina in her family's gondola to the

Volpi Palace on the Grand Canal. The gondola glided over the submerged entrance steps into a torchlit entrance hall with a marble floor that we could see underwater. Servants assisted us out of the gondola at the foot of the grand staircase and took the ladies' wraps when we reached the top. Marina looked lovely in a yellow chiffon ball gown, and Stella was radiant in a black and white satin with long white matching gloves. Her entrance drew every eye in the room as we were escorted to meet the Count and Countess Volpi. The yellow and white ballroom itself was magnificent, with huge windows that looked out onto the canal. The Venetian glass chandeliers were all ablaze, an orchestra played at one side of the ballroom, and a magnificent buffet of Venetian seafood delicacies was set up on the other side. Waiters circulated with hors d'oeuvres. It was not a sitdown dinner, but there were little ballroom tables and chairs placed around the perimeter of the ballroom, in the rooms off the ballroom, and on the terraces for those who wished to take a plate and sit. Titled and upper-class Italians as well as all the important names connected to the Biennale and quite a few Italian film stars, none of whom I recognized, made up the majority of the people at the ball. I felt as if I had stepped back in time to a more gracious age, albeit a decidedly snobby one. Later in the evening, Stella whispered to me in passing that Marina and I should not worry about seeing her home, as she'd met friends going back to the Lido who would take her. Sometime later, as Marina and I were leaving, I looked back and Stella was still in full swing waltzing with Rex Harrison.

Two mornings later my phone rang at around 9:00 A.M., and the manager said that the mayor was on his way up with several other gentlemen. I said, "What are you talking about? What mayor?" And on cue the bell rang. Janet opened the door and in came Mike Todd with two assistants and a small elderly man who turned out to be the mayor of Venice. Again on cue, the phones in both bedrooms began to ring. Mike said, "Don't bother, they're for me," and motioned his two guys to get them. Janet and I just stood there as he turned back to the mayor, took him over to the window, and demanded as they looked out on the canal: "Now you gotta promise me it won't rain on the Regatta! . . . OK? . . . Promise!"

The mayor just wrung his hands and said, *"Va bene, va bene, Dottore. Non fa piovere* (Okay, okay, sir. It won't rain.) . . . *se Dio vuole."* The last three words, "if God's willing," were said under his breath as he looked up to God and back at us.

Mike then clapped his arm around the mayor's shoulders, walked him to the door while saying, "Good, good. I'm depending on you now, okay?" and gave him a hearty handshake and a *grazie.*

As the little mayor backed out the door, trailing a string of *va bene*s behind him, Mike walked back to us saying, "Farley, sit down, I've got a proposition for you." We all sat down as he told me about a very special promo in Todd-AO that he was shooting for his next film, *Around the World in 80 Days.* He was traveling around the world himself, filming special events in every city that he visited. He was here to film the Venice Regatta, which was taking place this week. He would then intercut the events with nonspeaking surprise appearances by top-name celebrities from all over the world. When Stella told him I was in Venice, he thought I'd make a perfect surprise gondolier.

I thanked him and told him I was flattered, but I was under contract to do a film in Italy and I didn't think it would be legal for me to do anything else. "Farley, relax," he said. "This isn't a film. It isn't even a speaking part. There won't be any contract. It won't interfere with anything else you're doing. It'll only take a few minutes. Come on, what do you say?"

I was tempted but still pondering the legalities involved when he said, "I'll give you a thousand dollars in lire, and there'll be no record of it."

Janet poked me in the ribs, hard, and Mike laughed when I said, "Ouch!" "She's right," he said. "Let's go get this over with."

Fifteen minutes later we were standing in front of the Danieli Hotel on the Grand Canal, where he had four young gondoliers my size lined up. I stood back to back against each of them, and Mike picked one. We went into the men's room in the lobby of the hotel, where I put on the gondolier's outfit. Back on the canal Mike had an attractive young Danish couple waiting. The camera and its operator were already in place in one of the other gondolas, and they shot over my shoulder as I helped the couple into my gondola. Then he had them put the camera on land, and cut to the reverse shot of me smiling at the couple as they sat. That was all there was to it. I then went back into the men's room to change clothes. When I got back outside, Janet waved a thick envelope at me. Mike gave me a bear hug and said he hoped we would work together for real sometime soon. Then he and his crew were off into the crowd. When he was killed so unexpectedly in 1958, a year after he and Elizabeth married and had a little girl, the world lost one of the most dynamic entrepreneurs I've ever met.

The day of the Regatta arrived, and it was perfect. I started out with Marina at her family's palace, which was on the canal almost directly opposite my hotel. The Grand Canal was jammed with small boats that had to leave room in the center for the procession of the fantastically decorated longboats. I think the largest of them had eighteen or twenty oarsmen. The procession started in Castello near the gardens where the Biennale took place, entered the Grand Canal after passing San Marco, and proceeded up the canal as far as the Rialto Bridge. It was majestic and outrageously colorful. The palaces along the canal all held open house for fellow Venetians and their friends.

Marina and I only made it from her palace to Peggy Guggenheim's not too far up the canal. Everyone had spreads of food that varied from assorted cheeses to cold cuts, a much more enticing assortment of cold meats than that name usually signifies, accompanied by an unending supply of *prosecco,* the Venetian equivalent of everyday champagne. Peggy had tables out in her garden on the canal, which was overseen by a Marino Marini statue of a young man on a horse. Naked, his arms raised to heaven, the young man sported an impressive erection.

When I walked over to it, Peggy followed. "Are you scandalized?" she asked impishly.

"Not a bit." I laughed.

She explained that the erect member could be unscrewed and taken off when she was having guests who might be.

"And who would they be?" I asked her.

"I haven't the foggiest," she answered, "and if I did, I'd never invite them."

Marina showed me a Venice that the average tourist never gets to see: struggling painters' one-room studios; tiny trattorias that only neighborhood Venetians knew about; off the beaten track little churches with frescos and paintings that were priceless treasures. I felt she might have liked our relationship to move to another level, but as much as we enjoyed each other's company, and as much as I liked her . . . *like* remained the operative word. Aside from Marina, my free time in Venice was spent seeing Stella, until she left after the Biennale. Through no conscious effort of mine, my sex life was an uneventful bore. Then, the movie company and Visconti arrived in town.

Il Conte

Working within Hollywood's studio system had not prepared me for Luchino Visconti. This scion of the family that had ruled the duchy of Milan for two centuries knew only one way to work—his way. An aristocrat who was also an avowed Communist and openly homosexual, he was accustomed to having crates of fine leather gloves or handmade cashmere scarves or other luxuries sent to him to pick and choose from wherever he was. On *Senso* his first assistant director was the renowned Francesco Rosi, whose films include *Salvatore Giuliano* and *Moment of Truth,* and his second was Franco Zeffirelli, whose first two movies, *The Taming of the Shrew* and the exquisite *Romeo and Juliet,* were still a decade away. Franco was also Luchino's lover at the time, a relationship that was as much in the open as it was tumultuous. As a filmmaker, Visconti was a perfectionist who rarely got more than two or three setups finished in a day. He refused to be rushed by anyone or anything. At that rate, it was inevitable that my three-month contract would go on for over seven months. It would have been even longer had I been able to return to Italy when Luchino finally decided how he wanted the film to end.

My co-star Alida Valli was multilingual. We did our scenes in English, and she did her scenes with Massimo Girotti, who played her cousin, in Italian, and her scenes with Heinz Moog, the Austrian actor who played her husband, in German. Whenever producers showed up on the set hoping to speed up the process, Luchino treated them to impressive displays of artistic temperament that sent them scurrying. When we finished shooting the opening sequence of the film in La Fenice, Venice's breathtaking little opera house, the company moved to Vicenza to shoot in a Palladio villa that was used as the country home of the Count and Countess Serpieri, the parts played by Heinz Moog and Alida.

Vicenza is a small mountainside town about an hour north of Venice where many wealthy Venetians summered in order to escape the heat and stench of La Serenissima in the summer months. The incestuous life of our merry band of players living together in the small postwar Jolly Hotel outside Vicenza for three months nearly drove me mad. But the results are splendid and I am very proud of my work in *Senso*.

La Fenice

The company was staying at the hotel La Fenice et Des Artistes across the square from the opera house, but since I was finally receiving my per diem, I decided to splurge and remain in our luxurious digs at the Grand. I swore Janet to secrecy, always a chancy thing to try, because I didn't want to be perceived as the ugly American, above staying in a normal hotel room like the rest of the company. As soon as the stagehands had begun work at the opera house, Franco Zeffirelli called me to meet him at a little beauty parlor that all the opera singers used not far from the theater. I assumed it was to get a haircut and to discuss how to let it grow for the period. When I arrived, he surprised me by saying that since I was playing an Austrian, Luchino was hoping that I would agree to have my hair bleached blond, "like Laurence Olivier in *Hamlet*" was the line meant to bait the hook. Today, actors change hair color as readily as people change hats, but in 1953 it was still a big deal for a man. After mulling it over for a few minutes, I thought, What the hell, I can dye it back when we finish the movie, and agreed. Franco was delighted. After conferring with the hairdresser, he left to tell Luchino the good news. They sat me down, covered me up, and applied some thick malodorous gunk to my head. I closed my eyes and relaxed.

I don't know how much time had passed when my scalp began to sting. I bore that in silence for a bit, but when it got too painful I started yelling at them to get the stuff out of my hair. I didn't have to speak Italian to get my point across. They understood something was wrong. While the lady was rinsing my hair I heard her yell at someone to get Signor Zeffirelli. By the time Franco arrived, I was trying my best to deal with the fact that my hair was the color of strawberry sherbet.

Franco took one look, said "*O Dio mio!*" and launched into an excited exchange in Italian with the hairdresser and her assistants. That took a while. I was beginning to be aware that each moment is lived to its fullest in Italy. A bit later, as we walked to the theater, he explained that my scalp was obviously very sensitive to the compound that the hairdresser was using to strip the color from my hair. If she had left it on any longer, I could have been burned. I asked why they didn't just color it now to a dirty blond or light brown. He said that they were afraid my hair could fall out if they messed with it anymore. We went backstage to talk with Alberto, the head of the makeup department on the film, whom everyone adored. While he and Franco were talking, Luchino walked into the room. He stopped dead in his tracks and looked at me without batting an eye for a moment, then walked over to give me a warm welcoming hug, as he said, "*Caro* Farley, *finalmente, benvenuto* . . . Finally, welcome." He then pulled Franco aside and began an intense one-sided conversation that grew slightly in volume until he stalked out. At the door he turned to throw a "*Ciao, bello. Ci vediamo a presto* . . . see you soon," over his shoulder as he left giving Franco a final glare.

I had to press Franco to tell me what had been said. He finally gave a tight laugh and said, "He told me to get you fixed, and to do it soon and do it well, because you looked like a goddamned lollipop."

Alberto, who spoke a little English, clapped an arm around my shoulder and told me not to worry. He had a solution that would make this just a bad memory in no time at all. He had a way with him, because I really did start to relax. He also gave me a cap to wear as Franco took me into the theater.

We went through the door into one of the boxes for my first look at the opera house. La Fenice was breathtaking. Aside from my one time at Covent Garden, my only other frame of reference for opera houses was the old Metropolitan Opera in New York, which seemed like a vast unlovely barn compared to this little blue and gold jewel box. Many of the seats in the orchestra had been removed in order to be true to the period of the movie, which was 1866, when the young available men stood in groups or milled about the orchestra preening and flirting with the young women in the boxes. In our case, this group in the orchestra would consist of a potentially combustible combination of Austrian officers and upper-class Italians. As I stood there drinking it all in,

Visconti strode in from the lobby down to the center of the orchestra, shouting in Italian. He was followed by a protesting older man, the theater manager. Franco whispered that Luchino was demanding that the big Venetian glass and crystal chandelier be lowered to the floor in order for them to change it to candlelight, which was authentic for the period. The manager was trying to convince him that it was too dangerous. The chandelier had not been lowered since its conversion to electricity decades earlier. He was not sure that the old mechanism would even still work, much less support the weight of taking it up again. Visconti's tirade built to epic proportions as he somehow managed to compare the importance of this event with Italy's victory over the Austrian occupier at the time of *Senso*. The manager manger eventually gave in, and almost on cue, all work in the theater stopped. Heads appeared everywhere to watch as the chandelier was fitfully lowered. A big cheer, which Luchino gracefully acknowledged, went up as it finally settled. Franco said softly, "That was a good lesson to learn, Farley. He always gets what he wants, and he is almost always right."

We only had two weeks to complete the scenes at the opera house in Venice, because their season was about to begin. It seemed to be going slowly, but I was not yet used to the Italian way of working, much less Visconti's way of working. The scenes in La Fenice included most of the main characters and a full house of extras, as well as a full Verdian orchestra in the pit and a stage filled with opera singers, chorus and principals.

The staging was complicated and difficult and began with all the principals' entrances. I enter the orchestra to stand with a group of young Austrian officers; the Count and Countess Serpieri, Alida and Heinz, enter and settle in their box; and finally Massimo Girotti, who played Alida's cousin Roberto, a wanted Garibaldi partisan, appears in the midst of the crowd of Italians in the orchestra. All this is happening as the theater fills up with spectators and the orchestra enters, opens their scores, and tunes up. Finally, the chandelier is lit and hoisted as the house lights dim, and *Il Trovatore* begins. In the end, this scene was not used in the movie.

It begins instead close to the end of Act III of the opera as we see leaflets and red, white, and green rosettes, the colors of the new Italy, being silently passed from hand to hand in the upper reaches of the opera house, which is largely occupied by standees. As the tenor and chorus thunder out the call to arms, *"All'armi, all'armi!,"* a young girl's voice rings out from the gallery, "Foreigners, get out of Venice!" From the top of the theater a shower of red, white, and green streamers, rosettes, and leaflets rain down on the Austrian officers as the audience erupts. During the general chaos, Roberto and I have an encounter that results in a challenge to a duel. The plot is set in motion.

I arrived for my first morning of filming and went right to Alberto, who had something approximately the size of a deodorant stick with gooey black stuff in it that he applied to my hair. After he was through combing it in, it looked surprisingly natural, although it was hell washing it out each day. As Alberto had assured me, it also seemed to hasten the process of my hair darkening to its natural color. Janet took great delight in calling me Pinky for those two weeks, but the Italians were too polite to mention it.

Visconti was passionate about perfection in every area. No detail was too insignificant for his attention. The amount of food on a plate, or a partially consumed glass of wine, or the degree to which a candle had burned down all had to be absolutely right for the time frame of the scene. The angle of the sun's rays coming through a partially covered window had to be exact for the time of day in the story. If I sat on the floor at Alida's feet with my head in her lap, he wanted her loosened hair to fall over her shoulder just so. He was concerned with the fold of my cape and how much of my leg it covered. He knew exactly how he wanted her hand to be placed on my cheek and how much of the moonlight or sheet covered our bodies in bed. Every frame was a painting.

He orchestrated the emotions he wanted with the same precision. There was no leeway. On what word did a slap take place and with what hand? Where in the shadows did I place her in order to shield her from seeing too much of the dead body of an Austrian soldier along the canal? He felt so passionately about all of these things that I found it contagious. Luchino was very specific about what he wanted from me in each scene, emotionally and physically. After a few days, Franco was able to stop interpreting, because I instinctively understood what Luchino wanted even though he was demonstrating in Italian. I was used to working in a much faster way in Hollywood, and his specificity not only didn't hinder me, I got to like the challenge of it. In the course of the film, he was sometimes stern and unyielding with me, but I never was on the receiving end of his legendary temper. He was often curt, sometimes cruel, and occasionally lost his temper with Alida. He never lost his temper with her in front of me, but all film locations are rife with gossip, and in Italy this was as much a sport as a way of life. Sooner rather than later, everyone heard everything.

With the exception of the opening in the opera house, every scene I had in the film was with Alida. Even in the several scenes that included a third person, she was my focus. Alida was a professional and, as a good actor must be, she was always there in the moment. Off camera, she was remote to the point of coldness, and I've always felt her performance reflected that aloofness. Her passion always seemed more cerebral than visceral. I often wondered how the film would have turned out had I been able to play the love scenes with Ingrid Bergman, who had been Visconti's first choice for the part.

We finished at the opera house and were preparing to move to the next location, the Palladio villa near Vicenza, when Janet dropped the bomb that she was leaving. She had been corresponding with an ex-husband, and she wanted to go home to see if it was worth trying to rekindle something. Janet may not have been a good secretary or interpreter, but she was a fellow American, and we did have a good time together. After working all day with people who spoke next to no English, it was a huge relief for me to be able to relax and laugh with Janet. Franco spoke excellent English, but he also had a complex relationship with Visconti. I felt it would be unwise to rely on him off the set for anything other than group social activities. I asked if she could just come to Vicenza and help me get settled, but she had already booked a flight home and was taking a morning train to Rome. "Thanks for the notice," I snapped at her as I walked out the door.

I was walking off my anger along the Grand Canal when a voice called out, *"Farley, che fai?" . . . Dove vai?* What's up? . . . Where are you going?" It was Franco. He fell into step beside me. I told him I was walking off a head of steam because Janet had quit with no notice. When he asked why, I told him. He wryly observed that I shouldn't begrudge her a chance at getting back with the right man. I snapped, "The right man! He's her third ex! And they were only married for six weeks!" He started to laugh, and I finally joined him.

He told me that he was on his way to meet Francesco at a place nearby that was like a working man's private club. It was a hangout for the Venetian gondoliers, who were like one big family. The food and wine were fresh, inexpensive, and delicious. It was for men only and no tourists were allowed, but he was sure they would honor me as a special guest. At some point in the evening, different men or groups of men would spontaneously sing opera. Luchino, one of Italy's most important opera directors, had introduced him and Francesco to the place. Would I like to join them? I said, "You bet," and we plunged off into the dark side alleys of Venice.

We were less than ten minutes away from the Piazza San Marco when we crossed a small bridge and walked under it to an unmarked heavy double door. Inside we were greeted with the din of happy male voices mixed with the smell of cigarette smoke and good food. We entered a vast room containing long tables loaded with food and liters of wine, flanked by benches filled with men of every size, age, and shape. By the time the owner made his way over to us to welcome Franco, I spotted Francesco on the far side of the room, and we made our way over to his table. Waiters threaded their way through the crowd balancing trays of glasses and silverware, pitchers of wine, and baskets of bread. There were also platters of different pastas, delicately fried *frutti di mare,* and assorted vegetables. After we finished our first and second courses, out came trays of cheeses and fruits and more wine. We were having a great time as the two Francos tried to top each other with stories about Visconti at his most outrageous, when without warning the singing began. It started at the other end of our table. A sweet-voiced young tenor climbed up on it and sang the duke's aria, *"La donna è mobile,"* from *Rigoletto*. The room quieted immediately. A couple of accordions at different places in the room joined the aria. Next, two men at different tables across the room climbed up and sang Rodolfo and Marcello's fourth act duet from *La Bohème*. The singing went on for at least ninety blissful minutes, with duets, solos, quartets, and sextets from Italian operas being sung from everywhere in the hall, some in groups and some scattered about. Being a part of this evening made me feel as if I had become one of the group, an honorary Italian, and I think my ability to understand and to speak the language started to improve.

Janet's departure, which left me without an English-speaking buffer, was the beginning of my really bonding with Franco and Francesco on the film. They began to treat me like one of them. It was a good feeling.

A Sad Little Jolly

The Jolly Hotels were a chain that sprung up all over Italy shortly after the war. They were modern and functional but charmless, rather like a vertical Italian version of the Howard Johnson motels that sprang up across America in the 1950s. There were a number of *pensioni*, small B & B's, in town, where some of the crew stayed, but our Jolly was the only real hotel in Vicenza, and the only one within a half-hour's drive from our location, the Palladio villa. Luchino, his assistants, and the department heads stayed in the hotel along with all the principal cast members and their significant others. There is a lovely Italian word, *accogliente*, which means warm, inviting, cozy, and welcoming. Our sad little Jolly was none of the above. It was at odds with everything we associate with Italy: warmth, earth tones, classic taste. A five-story-high cement block structure with white stucco walls, white marble floors, and harsh modern lighting, it had all the modern conveniences in rooms that were small and cell-like. This was home for the next month and a half.

Dinner was served promptly at nine each evening, and the food was not too bad. Our long table consisted of Luchino, the two Francos, Massimo Girotti and his wife, and Rina Morelli, a wonderful character actress whom Luchino used whenever he could. In *Senso* she played Alida's companion. Rina spoke some English and had a wicked, bitchy sense of humor. She loved to gossip, and took great delight in shocking me. From Rina I learned why Alida never appeared at dinner. She supposedly was having an affair with Giancarlo Zagni,

Luchino's third assistant, "and since Luchino fancied him as well . . . ,' she let it trail off with an amused shrug. In the course of our stay there, I learned enough about Alida, and everyone else in the company, from Rina to write a book, and it would have made a great read.

Alida studied acting at a motion picture academy that Mussolini had set up in Rome just before the war. She became a star in the escapist *telefono bianco* (white telephone) films popular during the war. Her first love was an Italian Air Force pilot who was shot down over Africa by the British. She was married to Oscar de Mejo, an Italian painter/jazz pianist, when David O. Selznick discovered her and brought her to Hollywood in 1946. She almost did not get her visa to go with Selznick because of a rumor that she had an affair with Goebbels, Hitler's minister of propaganda. After her marriage to de Mejo, she had gone into hiding for two years rather than make fascist propaganda films for the Italian government. Her husband was a bigger success in Hollywood than she was when he wrote the song "All I Want for Christmas Is My Two Front Teeth." She fell madly in unrequited love with Frank Sinatra when they made the flop *The Miracle of the Bells.* Now she was betraying Visconti by having this affair with his third assistant. But after all, Luchino was still fooling around with Massimo Girotti behind his wife's back, and also behind Franco's back. The gossip was like a stream of consciousness that picked up again each evening exactly where it had ended the previous evening. The penance I paid for being plugged into all this company gossip was that "Fritzie," Rina's aging, corpulent, and flatulent dachshund, was always seated on a chair between us at dinner. Fritzie was so overweight that he resembled a bratwurst with feet, but he always managed to heave himself into a sitting position to drool and beg for my food.

Visconti's work process at the villa was as extravagant as the most voluptuous images in his films. At La Fenice, the schedule had been dictated by the time left before the opera season began, but there were no time constraints at Villa Godi Malinverni. He did not decide what scenes to do each day until inspiration struck in the early morning. Every area in which we might work had to be freshly dressed, set up, and ready to go each day. That included food, fresh flowers, and the myriad things that make a set ready, except lighting. That always had to be set up after the location was chosen because we only had a limited number of lighting instruments.

My first call to work at the villa was also a dangerously close call. Alida and I had a long tracking shot to do when she takes me from her bedroom to hide me in the granary. As we were passing a massive antique table, I heard a loud snap and instinctively pulled her aside with me. We just missed being hit by a pipe hung with lights that split the table in two when it hit. Shooting ended for that day.

After two days, I realized that since my work at the villa was limited to a couple of scenes in the countess's boudoir and a love scene in the granary, I was going to spend a lot of time just sitting around doing nothing. As lovely as the bedroom assigned to me as a dressing room was, I had no intention of just hanging out there while the rest of the film was being so painstakingly shot. I knew Visconti wanted that, but what I wanted was a car and the freedom it would give me. I told Franco how strongly I felt and he promised to speak to Luchino about it.

That evening, Luchino, Franco, and I had a summit before dinner. Luchino spoke first. Through Franco, he explained dramatically that it would make him very happy if I did not go driving around the countryside by myself. Driving in Italy was not like driving in America. The country roads were dangerously curvy and rough, and the highways were paved with the blood of young Italian men because they all thought they were racing driver champions. The cities were no better. There everyone drove like they were in a bumper car ride in an amusement park and paid no attention to stop signs or red lights. He loved me too much to see my life ended at this early age when he foresaw so many good things for me in the future.

I was 25 percent bamboozled, 25 percent flattered, and 50 percent still determined to have a car. I pleaded my case. Growing up in California meant that I had learned to drive almost as soon as I got out of the eighth grade. Since the time of my first movie, I had always had my own car, which I drove along the dangerously curvy and narrow Mulholland Drive, which connected the studios via the treacherous, twisty canyon roads. During the rainy season, there were mudslides around every other curve and produce trucks from the San Fernando Valley coming at me like a train if I missed the boulders on the roads. Franco gave me a "not bad" look, but Luchino just sat there glowering, so I forged ahead. "And besides, just a couple of years ago, I drove all through Italy, Austria, Germany, France, Spain, and England in a little Hillman Minx. I went over the Alps, over the Pyrenées, and never even got a scratch. I also . . ." *"Va bene, va bene . . .* okay, okay," he interrupted me curtly as he got up. "*Ci pensi tu, Franco . . .* Franco will see to it," and he stalked off.

Franco grinned at me wickedly and said "Good work" when Luchino was out of earshot. I asked him to get me a little red sportscar like the one that Aldo, our cameraman, drove. He raised his eyebrows at me; "I would not push my luck, Farley." Several days later, he gave me the keys to a car that had arrived from Milan. I raced out to see my car. There sat a big, black, vintage Buick sedan, out of a 1930s gangster film. At lunchtime, I drove it up to the dirt-floor tavern in the countryside near the villa where the company ate each afternoon, literally scraping the walls of the houses on both sides of the road as I went through the nearby little village. The whole company was waiting for me outside the tavern when I pulled up. I backed in smoothly next to Aldo's red Alfa and got bravos.

Luchino and Franco both had huge grins when I walked over to them. I admitted to Luchino that it was a great joke and asked when my real car was arriving. His grin vanished as he said firmly that this was it. It was too dangerous for me to have a speedy little Italian car that trucks could squash like a bug, and this was the only solid American car he could find, and that was that. *"Basta! È finito!* . . . Enough! It's finished!" He turned and walked into the tavern. I started after him when Franco grabbed my arm and said, "It won't change, Farley. Don't press him." Reluctantly, I gave in, and after I got used to maneuvering along the country roads I started to have fun with the car. It guaranteed me a big welcome wherever I went while exploring the countryside in search of the many other Palladio villas near Vicenza. I became something of a celebrity in our little village, because one day while scraping my way through, a ritual that the locals now came out for either to shout encouragement or to watch potential disasters take place, I came to a nose-to-nose standoff with a government oil truck. When he gestured at me to back up, I shook my head no. I had become pretty deft at getting through the town without incident, but I was not about to try it backward. The two of us got out of our vehicles. I had learned by now never to utter a word of Italian in situations like this. You win much more quickly by sticking to your point in English. After much shouting and gesticulating in English and in Italian, accompanied by loud partisan encouragement for me from the delighted bystanders (Italians will always side against the government in a private squabble), I finally forced him to back up to the outskirts of the town where the road widened and I could get by. From that day on, I was a local hero.

Dinners at the Jolly may have been mediocre but the lunches at that little country taverna were incredible. I don't know how the sweet older couple who ran it managed, although I'm sure the daily presence of the count inspired them. In the entire time we were there, we never had the same meal twice. The antipasti were always freshly homemade surprises; the primi piatti were a new kind of pasta with a different sauce every day or different hearty soups; the *contorni,* vegetables, were prepared in such a variety of ways that it seemed to be something different each time; the main courses ranged from whole roast suckling pig—I still dream of the cracklin'—to the chickens that pecked underfoot the day before, to trout caught that morning from a nearby stream. For dessert there was always a platter of superb local cheeses and fresh fruit. All of this was washed down by uncomplicated homemade wines that were perfect with the food, followed by strong caffè to jolt us awake enough to return to work sated and invigorated. The meals were such that I did everything I could to get back for them each day, even when I wasn't working. She was missing out on some terrific meals, but Alida still never ate with the company.

One afternoon, after a particularly satisfying meal, Franco told me that

Luchino was thinking about changing the afternoon schedule. Would I come back to the villa to be there in case he needed me? I did, of course, and fell sound asleep in my dressing room. I woke up sitting in a chair outside in the rain with our makeup man slapping my face. Alberto had come to my room to tell me that I was not going to be used, and he smelled gas as he came down the hall. He raced in to find me unconscious and not breathing, and scooped me up to carry me outside, where he administered some kind of CPR that probably saved my life. Apparently a draft had extinguished the flame on the heater in my room, and the room had filled with gas. Except for a lingering headache, I felt fine almost immediately after I regained consciousness.

That night at the Jolly, Luchino asked if I would like to take a long weekend off and go to Paris for a change of scenery. I jumped at his suggestion. He arranged cars and tickets for me and booked me a room in his favorite little hotel, the Lancaster, on the Right Bank near the Étoile. It was a gem, furnished with exquisite antiques. I couldn't have felt more privilaged. After checking in, I tried to get in touch with Ethyl and Buddy, with no success. As I started to unpack, thinking that I should have called before leaving Italy, and wondering what I would do if they were not here, there was a knock on the door. I opened it to one of France's most popular and admired leading men of the 1940s and 1950s, Jean Marais. After he introduced himself, I guess I just stood there looking stupid because he said, "May I?" gesturing into the room.

"Of course," I said, jumping out of the way. I closed the door, followed him in, shook his hand, and introduced myself.

He laughed as he said, "I know who you are, Farley. I've seen your Hitchcock films, and also the one directed by Nick Ray. You are a good actor." His English was on a par with my French, so this entire exchange was much more awkward for both of us than I've made it sound. He went on to say, "Luchino has made me promise to help make your stay in Paris a great success. What would you like to do?"

The lightbulb finally went on. Luchino! He must have known Marais through Cocteau. As a young theater director, Luchino had done several of Cocteau's plays in Rome, and Marais's early career had been guided by Jean Cocteau, who wrote both plays and screenplays for the sensationally handsome young actor. My thoughts raced for a moment. I was not eager to be a part of one of Luchino's manipulations, but I also didn't want to be rude to Jean Marais. Finally, because I couldn't think of what to say and the silence was awkward, I finally blurted, "Do you know Zizi Jeanmaire?" He said no, but he certainly knew who she was. I asked if he thought he could help me find her, since I had no idea of how to begin and I would really love to see her. He said that he would make a few calls and be back in an hour or so after I had finished settling in. "Would that be okay?" I assured him that it would, and he left. After I had finished unpacking and tried Ethyl and Buddy again with no luck, I sat there wondering if Luchino had an ulterior motive for having set this up. Before I could come to any conclusion, Jean Marais was back with an address on the Rue Ravignan, and off we went.

Next thing I knew, we were knocking on an apartment door in Montmartre. The door was opened by Zizi, who did a classic double-take, then jumped into my arms squealing, "Oh, my good thing!" I introduced her to Jean, whom she had recognized on sight, and she led us into the living room where she introduced us to Paul, a young dancer with whom she was obviously involved. Paul went to get some glasses and a bottle of wine. Several glasses of wine later, we went out to a little place nearby for something to eat. We had escargot, steak frites, and a salad of frisée with lardons, accompanied by liters of good house wine and baskets full of peerless Parisian bread. With Zizi's help, or it may have been the wine, the language barrier seemed to melt away long before the evening was over. From there, Zizi took us up to tiny little club up near Sacré-Coeur, the white church that sits at the top of Montmartre and stands out as one of the landmarks of Paris. An old Russian guitar player who had been a legend in Paris since the Russian Revolution was performing there. He was as much a landmark as the church, and supposedly could give Segovia a strum for his money. Jean knew of him, but had never seen him. So we were all up for the idea. The guitarist did not disappoint. He was a big grizzled bear of a man with a full beard and a wild head of hair that somewhat resembled the untrimmed tops of his guitar strings. He played classical music and Russian folk songs so beautifully it brought tears to my eyes. He came over to envelop Zizi in an enormous hug, and politely bowed as we were introduced, but we could not talk him into sitting down for a glass of wine.

The owner of the club, who also sang there, was a woman named Genette Auger, also known as Geneviève. She became a semi-star on late-night TV in this country, along with the British music hall favorite Hermione Gingold, as a regular guest on the *Tonight Show* with Jack Paar in the late 1950s.

The next day, the smell of *café filtre* and hot croissants woke me at noon. Jean put the coffee down next to the bed and opened the curtains, and I realized that we were on his luxurious houseboat on the Seine. I didn't remember all the details of the night before, but I remembered enough to know he had been caring and very sweet. I decided that getting us together had not been a self-serving manipulation on Luchino's part. It had been a successful attempt to bring together two people he cared about. After I had showered and dressed, I joined Jean in the main cabin for more coffee, and we sat and talked for hours. He told me how he had always hated the in-crowd and the social scene in Paris, which was why he lived on a houseboat. It afforded him more privacy. We talked about his early career and how it wasn't until he became involved with Jean Cocteau both personally and professionally that he was able to tap into the talent that made him so successful. As a director, Cocteau had managed to break through the self-protective barriers that many good-looking actors build to hide behind. Before that Jean had felt that the only thing that he brought to his work was his looks, and he had not liked that feeling.

At one point, I called Ethyl and Buddy again, and Ethyl answered! When she heard I was in Paris for a long weekend she said, "You get over here right now!" I told her I was having lunch with Jean Marais. She said, "Oh my . . . come to dinner, then, and by all means, please invite him. I've been in love with him ever since I saw *Beauty and the Beast.*" I promised to try. But Jean had plans to attend the opera with friends that evening. Too bad; I think he would have lived up to Ethyl's fantasy.

I spent that evening and the next day and evening with them as we caught up on one another's lives and just enjoyed being in Paris together. I had to get back to work. As I was packing to leave for the airport, there was a knock on the door. It was Jean. He had come to say goodbye and to tell me that he had talked to Luchino to tell him how lucky he was to have me in his film. We promised to stay in touch.

Back in Vicenza that evening, Luchino said that I looked rested and that he hoped I had enjoyed myself. I said that it had been a wonderful break and thanked him for introducing me to such a lovely little hotel. I had decided to let him be the one to bring up Jean's name. He didn't, so neither did I.

Two days later, it was late Friday afternoon, and Alida and I were finishing a scene in her boudoir, when three representatives in black suits from Lux Films appeared on the set. Luchino called a break. As I headed for my dressing room, Franco pulled me off to the side and said, "Stay. You will enjoy this."

I watched the tight little huddle on the set for a couple of minutes, and then Luchino's voice and gestures started getting louder and more dramatic. He wheeled and strode off through the bedroom we were shooting in, threw open the doors, marched down to an unlit alcove off the antechamber, grabbed the armful of flowers out of a large vase on a table in front of a mirror, marched all the way back to the executives, and dashed the now-wilting flowers to the ground at their feet. He then proceeded to jump up and down on the flowers while bellowing at the executives: "*Merde, merde, merde!!!* How do you expect me to work like this? I am an artist, not a banker!" This slightly paraphrased line I recognized from Chekhov's play *The Seagull.* The executives were trying to get their "*Scusi, Contes*" in as they backed out of the room stumbling over one another in an effort to escape his wrath. As soon as the doors closed behind them, he yelled to no one in particular, "We will resume work in ten minutes after this mess is cleaned up." None of us knew it at the time, but *Senso* was to bankrupt Lux Films.

One morning I arrived on the set to see Luchino walking back and forth in deep conversation with a man who for one crazy moment I thought was Erich von Stroheim. Then I realized that the bald head, the jodhpurs, the boots, and the riding crop were what had fooled me. I sat down ready to work, and Franco sat down quietly next to me. He said, "Farley, it might be a good idea for you to wait in your dressing room. I'll come get you when Luchino is ready." When I asked him why, he leaned in and whispered, "The man Luchino is talking to is Palmiro Togliatti, the head of the Italian Communist party. He might want to have a picture taken with you. That would not make your Senator McCarthy happy if he happened to see it, right?" He was absolutely right, and I slipped away to avoid any potentially embarrassing moments.

It was November, and we were nearing the completion of our work at the villa when I had a brainstorm. In order to avoid any repeat of the Jolly Hotel togetherness experience, I would rent a house in Venice when we returned to resume shooting there. I called Stella in New York and got the name of the art dealer at whose house we had dinner the evening I met Peggy Guggenheim. She gave me his number in London, and I called. Not only was he in, he said that he would be delighted to rent me his house as long as I had no objection to the two servants, Marco and Maria, who lived there full-time. They both spoke reasonably intelligible English, and Maria was a wonderful cook. I had no objections. It sounded ideal. I was delighted. We made a deal, and it was done. He would tell Marco and Maria of our arrangement, and I would call to let them know when to expect me. When I asked Franco to let Luchino know, he said he would.

At our last dinner at the Jolly, it may have been my imagination, but everyone seemed more lighthearted than usual. Luchino stood to thank us all for our good work and to say how much he looked forward to finishing the sequences in Venice before we returned to Rome. He then looked at me and said, "Unfortunately, we will not have the pleasure of Farley's company as much as we did here, since he has rented himself a house in Venice." It was obvious that he was not thrilled by what I had done, and would have preferred to have me more under his control as I had been in Vicenza.

I thought quickly and said that one of my reasons for renting a house was so that I could invite them all to help me celebrate one of our most important American holidays, Thanksgiving. Luchino gave me a level look and said, "I'm not so sure that discovering America was a good thing."

Next to me Franco murmured under his breath, "Capitalism."

I quickly improvised a little speech about what kind of a holiday Thanksgiving was. It had nothing to do with the discovery of America. It was a holiday in memory of a time when the early settlers invited the Indians to share the bounty of their first major harvest. Everyone sat down together like brothers for a communal feast in celebration of times to come.

Luchino absorbed the translation of that and finally smiled as he said he would be pleased to come. That night, drifting off to sleep, I was jolted wide awake by the thought, "Where the hell am I going to find cranberry sauce in Venice?"

Cats

Sunday evening, as I got off the train in Venice, I spotted a distinguished middle-aged man waiting in the fog at the end of the platform, holding up a sign with my name on it. I had called the house to tell Marco and Maria when I would be arriving, and much to my surprise he was there to meet me. He insisted on carrying my bags to a boat he had waiting, and we were off. We arrived, and they showed me to my bedroom on the second floor. It was a lovely big room, all windows on one end that looked out onto a pretty walled garden. There was a very large adjoining bathroom at the opposite end next to the bed. One wall was all books and the other was filled with Venetian lithographs surrounding a fireplace. I could not have designed a place in which I would be more at home. Upon my arrival, Maria had asked what I would like for dinner, and I had asked her to please make it something very simple. I was not as hungry as I was tired.

After I had settled in, there was a soft knock at the door, and Marco entered with a glass of *prosecco* and told me that supper would be ready in about twenty minutes. When I went downstairs I was greeted by a lovely meal of *risotto ai frutti di mare,* cold chicken, green salad, and assorted cheeses. It was perfect.

I was awakened the next morning by Marco when he brought in my breakfast. He set it down on a table by the windows and opened the drapes. Then a scene appeared that I could happily wake up to every morning for the rest of my life. Dozens of cats of every size, shape, and color, or mixture of colors, had managed to squeeze onto the ledge and were pressed against my windows. They obviously slept there for the warmth of the house that passed through the panes of glass, and they took the drawing of my curtains as their clue to begin the day. Watching them get up to yawn, stretch, and groom themselves and one another before jumping down to the top of the garden walls was a start to my day that I have never been able to equal. Marco and Maria were gems, and their English was far superior to my Italian. I convinced Marco that I was not a breakfast-in-bed type. All I wanted was a glass of juice outside my door. When the glass vanished, I was up. I would take my juice, draw the curtains, and sit to enjoy my cats before showering. After dressing, I would go down to the dining room.

I discovered that Marco was an avid movie fan, and I loved talking movies with him as I breakfasted. One morning I mentioned what a brilliant actress I thought Anna Magnani was. He would have no part of it. He hated the whole neorealistic trend in Italian films. "It was all too ugly and dirty!" I was scoring a pretty good point in my pro argument when he cut me off by unexpectedly clearing my breakfast dishes. As he turned to back out the pantry door, he declared with great finality, "Well, she's no Lana Turner!" I had to laugh even though I understood the feelings that shaped his sensibility. Italy went through some bad times before, during, and after the war, and he missed the days of their escapist films in the 1930s and early 1940s. *Telefono Bianco*—White Telephone—was what the genre was called. It was pure escapism, comparable to the Astaire and Rogers series in America during the Great Depression.

I only had one scene to shoot this time around, so I wasn't surprised that more than a week passed before I heard from anyone connected to the company. During those days I discovered the enchantments of Venice in the winter. It was almost devoid of tourists, and the constant fog gave the city a new layer of mystery. Saints and gargoyles would suddenly and spookily materialize as I approached. At night, the colors from a lit flower shop across a square appeared, first as a faint glow of colors that as you got closer, would brighten and slowly swim into focus.

On several mornings, I got up early to go to the market with Maria. It was a unique spectacle, with boats arriving from the mainland piled high with fruits, vegetables, meats, and every other kind of supplies imaginable that had to be off-loaded to individual vendors from Venice's market. The various vendors all knew Maria by name, and God forbid that any one of them tried to sell her anything that did not live up to her standards. She was capable of a performance that Magnani would envy. Shopping with her helped me to understand the Italian joy of fully participating in all the interactions of life.

After over a week with no word from the company, I called Franco at his hotel. He apologized at once for not contacting me, but something terrible had happened and shooting had been delayed. Aldo, our cinematographer, whose red sportscar I had coveted, had been killed in a car crash while driving down from Vicenza to Venice. He had been with Luchino ever since his first film. Luchino was beside himself with grief and having a very difficult time deciding how to replace Aldo. Franco promised to contact me as soon as they had a replacement.

Possibly because I had been fortunate enough to work with several of Hollywood's legendary cinematographers, Gregg Toland, James Wong Howe, and Joe Ruttenberg to name three of them, I knew what an essential part they played in the realization of a director's vision. Aldo had been with Visconti for so long that he had developed the ability to anticipate the Maestro's wishes and needs. Not only that, an unspoken love had grown out of their mutual respect. There is no way to forge that kind of bond instantly. It can only grow out of working together in a variety of circumstances both good and bad.

I was also terribly upset, possibly because I was aware of how much cinematographers contributed to the quality of a film, but also because he was such a sweet and caring man. In the short time I had known Aldo, I had come to care about him as much as everyone else did. Not only did he know how to make beautiful pictures, he knew how to say the right thing to everyone. When I did a scene, he would say, "Farley, when you speak it is like Shakespeare."

With more unexpected time on my hands, I took a chance and gave Peggy Guggenheim a call. Much to my surprise, she was listed in the phone book. She also just happened to be in Venice and answered the phone herself. She invited me over to dinner the next evening. It turned out to be the first of many evenings that she and I and her beloved pack of Lhasa apsos spent together that cold and foggy November. The dogs originated in Tibet and were believed to receive the souls of their masters when they died. Peggy and her doggies lived together in one big room, the only one with heat in the palazzo. The rest of the rooms were closed down for the winter. It was there that Peggy reminded me about the restorative or at least warming quality of Italian grappa, which in those days was more like marc, the shot of liquid fire made from the dregs of grape pressings, that many a French workingman uses to kick-start his day. Now grappa has been refined to the level of a French *eau de vie* and is quite fashionable.

I never tired of hearing stories about how, at age thirty-eight, she began collecting artists and their works. She also told me about the time when she and her second husband, Max Ernst, the Dadaist/Surrealist painter, were hanging her first show in Paris as the German troops marched into France. Peggy had had shows in New York and in London, but Paris was then the center of the art world, and she was damned if any war was going to ruin her first chance to show there. She and Max ignored all the unofficial and official warnings to leave until the highest government officials remaining in Paris appeared at her gallery one morning and ordered them to leave. The German army would be in Paris within forty-eight hours, and France could not be responsible for her or Max's safety, much less the safety of the paintings. She and Max finally heard the warning. They packed all the paintings into the back of an old truck and fled just hours ahead of the Germans' triumphant entry into Paris. They were heading for Portugal via northern Spain. Somewhere near Bordeaux, they admitted to themselves that they could not risk entering Fascist Spain with the paintings and struck a deal with a French farmer to bury them under the floor in his dilapidated old barn. She went back after the war when Americans were very welcome all over France. The old farmer and her paintings were still there and still in great shape.

One morning while exploring the city, I came upon the restaurant that Franco Zeffirelli had taken me to, where the gondolieri hung out and sang opera. I tried the door, and it opened. The owner, who was working at a table near the front door, recognized me and got up to greet me. After a minute, I asked him if he ever made an exception to the no women rule. He frowned and started to shake his head, but I kept on going and said that I was only asking because I was wondering if perhaps one evening I could bring a Signora Peggy Guggenheim who owned an important . . . he interrupted me excitedly. Of course he knew who la Signora Guggenheim was, and she was not just a woman, she was "*una vera padrona* . . . a patron saint" to the people of Venice. He would be honored to have her in his place, and . . . now it was my turn to interrupt. I thanked him and promised to call before bringing her. He was overjoyed at the prospect.

It was the first time I was aware of what esteem Peggy was held in by the people of Venice. This only grew through the years. When I next saw her in the early 1970s, she had been made the Venetian equivalent of a Dame. I can only imagine how they revered her when, upon her death, she left her entire collection to the Solomon Guggenheim Foundation with the stipulation that it be maintained in perpetuity in Venice. She had a ball being the only woman there the night we joined the gondolieri for food, wine, and song. I think she was particularly pleased and flattered when the same handsome young tenor whom I had heard with the Francos came over, knelt, and dedicated "*La donna è mobile*" to her.

Ever since I felt comfortable enough to do it, I had started pestering Luchino about getting me a copy of *Ossessione* to see. I was not only curious to see his first movie, but I was eager to see how he had translated *The Postman Always Rings Twice* into an Italian subject. It had been the film that initiated Neorealism and anticipated the rebirth of Italian cinema after the war. What we were doing now was so epic, I just had to see that first film. I knew how busy he was, so I had not pestered him for a while. One morning on the set, he asked if I had plans for the evening. When I said that I didn't, he said, "Good. Tonight you will see *Ossessione*."

I thought that meant that he had gotten a 16-millimeter copy of it to project in one of the public rooms in his hotel. No way. He had commandeered the local movie house for the evening and screened it for me, and of course any other members of the company who wished to see it, which was everyone except Alida. It was a terrific movie. All I had loved about the Hollywood version was wiped out by the raw intensity of this version, with the possible exception of John Garfield's superb performance. Massimo Girotti was equally superb in the Garfield part, and Visconti had stripped Clara Calamai, in the Lana Turner part, of any of the glamorous crutches that had been Miss Turner's trademark. The other changes that he made to transfer the action from California to the Po Valley only seemed to intensify the tragic inevitability of the story. The movie's style was as far removed from what he was now doing with *Senso* as an MGM musical was from a Warner Brothers gangster movie.

Mambo

Visconti had engaged the services of Robert Krasker, the British cinematographer whose work on Laurence Olivier's film of Shakespeare's *Henry V* was so impressive. Krasker was on his way, and we would be ready to resume work as soon as he and Visconti were able to screen the footage that had already been shot. I was home expecting that call when one came from Robert Rossen, a well-known American screenwriter (*The Strange Love of Martha Ivers, Blues in the Night,* and *The Treasure of Sierra Madre*) and director (*Body and Soul, The Brave Bulls,* and *All the King's Men*). As a result of the blacklist, he was now working exclusively in Europe. He had a project pending and wanted to know if I had a free day in my schedule to meet him for lunch at Harry's Bar.

We met the next day for what turned into a very long lunch that began at 1:30 P.M. and lasted until 6:00 P.M. He was doing a film in Italy called *Mambo.* It was to star Shelley Winters, Vittorio Gassman, Silvana Mangano, and, he hoped . . . me. I haven't given you the slow buildup he gave me that day, which included the story, my great part in it, and all the rest, which had kept me interested through the first two Bellinis. I've cut to the punch line, his naming the actors, which was delivered with the third drink. "You've got to be kidding," was my answer.

He wouldn't give up and went on about how right we all were for the parts and what terrific actors we were, and soon he capped it with "Think of the great press we will get!" My response was: "That's exactly what I am thinking about! What are you, crazy?"

Rossen was a good screenwriter and a good director who understood the frustration I had felt at being typecast by Goldwyn as the sensitive, tortured young man. He assured me that his film would go a long way toward changing that perception of me. But his idea was just too perverse. Shelley and Vittorio had separated, and she was revving up for a divorce. God only knows what publicity stunts she was planning. I was a former lover and still her friend. Vittorio, a notoriously temperamental womanizer, was about to be her ex-husband. *Bitter Rice* had made Silvana Mangano the hottest new sex symbol in the Italian cinema. The ravenous Italian gossip press, for which the word *paparazzi* was coined, would hound us mercilessly. I could see why it appealed to Rossen as great publicity for the film, but all the Bellinis in Italy would not be enough to convince me to be a part of that particular three-ring circus.

The Turkey

The jellied cranberry sauce and mincemeat that I had ordered from New York arrived along with a recipe for a Thanksgiving dinner. I shopped with Maria, who figured out how to substitute Italian products like squash for yams. The problem was the turkey . . . *il tacchino*. In 1954, it was impossible to find a plump, well-fed turkey in Venice. All one could find was a scrawny bird that had much more in common with a scrawny oversized chicken than it did with a Butterball or its 1954 equivalent. Then I had a brainstorm. There was an American air base near Venice. I rented a car the day before Thanksgiving, found my way to the base, and talked my way into a meeting with the CO. He heard me out and finally agreed to help me in my effort to confront Count Luchino Visconti with the fruits of capitalism. He called his commissary, and within a half-hour presented me with a bona fide American turkey. I handed it to an astonished Maria late that afternoon She and Marco outdid themselves with *il tacchone*, as they christened our bird . . . *-one* is the Italian suffix that means very big. So our *tacchino* became a *tacchone*.

Luchino and the Jolly Hotel contingent arrived as a group. After they entered, Luchino grandly but benevolently announced that even though he disapproved of capitalism, their great love for me brought them here today. He explained to all that it was a holiday commemorating the one time that the early American settlers had treated the Native American people like equals. It seemed best simply to accept his benediction and go into the sitting room for drinks.

After several glasses of champagne, someone suggested that we play the Truth Game, something I'd managed to wriggle out of whenever it took place in Vicenza. But this was my house, and I was trapped. This is the Italian version of Truth or Dare, which the Italians, or at least this group, played for much higher stakes than we do. It started off innocently enough, but when it was her turn, Massimo Girotti's wife upped the stakes. She smiled at Luchino and asked him sweetly, "When did you last have sex, Luchino?"

He smiled back just as sweetly and replied, "Yesterday afternoon with your husband, my dear."

Marco, who was standing nearby with champagne, jumped in with, "*Signori e signore*, Thanksgiving dinner is served."

Other than a little too much truth, and the fact that no one could understand the concept of either jellied cranberry sauce or mince pie except the Brit Bob Krasker and me, Thanksgiving Day was a smash. Maria's dressing, which bore a close resemblance to polenta, was a particular triumph.

The following week Alida and I filmed the one scene we had left to do in Venice. It was a love scene that took place in a cheap rented room near the Austrian Army barracks in the city. In the film the scene was meant to illustrate Livia's willingness to abandon caution and to risk her good name, despite her aristocratic upbringing, because of her growing obsession with Franz.

The company prepared to move to Rome to shoot the end of the film. Alida and I had one more scene together. It was our most important and emotionally complex scene in the film.

The Shiner

I had barely settled into my room at the Hassler, which overlooked Rome from the top of the Spanish Steps, when someone started pounding on my door. I opened it . . . and in fell a hysterical Shelley. She was sporting a perfect bull's-eye of a shiner. I called room service to order a raw steak and went to work calming her down. It took a while, but after I got her resting on my bed with the steak draped over her eye, she finally slowed down enough to get her story out.

She'd come to Italy to do Robert Rossen's movie *Mambo,* in part because it gave her a chance to tie up some loose ends with Vittorio. Even though their relationship was amicable, she felt that the marriage needed to be ended formally so they could get on with their lives. In other words, she wanted a divorce. He was performing *Hamlet* in Genoa with his company, and she had gone there to see him in it as a surprise. The only problem was that she had hated both the production and his performance. She went backstage after the show with the good intention of keeping her mouth shut, a difficult goal for Shelley. When he asked her what she thought about his performance, she told him, "It was terrible." He responded by presenting her with a black eye. She had come straight to Rome and checked into the Excelsior, where she heard that I was in town and tracked me down. I got her moved into the Hassler, but aside from dinner that first night, the only other time I got to see her was when she heard that Gassman was doing a telephone interview about his separation from her with *Il Tempo,* one of Italy's major newspapers. She made a deal with the reporter doing the interview: she would be present when his interview with Gassman took place, and she would comment on everything Vittorio said. The reporter jumped at the opportunity to get this two-sided interview. Of course, she had not told me about her plan of journalistic one-upmanship. She just told me that she needed my moral support because she was doing an interview that could affect her divorce.

Wanting to help, I agreed. During the interview, when Vittorio got dramatic about how much he missed his fourteen-month-old baby daughter, Vittoria, Shelley added: "If he misses her so much, how come he doesn't know that she's eighteen months old?" She had a topper ready for everything he said about their relationship and separation. The press ate it up, and she came out of the interview looking like the poor little wronged woman. In this case, it was true that she was somewhat wronged. But poor? . . . little? . . . Never!

Shelley could still not understand why I refused to do *Mambo*. She kept begging me to change my mind, saying, "Think of the publicity we will get. You just can't buy that kind of publicity. They'll be reading about us all over the world! Besides, I'll feel so much safer with you there with me." I tried to explain how happy I was being involved in a quality project with a wonderful director. I didn't want to follow it by being involved in a project that was destined to become a press-feeding frenzy. As usual, publicity always trumped common sense with Shelley, and I could not get through to her. I'll never understand how she and Vittorio survived the film together without bloodshed. It turned out to be a pretty bad movie. Even though I was irritated with her that day at *Il Tempo* for tricking me into her planned effort to one-up Vittorio, I had to admire her chutzpah.

While reading the newspaper that afternoon, I found out that Ava Gardner was in Rome shooting *The Barefoot Contessa* with Humphrey Bogart and Rossano Brazzi. Before I had a chance to call her, she called the Hassler to say that she'd just found out that I was in town and invited me over to a Sunday-afternoon party in her suite at the Excelsior. As soon as I got there, she dragged me away from the crowd into her bedroom to talk. She was as funny and gorgeous as I remembered her. She was in the middle of complaining about what a piece of crap the film was, and how lucky Rita Hayworth was because she turned it down, and how difficult Sinatra was being over their split-up, when the phone rang. It was Frank. She listened for a bit, then said, "Frank, I can't talk anymore right now, call me later . . . I said not now, later! Because I'm with Farley! That's why!" She banged down the phone, looked at me, and started to laugh. "Come on, honey, let's go get you a drink." We went out into the living room, found the bar, and there, of course, was Bogart. I think Betty was making a film back in Hollywood. Bogie was even more colorfully outspoken with his opinion of the film than Ava had been. The only one who came out of the film well was Brazzi. It made him a viable Hollywood star.

Luchino did not get to the big scene between Alida and me until after

Christmas. So I flew to London to get away from all the craziness in Rome and to see some theater. But most of all, I wanted to spend a little sane time with Peter and Mary, who always had a real old-fashioned English Christmas, complete with roast goose and Christmas pudding, for family and stray friends. It was a wonderful restorative. In no time at all, I felt grounded again and back in the real world.

On Twelfth Night, I got the call I'd been waiting for. Luchino was ready to shoot my final scene in *Senso.* The scene, which took place in Verona, was shot in a gorgeous little movie studio that was built into one of the ancient walls that surrounded the city of Rome. At the time, I thought, Leave it to the Italians to have a romantic movie studio. I had been brought up on the industrial-looking soundstages of Hollywood, where nothing was real except anxiety, insecurity, and fear.

The final scene was the most emotionally complex one I had in the movie. In it, the countess leaves the villa during the battle and undertakes a dangerous and stifling carriage ride to Verona in search of Franz. The city streets are filled with drunken Austrian troops celebrating their victory over the Italian army at Custoza. When Livia locates Franz, he is living in luxurious squalor with a young prostitute on the partisan funds meant for Garibaldi that Livia had given him to bribe his way out of the Austrian army. These funds had been entrusted to her to deliver to her cousin Roberto to be used to arm the Italian partisan troops. Franz is drunk and filled with feelings of self-loathing as well as anger at Livia. He lashes out, forcing her to pour wine for the prostitute, and demands that she recognize him for the useless coward that he is.

Luchino told me in detail what he wanted in this scene. I assumed that he had done the same with Alida. I also assumed that it would take several days to complete. We rehearsed it in the morning and did two takes in the afternoon. When we finished, Alida departed without so much as a fare-thee-well. As soon as Franco had checked both takes and declared them a buy, I got a big cheer and a prolonged round of applause from everyone else on the set. Luchino swept me into a major hug and asked me to have lunch with him the next day. He said that Franco and Francesco wanted to take me to dinner that evening, but he would have me all to himself the next afternoon.

That evening the two Francos took me back to the trattoria in Trastevere where we had all first met. Alberto and the other members of the crew with whom I'd become close were there. Even though I was more than happy to finish the film and get on with my life, I had pangs of separation anxiety at the thought of saying goodbye. These fellows had become my *cari amici* . . . my dear friends. I was going to miss them. The Italians don't say *miss.* They say, We will feel your absence, which covers it beautifully.

The next day Luchino took me to lunch at Ranieri, which at that time was the best restaurant in Rome. Over lunch, he told me about some of the problems he had been having with the Italian government censors over *Senso*. They were being extremely difficult, and he was worried that if they had their way, our beautiful film would be ruined. I must have looked stricken, because he hurried to assure me that they were not talking about my scenes, it was mostly the battle sequences and the scenes that concerned them that he was worried about. I said I was worried about his film, not just my scenes, and asked him if the battle wasn't, in effect, the framework of the movie? He looked at me for a long moment before saying, "Thank you, Farley."

We then talked about the ending of the film. He had not decided if Franz's execution should be seen. His plan was to show Livia's final descent into madness after she turns Franz in to be shot as a deserter. He would end the film on the countess running through the streets of Verona, colliding with drunken Austrian soldiers and their prostitutes, screaming Franz's name over and over. I loved that idea. It was the perfect ending.

Three months later I got a call from Lux Films to come back to Italy in order to do the execution scene. I was filming *The Girl in the Red Velvet Swing* at 20th Century-Fox, and they could not give me the time off to go to Italy. As a result, Franz's execution, which was shot against the blood-soaked walls of the Castel Sant'Angelo in Rome, where countless executions had taken place through history, had to be done in a long shot. This particular sequence has often been singled out by critics because of the dramatic effect Visconti achieved by not showing Franz's face. That scene and Livia's carriage ride to Verona where she discovers Franz and his prostitute were shot by Giuseppe Rotunno, Aldo's assistant cameraman. After our work in Venice at Thanksgiving, Visconti and Robert Krasker had a falling-out, and Krasker did not finish the film.

Hollywood Ending

I arrived back in Hollywood exhilarated and exhausted from my nearly nine-month experience on *Senso*. I felt ten years older, but in all the right ways. Obviously, I had grown up during those months in Italy. My agent, Charlie Feldman, asked me to meet him for lunch as soon as I was rested. He wanted to hear everything about working for Visconti. More good films were being made in Italy by a whole new crop of talented directors, and he felt it was inevitable that more American actors would be receiving offers to work there. Over lunch, he asked how Tennessee had behaved on the production. I had completely forgotten that Tennessee was even involved. I told Charlie that I had met him on my first night in Rome, and then I never saw or heard about him again. The only writer that I heard mentioned during the filming was Suso Cecchi D'Amico. We both laughed at the irony, because it was Williams's name that had sold me on the whole project in the first place. Then over coffee he dropped the news that Darryl Zanuck had a two-picture deal for me at Fox, and he was willing to pay me very handsomely to do them. Charlie felt that if I still intended to leave for New York, it would be good for me to go with two big American films coming out rather than hoping for the best from a foreign film that might not ever be released in the United States. I warily asked what these two films were. He told me that *The Girl in the Red Velvet Swing* was going to be a lavish production based on a real-life murder/sex triangle that involved the famous architect Stanford White and the young millionaire Harry K. Thaw, who shoots White over Evelyn Nesbit, a sixteen-year-old model who became the Gibson Girl. Ray Milland, who won an Academy Award for *The Lost Weekend,* was playing the architect, and a young English actress who was getting "the build-up" as the next Elizabeth Taylor was playing Evelyn Nesbit. "Who?" I asked. "Her name is Joan Collins. This will be her first major American film, and she really is a great beauty," he told me. The scriptwriter, Charlie Brackett, was an old pro, and the director, Richard Fleischer, was solid and dependable. My part, Harry K. Thaw, was the psychotic millionaire who marries the girl and kills her former lover, Stanford White. It sounded intriguing.

"What is the other one?"

"It's a mystery. I don't know much about it yet, but you'll get top billing and the other featured actors in it are Anthony Quinn and a young actress named Anne Bancroft, who I hear is very good. She studied at the Actors Studio in New York."

Charlie always knew how to bait my hook, and I had always been a fan of Tony Quinn's work. I said I'd think about it. I then did some research on the actual case of the murder of Stanford White and decided that it would be a happy change for me to play an obsessed madman after all the sensitive-young-man parts I had been stuck with while under contract to Goldwyn.

My first day on the set I discovered that Cornelia Otis Skinner was playing my mother. While in Rome, I had stumbled on a tiny English bookshop run by two British matrons and their pug dog. Coincidentally, I'd bought a book there to read on my flight home about two innocent American girls abroad called *Our Hearts Were Young and Gay.* Miss Skinner had written it with her friend Emily Kimbrough. A renaissance woman, she was a successful playwright and author of numerous essays and collections of light verse. She was a unique comic talent and a gifted character actress. She toured all over America in the late 1920s performing a one-woman show of short character sketches she had written. I headed straight for her dressing room to introduce myself. She was a dignified middle-aged lady with a sly sense of humor. I liked her at once and grew to like her even more as the movie went on. I couldn't bring myself to call her Cornelia, and Miss Skinner seemed too impersonal. At the end of our first day working together, without planning it, I said, "See you tomorrow, Miss Skinner, sir." She did a slight take and gave me a little smile and that was it . . . Miss Skinner, sir.

Joan Collins was a very different cup of tea. A gorgeous girl with raven hair, a peaches-and-cream complexion, and dazzling blue-green eyes, she had both stage and screen experience in England and was in no way intimidated by the Hollywood buildup the studio was putting her through. I don't know whether or not she enjoyed it, but she was smart enough to embrace it for what it was worth and not let anything go to her head. I liked her enormously. How could I not? She was beautiful, talented, grounded, and loved a good dirty joke.

I had very little to do with Ray Milland in the movie except shoot him in the face three times at point-blank range. I wish we had had some scenes together. He was a very good actor as well as very much a gentleman. I would have enjoyed the chance to work with him.

I've never seen *The Girl in the Red Velvet Swing,* so I have no idea of how good or bad it is. However, up there with *Strangers on a Train,* it was one of my more enjoyable filmmaking experiences in Hollywood. No one behaved like a prima donna, there were no mishaps with guns on the set, and my hair had grown back to its natural color. Richard Fleischer didn't deviate from his shooting schedule; and all the actors liked one another and working together.

By the time we had finished, *The Naked Street* was ready to begin. All I have to say about my final movie at 20th Century-Fox is, "Thank God for Tony Quinn and Anne Bancroft." The writer, Maxwell Shane, was not very good and was an even worse director. Tony was a unique actor, as was Anne, and we all struggled to inject some kind of drama into a script that was preachy, trite, and pedestrian.

Anne and I would spend our lunches talking about the theater and life in New York. This was her tenth film, and she was not happy about any of them. I felt that she was too special and too good for Hollywood to ever figure out how to use her well and suggested that she go back to the theater. Perhaps I was projecting my own intentions, but in any case, she did return to New York and was soon to win a Tony for her work in *Two for the Seesaw,* followed by another one for *The Miracle Worker.*

When Anne did go back to Hollywood in 1961, it was to re-create her role as Annie Sullivan in the film version of *The Miracle Worker.* For that, she had the play's Broadway director, Arthur Penn, to thank. United Artists had hired Penn to direct the film version of his stage success. He wanted Anne and Patty

Duke to repeat their roles. U.A. offered Penn a lavish two-million-dollar budget for the small, black-and-white film if he would use either Elizabeth Taylor or Audrey Hepburn as Annie Sullivan, but Penn, backed by author William Gibson, turned them down. The film won Academy Award nominations for Penn and Gibson. Anne and Patty took home Oscars for their performances. Anne was now a movie star. Shortly after that, she married the great Mel Brooks. Anne became a film icon for her performance as Mrs. Robinson in Mike Nichols's decade-defining hit, *The Graduate.*

Tony Quinn continued to do good work in all mediums. When he and *Zorba the Greek* found each other, he became famous the world over. On the set of our movie together, going over our lines one afternoon in Tony's dressing room, I noticed a terrific photograph of him. His head shot in profile looked as if it belonged on a Mayan or Aztec frieze. I asked him, "Do you have any copies of this?" He said he did, and I asked if I could have one. "Are you sure you want one?" He was obviously flattered and a little flustered.

Tony went on to play Stanley to Uta Hagen's Blanche in the national company of *A Streetcar Named Desire.* I heard so many good things about their production that I flew to Chicago to see it. They were very different from Marlon Brando and Jessica Tandy in the Broadway production, but they were spectacular. It's a testament to the strength of the Tennessee Williams play that different actors can make it an equally exciting and involving experience. After that, Tony made some of the biggest films in his career both here and in Italy in the late 1950s and the 1960s. His parts were all based on his masculine earthiness, which was used to great advantage in *Zorba.* There was no one else quite like him, and he always did his thing with great style and panache.

Act III

The East Coast

The film was over. I was done. It was finally time for me to go to New York and begin my new life. Shelley was already bicoastal and had gotten a lovely apartment in an old prewar building on Central Park to complement her house in Beverly Hills. One way or another, our paths would continue to cross. I said goodbye to my parents and the other people who were near and dear to me and finally moved to New York. At last my apartment in the East Sixties, which I had rented before *Senso,* was going to be occupied.

I had barely settled in and started to work out a schedule of classes when Charlie called from Hollywood. Marlon Brando had just turned down a script at Twentieth, *The Egyptian.* I was Zanuck's next choice. This time I said no. I had made a clean break, and I was sticking to my plan. Two hours later he called again. Zanuck had upped the money and carried on about what a big movie this was going to be, starring Jean Simmons, Gene Tierney, and Victor Mature. The director was Michael Curtiz, an old pro with dozens of films to his credit and a great track record for success. After several more calls and a lot more pressure, I agreed to think about it and asked for a copy of the script. The script was undergoing rewrites, and they had nothing to send at the moment, but the cast had to be set so they could begin publicity as soon as possible. "Hmmmm, not a good sign," I thought as I went out to buy the book on which the film was based. It was a quick read, perhaps because I didn't think it was any good. I knew at once that I wanted no part of it, and told Charlie so. Next thing I knew, several of the producers involved started calling, and each time I said no, each of them said in disbelief, "But it's a Darryl F. Zanuck production!" I told each of them that I was suitably impressed and properly grateful but not interested. It took many more calls for it to sink in, but they finally gave up.

A handsome British newcomer, Edmund Purdom, had stepped in at the last minute to mouth Mario Lanza's singing in *The Student Prince* when Metro decided that Mario was too fat to be seen. Operettas had not been in fashion since the late 1930s, when Nelson Eddy and Jeanette MacDonald were dubbed "America's Sweethearts." Mr. Purdom went right from that into the part I had been offered in the "Darryl F. Zanuck production," *The Egyptian.* Neither film worked to launch his career. A couple of years and several other sumptuous costume epics later, his Hollywood career faded as quickly as his one-year marriage to Tyrone Power's ex, Linda Christian. Miss Christian never made it as an actress in Hollywood, either. She surprised everyone in 1964 with her performance in an Italian/Spanish co-production, *The Moment of Truth.* That film, which many consider the definitive film about bullfighting, was directed by Francesco Rosi, Luchino's first assistant on *Senso.*

In almost every way, life in New York exceeded all my expectations. I loved the freedom of being in a city where I could walk everywhere, from Central Park to the Garment District to Wall Street. It was like being able to walk to different countries. I had an infinite variety of behavior to observe and learn from.

Shortly after I settled in, the actress Geraldine Brooks called me about a party she was arranging to introduce Anna Magnani to the New York theater crowd. I'd dated Gerry in Hollywood when we were both living there, and we had remained good friends. In 1950 she had gone to Italy to play Magnani's younger sister in a film called *Volcano,* and they had become friends. Magnani was coming to New York for a week on her way to Hollywood to make her first American film, *The Rose Tattoo.* Gerry said that Anna was very nervous about having to do a film in English, and she wanted to spend some time just hearing the language before she had to begin filming. The party was being hosted by some wealthy friends of Gerry's father, who was a well-known costume manufacturer and designer. Gerry knew how much I loved Italy and Visconti, and Anna had done a couple of films for Luchino. In the hope of putting Magnani at ease, she invited me over early the night of the party. Magnani was everything I hoped she would be: warm, funny, volatile, and definitely larger than life. Having Visconti in common helped us to feel comfortable with each other almost from the moment we met. She and Gerry had decided that when the party started, she would stay in the bedroom and Gerry would bring in the people who wanted to meet her, a few at a time, so that Anna, with her limited English, wouldn't feel overwhelmed.

Everybody in the New York theater showed up. The place was jammed beyond all expectations. I was at the bar talking to Julie Harris a while later when Gerry came over to pull me aside, "Farley, you have to help me. Anna needs to see you. She hurried me through several rooms, past an endless line of people, to the bedroom. We stopped outside the door for a moment where she whispered, "She wants to go back to her hotel, and wants you to take her," and pulled me into the room after her. Anna and her manager were standing there at the ready. She grabbed my arm, Gerry opened the bedroom door, and out we went, followed by her manager past the endless line of startled actors and other theater luminaries. The private elevator near the entry hall was waiting, and as we scuttled in, Gerry hissed, "Her limo is downstairs." As the doors closed, I could see the mob moving in on Gerry.

I climbed in the backseat with Anna, and her manager got in front with the driver. As we pulled away from the curb, I heard him say, "Plaza Hotel" to the driver. Then Magnani erupted. She leaned over, and while cuffing her poor manager about the head, she berated him for getting her stuck in that mess, sitting on the bed like some English queen receiving people. It was a splendid Italian tirade. When she wound down, she looked over at me and caught me grinning in appreciation. I thought I was in for it, but she suddenly laughed and slapped me on the knee. "Farley, you come and we watch TV, okay? In the lobby at the Plaza, she told her manager to call Gerry and give her four names to bring over to meet. *"Nessun' altro!* (Nobody else!)" I remember Julie Harris and Danny Kaye were two of the names. We went up to her suite, where she immediately turned on the TV and pulled a chair right up to it, fascinated.

In the mid-1950s, summer stock was still the place where apprentice actors went to learn their craft; established actors went to expand their abilities in roles they might not normally be chosen to do, and stars went to keep themselves in the public eye. In the 1960s, stock began its painful decline under the onslaught of prepackaged musical dinner theater. I decided that the best way for me to learn about theater was to get onstage. Summer stock was a place where my name assured easy entry, as opposed to Broadway, where a young movie star with no stage experience ranked pretty low on the list of desirables. All I needed was the right play, the right co-star, and a good director.

In Hollywood I had gotten to know a talented composer named Sol Kaplan. His wife, Frances Heflin, was actor Van Heflin's sister. Fra, as she was known by all who loved her, cut her acting teeth on Broadway in plays that include *I Remember Mama,* in which she played one of the children, and *The Skin of Our Teeth,* directed by Elia Kazan, starring Tallulah Bankhead, Frederic March, and Florence Eldridge, with Montgomery Clift and Fra playing the children. Fra may also be remembered as Mona, mother of the oft-nominated Emmy Award–winning actress Susan Lucci, on *All My Children.*

Sol and Fra had moved to New York from Hollywood when Sol's rising career as a film composer was cut off by the blacklist. They, along with their two young children, Jonathan and Nora, became my New York family. And their big, warm apartment on West End Avenue became my second home for many love-filled years. Jonathan, who is a very talented and successful film and TV director/producer, lives in Los Angeles. Nora and Mady, the youngest, are both terrific actresses who wisely left the business for less precarious careers. They are still my family.

That first summer in New York, Fra and I decided to tour the East Coast summer stock circuit in *The Hasty Heart,* a sentimental World War II comedy/drama by John Patrick. We piled Jonathan and Nora into the car and took off for our first engagement. I loved traveling with Fra and the kids. Just driving through the lush green eastern countryside, playing word games with the kids, was great. The beauty of New England, with its pristine small towns clustered around their white steepled churches, made an instant East Coast convert of me. Our demand to share a dressing room shocked many an uptight theater manager. Not only were we not married, we had children in there with us. The tour was a great success, and we played to packed houses with appreciative audiences. The first time I got a laugh onstage, I knew what live acting was all about. Having that many people connected to you, sharing your emotions, is an exhilarating experience. The only thing we were not happy about was that we had to perform with a different group of actors at each theater with no time to rehearse. We barely had time enough to do a walkthrough so that we wouldn't trip over the furniture. Sometimes we had good actors, and sometimes they were so bad that Fra and I didn't dare look at each other for fear of losing it. One memorable night, we were so distracted by one actor's outrageous antics that Fra transposed the words "cocked" and "cap" in a line she had about me, saying, "You walked in and just stood there with your cock capped over one eye." It wasn't easy getting through the rest of that performance. We decided that next summer would be different, and it was. We assembled our own company for *The Rainmaker,* and had the sets designed to our specifications.

Just Off Broadway

Fresh from having toured in stock, I was eager to get started at the Neighborhood Playhouse to begin studying with Sandy Meisner. He put me in his "professional" class, which was quite small. I was in diverse company: Bob Fosse, who went on to Broadway and Hollywood acclaim as a director/choreographer; Gloria Vanderbilt, a multitalented lady who painted and designed fabrics; Jimmy Kirkwood, a comedian who went on to write a number of funny books and plays and eventually co-wrote *A Chorus Line;* and Tom Tryon, a handsome guy but a wooden actor who starred in the movie *The Cardinal,* and went on to write bestsellers. I had no sooner settled into class when I got a call from my agent. The producers of the Phoenix Theatre had offered me a leading part in a new play they were presenting called *The Carefree Tree.*

The Phoenix Theatre on Second Avenue at 12th Street was a leader in the off-Broadway movement that took root in the mid-1950s. Its founders, T. Edward Hambleton and Norris Houghton, were dedicated to presenting challenging new productions of high artistic quality at affordable prices. The Phoenix Theatre was in a Broadway-size house of about 1,200 seats. Such notable directors as Tyrone Guthrie, Michael Redgrave, and Jack Landau, co-founder along with John Houseman of the American Shakespeare Festival and Theatre, worked there in the formative years of the company.

The Carefree Tree was a Chinese fantasy of a play that was to be directed by Jack Landau, who had also designed the scenery. Alvin Colt, Broadway's best and busiest costume designer, did the costumes. A number of well-known theater actors were to be in the play, and the billing was alphabetical. The actress who played my love interest was Janice Rule, who first captured Broadway theatergoers with her beauty as well as her talent in *Picnic* in 1953. Everything about the project sounded good. I said yes.

Our rehearsal studios were over a famous dairy delicatessen near the Phoenix on lower Second Avenue in what used to be the heart of the Yiddish art theater district. I loved the neighborhood with its unique theater history, and the deli with its ancient waiters whose hands shook so much that the delivery of every bowl of borscht was a real-life drama. The rehearsal process, a three-to-four-week period during which we and the director explored the play and the life and direction of our characters, involves the actors laying themselves bare in order to get inside the skin of the character they are playing. Ideally the actors are guided, helped, and supported by the director, who has an overall vision of the play. With very rare exceptions, which is almost always the case when the director is from the theater, there is no comparable process in film. Instead, the film actor has to arrive with a fully developed character that, with a few instant adjustments, he hopes will integrate into the story. There are occasional exceptions; Robert Altman springs to mind, but his process is unique in big-budget films. Rather than rehearse a written script, he depends largely on his actors' ability to improvise their performances within a given framework. Most often his results are wonderful, spiced with some deliciously chaotic moments.

I fell in love with Janice. She was an exquisite redhead with the long-limbed, long-waisted figure of a dancer, which is how she had started in the business. One of a large "lace curtain" Irish family from New Jersey, she was feisty and competitive, with a deep throaty laugh. We were both smitten. Our play did not get great reviews, but we loved doing it and found each other. Janice's divorce from the playwright N. Richard Nash was soon to become final. It is ironic that Dick had written the play my company was to do in summer stock the subsequent summer, *The Rainmaker.*

When the "Chinese Boo Boo," our affectionate name for *The Carefree Tree,* closed, Janice moved in with me, and before long we were making wedding plans. In the few months it took us to reach the wedding invitation stage, we had also begun to reach a firsthand understanding of the Cole Porter lyric "our love affair was too hot not to cool down." It was a gradual awareness of the fact that it had been great, but it was time to move on with our lives and careers, not with married life. It's a fact of theatrical life that actors, when playing people in love onstage, frequently fall in love offstage. Later in her career, Janice gave up acting to study psychoanalysis. Her specialty was actors and the various emotional entanglements that ensue when the characters they are playing are emotionally involved. Since we remained friends always, we managed to share many a good laugh over what coulda, shoulda, woulda been.

The Tube's Golden Age

I had bought out my contract with Sam Goldwyn during the twilight of the Golden Age of Hollywood. That twilight coincided with the full flowering of the golden age of live television. It was fortunate for me because that first tour in summer stock and that first role in a prestigious Phoenix Theatre production had not opened any doors for me to Broadway's movers and shakers. They still thought of me as a movie star, not as a serious actor. My agent suggested that he look into television, where they could never get their fill of movie names. I'm glad I listened to him, because during the next five years I did approximately thirty live television shows with wonderful directors like Alex Segal and Sidney Lumet.

Live television was the most exhilarating, adrenalized experience I'd had to date as an actor. We rehearsed in sequence for several weeks. Then, after a dress and technical rehearsal, we performed it on air. There were no such things as TelePrompTers, tape stops, reshoots, fixes in editing . . . none of the technical advantages that are taken for granted today. When you got on that thirty-, sixty-, or ninety-minute express train, there was no getting off until it reached its destination. If you or another actor went up (forgot the line) or didn't make the entrance, you had to keep going until, one way or another, everything got back on track. If the show was under, they could fill time with a commercial. It could not be over. It had to end on time. Some of the shows were bad, many of them were good, and some of them were superb. All of them were fun to do. I worked with some of the most talented actors and directors in the business.

Janice called me one morning. She and Roddy McDowall, who lived right down the street from me, had had dinner with a director friend of theirs, Alex Segal, the night before. He was starting rehearsal for a live telecast the next day with a show about Sigmund Freud as a young man and had lost his leading man. They had convinced him that I was perfect for the part, and he was going to call me. I got off the phone and waited. Not more than a half-hour passed before Alex called. He and the producers would be overjoyed if I agreed to do the part. They were messengering the script to me, and would appreciate it if I could read it right away and let them know my answer. I read it, liked it a lot, called him back to accept, and spent the rest of the evening reading it over and over.

The next morning I arrived at rehearsal, met Alex and the cast, and was measured on the spot by the costume designer for my clothes. That done, I expected we would sit down for a read-through. Alex said, "No way, I want you all on your feet." This isn't going to be easy, I thought as I took my script and joined the others on the taped-out demarcation of the set. Alex yelled out, "No scripts, Farley."

"But I just got it last night, I don't know anything yet," I said with more than a touch of desperation.

"Don't worry about that, my assistant will cue you," he said. Cue me she did, every line, for days.

For several days all I could worry about were words. I didn't have a brain cell free to worry about blocking or motivation or anything else. In the second week, as the words began to fall into place, it seemed like everything else began to fall into place with them. I wasn't plagued by any of the usual uncertainty about my character's motivation or his relationship with the other characters.

As a director, Alex had a reputation as a yeller, but that didn't bother me at all. I was so happy about the ease with which I got inside the skin of young Freud that I completely forgot the agony of those first few days. I loved working with Alex, and I think that the feeling was mutual, because I did several more shows with him.

As Apollodorus, the emissary who smuggles Cleopatra into Caesar's quarters wrapped in an oriental rug and unrolls her at his feet in the *DuPont Show of the Month* production of George Bernard Shaw's *Caesar and Cleopatra,* I was in the company of some of theater's heavy hitters. My fellow cast members included Sir Cedric Hardwicke, Claire Bloom, Jack Hawkins, Cyril Ritchard, and Dame Judith Anderson.

The only problem I had was with wardrobe. My costume was a short white tunic and a big enveloping hooded cloak. The tunic narrowed and gathered on the left side to drape over my shoulder. At the dress and tech rehearsals I had trouble with that damned tunic. It kept slipping off my shoulder, a bit like Rita Hayworth's lace nightgown strap in the famous World War II *Life* magazine pinup. I got little sympathy, and worse, no help from the costumer, who was too busy with other problems to worry about my shoulder. My character appeared in only one act of the play, and I was damned if my costume was going to distract me or the viewing audience. Before we went on air, I borrowed scissors from wardrobe, cut off the entire top off my costume, and had makeup do my chest and back. When I whipped off my cloak, and climbed onto the railing around the terrace to dive into the harbor of Alexandria, I was topless. The costumer had a fit, but when the show was over, I got applause from the stagehands, congratulations from my fellow players, and excellent reviews.

I played Eddie Cantor's son in the *Playhouse 90* production "Seidman and Son." I had been told my father was going to be played by Lee J. Cobb. Eddie, whose films had helped to keep the Goldwyn Studio afloat during the Depression, was now an old-timer, but definitely a trooper, and very much a presence. At times I had to guide him around a bit, but he did a great job and was very sweet, thanking me for my help when we finished. My girlfriend was played by Mona Freeman, who was excellent as one of the young women in the film adaptation of *Our Hearts Were Young and Gay* by Cornelia Otis Skinner. She loved "Miss Skinner, sir" as much as I did, so we bonded immediately. Peter Lorre, one of Warner Brothers' outstanding character actors, was also in it. He had rocketed to fame in 1931 playing a psychopathic child murderer in *M,* director Fritz Lang's first talking film. I had lunch with Peter whenever possible. I listened avidly to his stories of the old days at UFA in Germany for as long as he was willing to tell them. He used to sneak up on me during rehearsal and, in that inimitable voice, whisper in my ear, "What are the creeps doing now?" I would always lose it, no matter how serious the moment.

I played twins, with twenty costume changes, in *Playhouse 90*'s production "The Clouded Image," which was based on Josephine Tey's mystery novel *Brat Farrar.* Our director was Franklin Schaffner and the rest of the cast included John Williams, Vincent Price, and Dame Judith Anderson. To everyone's horror, I took to calling the diminutive Australian actress "Big Judy." She loved it and invited me to her Santa Barbara home for a weekend when we finished. Unfortunately, this was one of a five-show back-to-back marathon that necessitated flying from New York to California for *Playhouse 90* and immediately back to New York to begin the next show.

Alex Segal directed me again in the title role in a ninety-minute adaptation of the Sinclair Lewis novel *Arrowsmith,* produced by David Susskind for *DuPont Show of the Month.* This time I was prepared for the way Alex worked. He could yell all he wanted; when things fell into place, they did so with amazing clarity. I thought Alex was one of the best directors I ever worked with.

I had the good fortune to be cast as Morris Townsend opposite the wonderful Julie Harris in *The Heiress.* Julie, with whom I was later to do a Broadway show, was absolute perfection in the part. We became good friends, and some years later she wrote a very flattering introductory piece about me for National Repertory Theatre's souvenir program.

In my next live TV show, *The Prisoner of Zenda,* directed by Alex Segal for David Susskind and DuPont, as Rupert of Hentzau I dueled with Chris Plummer with heavy broadswords until my arms felt dead, then threw my sword at him and dove out of a castle window into the moat. I was beginning to become a pro at diving from high places into bodies of water. At least this time I had no shoulder strap to worry about.

I also played Peter Ilich Tchaikovsky to Helen Hayes's Madame von Meck. I was intimidated at the prospect of working with Miss Hayes, whom many considered the finest actress in the American theater. We, along with the New York City Ballet and a Philharmonic-sized orchestra, were working at NBC's new state-of-the-art color television studio in Brooklyn. NBC had erected two enormous soundstages on the site of a former silent film studio at Avenue M in Midwood. We were in Studio 1, and next to us in Studio 2, Mary Martin was doing *Peter Pan.* As we finished our first day of rehearsal, Helen said to me, "They've given me a big limo, and I go through New York on my way home to Nyack, may I drop you?" I said, "That would be very nice if you're sure that I'm not taking you out of your way." She assured me that it would not. When she dropped me off at my apartment, she said, "Since we both have to be there in the morning, why don't I pick you up?" From that day on, we drove together to and from the studio. She was great company and confided in me that she found working in movies very difficult because nothing was ever done in continuity, and she hated having to summon up emotions in such a haphazard way.

One morning on the way to Brooklyn she asked if I would like to meet Mary Martin. "I'd love to!" I said. Mary Martin was up there along with Ethel Merman as one of Broadway's musical comedy greats, and her biggest hit, *The Sound of Music,* was still to come. That afternoon, when we broke for lunch, Helen took my arm and we went through a pass door to a loading area between the two studios. It was deserted except for a huge amount of crates and scenery from both shows. We stopped, and Helen listened for a moment before calling out in a child's voice that would have reached the last row of the balcony, "Where are you? . . . Where is my little fella? . . . I know you're hiding here someplace . . . Come on out!"

A disembodied voice rang out from a pile of crates: "I'll come out if you promise me that you believe!"

"I believe, I believe!"

"You have to clap if you believe!"

Helen started to clap, and from nowhere out popped Peter Pan. Two great ladies of the American stage collapsed into each other's arms giggling like schoolgirls. I hope it didn't show, but for a brief moment I was completely unnerved.

That evening, after Helen dropped me off, the phone started to ring as I was coming up the stairs to my brownstone apartment. I took the stairs two at a time, threw my groceries down in the hall, fumbled for my keys, got in, ran for the phone, and shouted "Yes" into the receiver.

A voice at the other end asked quietly, "Is Farley Granger there?"

"This is Farley Granger, who's this?"

"This is Noël."

"Noël who?" I asked impatiently.

There was a brief pause, then a burst of laughter, and the voice said, "Noël Coward."

"Oh my God, I didn't dream . . . I mean I never thought . . ."

He laughed again. "Don't be silly, dear boy, how could you possibly have known. I called at the last minute to see if there was a chance that you might be free for dinner. They are doing a play of mine on television, and I'd like to talk to you about doing one of the parts."

I said that I'd be delighted. I had only met him that one time on *Rope,* but it was very good to see him again. After we ordered a drink and got through the usual small talk, he said with a smile, "You must know, Farley, that I find you terribly attractive. I would like very much to go to bed with you."

I took that in for a long moment, and then told him carefully that although I was very flattered, I was involved with someone, which wasn't true, but I wanted very much not to hurt his feelings.

He let out a theatrical sigh and said, "Thank God that's out of the way. Now we can relax and enjoy ourselves." We spent a great evening together. We also talked about his play, which I knew, and I told him that I wasn't really right for the part. He agreed with me. It was the part of the young man in *Present Laughter.* I have no memory of who played it on television, but Nathan Lane was nominated for a Tony in George C. Scott's 1983 Broadway production of this play, and he deserved it.

I had also been getting a lot of the stage experience I needed at this time in my life because whenever I was not involved in a major television project, I kept busy doing plays in a year-round stock company in New Jersey run by Robert Ludlum and his wife. Their company was close to New York, just across the Hudson River in New Jersey. This was years before he became one of the leading mystery/spy novelists of our time. I got to do a wide variety of roles for him, including the leads in *Mister Roberts, Sweet Bird of Youth,* and *Picnic,* with Sandra Church doing the part in the last that Janice Rule had done on Broadway.

Sandra and I became friends. She was a lovely redhead and a very talented young lady. Not too long after this I took her to the opening night of Betty Comden and Adolph Green's off-Broadway show, and at the after-party she met Jule Styne, who was instantly smitten. Their subsequent relationship led to her getting the title role in Jule's great musical *Gypsy.*

Sidney Lumet, another fine director I worked with in live television, went on to become one of our best film directors. He was then married to Gloria Vanderbilt, who had become a friend when we were in class together at the Neighborhood Playhouse. Gloria confided in me a few years later that Sidney had tried his best to get me for a film he did with Sophia Loren. Unfortunately, he didn't have the same kind of clout that Hitch had with the studio. When Warner Brothers insisted on using one of their contract players in the part, he had to go along with them. In the late 1960s, Sidney and I talked about my playing Nicky Arnstein in *Funny Girl* with Streisand, but when he opted out of that one, my chance of working with Barbra went with him.

I met an amazingly talented diversity of wonderful actors and directors in those days of live television. Along with doing stock and studying with Sandy Meisner and Stella Adler, it was the best kind of training that an actor could get. When my Broadway break arrived, I was ready for it.

Jane Austen Hits Broadway!

My agents called to say that I had gotten an offer to play Fitzwilliam Darcy in a musical adaptation of Jane Austen's *Pride and Predudice* on Broadway. The show was to be called *First Impressions,* the initial title of Miss Austen's book. The producers included the composer Jule Styne. Our set designer was Broadway's current golden boy, Peter Larkin, and the costumes were being done by Alvin Colt. Abe Burrows, one of the forces responsible for the classic American musical comedy *Guys and Dolls,* and who in the intervening eight years had had almost as many hits, had adapted the book and was directing. Gisele MacKenzie, a name I knew only as the star of *Your Hit Parade* on television, was playing Elizabeth. Hermione Gingold, the eccentric star of dozens of British music hall revues, was playing Mrs. Bennett, the desperate mother of five unmarried daughters, who was portrayed so brilliantly by Mary Boland in the MGM movie. That excellent film starred the lovely Greer Garson as Elizabeth, and gave Laurence Olivier his third big hit in this country as Fitzwilliam Darcy. Those were pretty big shoes to presume to fill, but the idea was too good to resist. The huge success of *My Fair Lady* had proven that good period material, well cast and well presented, definitely had a place on Broadway. One of my best friends from Hollywood, James Mitchell, a marvelous dancer who had done the dream ballet in the film of *Oklahoma!* and was the lead dancer in *Brigadoon* on Broadway, was playing the cad, Mr. Wickham. So I would have a friend in the company.

One evening a week or so before we were scheduled to begin rehearsal, I got a panicked call from Hermione. "Gisele has dropped out of the show because she is pregnant, and the producers replaced her with that @#%$*+^#$%* Polly Bergen!!! I will never work with that @#$% again. She drove everybody crazy in *Almanac*, even Harry [Belafonte] couldn't stand her, and you know how sweet he is."

Hermione and Polly Bergen had done a show together called *John Murray Anderson's Almanac.* I never found out precisely what had caused these two women to dislike each other so vehemently, but Polly's reputation was not a secret. The fact that Polly was currently married to Freddie Fields, one of the top agents in one of Hollywood's most important talent agencies, gave her a sense of power that she did not work too hard to disguise. Hermione felt that she had either strong-armed John Murray Anderson or worked her wiles on him to get several additional numbers. And that it had been done at the expense of others.

I just let her babble on, knowing that at this rate she would exhaust herself. Soon enough, she stopped, and I could just hear panting. Finally she said, "Well, I'm quitting! What are you going to do?"

"Hermione, haven't you signed a contract? I did."

There was a long pause and then a wail, "OOOH, daahling . . . What are we going to do?" And she hung up.

I didn't know much more about Polly Bergen than I did about Gisele MacKenzie. In *Who's Who* Polly is listed as a business executive first and an actress second, which is curious for a performer of her repute. Of course, I had seen her on numerous television variety shows and knew that she had gorgeous eyes and a nice throaty voice, but she came across as more 1950 American nightclub than 1813 English landed gentry. I felt that an ideal Elizabeth should have the pure exuberant soprano of a Barbara Cook or Julie Andrews, but with Jule Styne and Abe Burrows at the helm, who was I to question their choice? I was too preoccupied about what was going to come out of my mouth when I did open it for my first try at singing on stage. Thank the gods for Rex Harrison, who so brilliantly broke ground for the song/speak style of delivering a number, although he set a standard that was every bit as daunting for me as Olivier's performance in the film.

We rehearsed at the Variety Arts Studios, which were in Midtown in the theater district. In the beginning, the book or scene rehearsals were in one studio, the musical and singing rehearsals in another, and the dance rehearsals in yet another. At various times in the rehearsal period, the director would combine these elements until he felt it was time to bring the whole thing together. Polly and Hermione, as mother and daughter, had many scenes together. But from the first day of rehearsal until Polly left the show, neither one of them ever spoke one word to the other that wasn't scripted.

Hermione always swept grandly into rehearsal with her little dog, Mr. Poodle, in her arms and would throw her ratty mink on the floor in the corner for the little fella to sleep on. He would then spend what seemed like hours at a time happily humping her coat. We principals had all gotten used to it, but as Abe began to integrate the singers and dancers, it was a daily treat to watch the newcomers' reactions. I'll never forget the efforts of the dancers to focus on their movement without stumbling over each other or breaking up when they first tried to ignore Mr. Poodle in action.

Out of Town

Our first opening out of town at the Shubert Theater in New Haven was chaotic, to put it mildly. Abe and Jonathan Lucas, the choreographer, had obviously asked for the moon, scenically, and Peter Larkin had tried to give it to them. There was much too much scenery to fit into the theater. One of the sets, a ballroom for which Lucas had done elaborate choreography that included the dancers weaving in and out of numerous standing columns, was a painted backdrop. I overheard Abe say to Jonathan, "I guess Peter really screwed us on this one." I wanted to ask, "Did either of you ever talk to him?" Whenever the unwieldy beast that is a Broadway musical succeeds, it has to reflect good communication between the disparate elements that make up the whole, and the director, the boss, is the one responsible. Often that doesn't happen until disaster strikes.

New Haven was a disaster for us. There was one magnificent set that got thrown out immediately, which probably saved many a dancer from injury. Abe and Jonathan had set one dance number in a harborfront tavern, which, to give the illusion of being at water level, was entered from above. On this set, the dancers had a number in which they had to balance themselves with their arms and legs fully extended inside oversized barrels and roll head over heels in choreographed patterns. During the rehearsals at Variety Arts Studios in New York, one of the most daunting challenges was to try to concentrate on rehearsing the scenes with the sound of barrels crashing and injured dancers screaming coming from the studio above us. Many a brave young male dancer had been taken to the hospital with broken bones while rehearsing this mayhem. In New Haven, no tears were shed when this number was cut from the show.

Another moment in the show that did not work on opening night in New Haven was a scene in which Darcy and Elizabeth competed at archery. Peter had ingeniously rigged the targets to partially expel an arrow after we drew and released the strings of our bows. That visual with an accompanying sound effect was to give the impression of actual arrows hitting the target. With the luck of the draw, I was to shoot the first arrow. The arrow popped out of the target before my bow was fully drawn. There were sniggers from the audience, but I soldiered on. After several more increasingly out-of-sync tries, I had the audience rolling in the aisles. That number joined the barrels in the tavern, out of the show. It was too bad. With the correct allotment of rehearsal time, which was by now in very short supply, that bit could have worked and been a lovely moment of one-upmanship for Elizabeth.

Everyone looked gorgeous. Alvin Colt's costumes were superb. Outside of the theater, I saw less and less of my friend Jimmy Mitchell. His "big number" had, so far, failed to materialize, and he was retreating into a major funk.

Our show curtain, a lovely example of Peter's ingenuity, was a huge open lace fan on which was painted, in silhouette, two men running from the figure of a woman pulling five young women after her. As the overture, orchestrated by Hershey Kay in the style of the period, harpsichord and all, finished, the curtain opened, which resulted in the fan closing, and the play began. Behind the curtain were two twelve-foot-high boxwood hedges on tracks. When closed, they overlapped, leaving an exit between the overlap. They were used to create an "in-one" or limited downstage area with a painted drop behind, for intimate numbers that were done while the scenery upstage of it was being changed. The problem we had was that the crew had not yet had enough technical rehearsal time to master their operation. Sometimes the hedges came on too slowly or jerkily and jammed, and sometimes they came on with a speed that terrified anyone near them. The dancers, who had much of the in-one action, were the most vulnerable to being hit by a runaway hedge.

Our reviews in New Haven were mixed. The critics there were used to bumpy opening nights and were somewhat forgiving of technical mishaps. Even our negative reviews were along the line of "Promising" and/or "With a lot of work and a little luck . . ." The creative powers that be met after the show and worked and argued and tinkered all night long, every night. I think it was Neil Simon who said, "Hell is being out of town with a Broadway musical." By the end of our run in New Haven, Jimmy still had not gotten his promised number and Jonathan Lucas, our choreographer, was gone. Jimmy fared no better with three subsequent choreographers. The rest of us could barely keep up with the daily changes in the show.

Our next and last out-of-town booking was the Forrest Theatre in Philadelphia. The Forrest was a lovely theater with one minor problem: when it was built, they forgot dressing rooms. They acquired space for them in a building across the alley from the theater. In order to get there, we had to go down to the basement, cross under the alley, and take an elevator up to the dressing rooms. I imagine that wasn't too much to ask of actors in a settled touring play, but we were a musical in a state of . . . flux. Consequently, everyone claimed the basement as home base. The wardrobe, hair, and makeup departments that usually had it to themselves had to share the space with the cast, some fifty-odd people. Some of the more sensitive souls tried to rig sheets for privacy's sake, but most of us threw caution to the alley and just got on with it. The basement was bedlam, definitely not a place to prepare calmly for a new running order each evening. We also rehearsed every afternoon in the theater.

In midweek I arrived at the theater to find that Hiram (Chubby) Sherman, who was not only wonderful as Mr. Collins but the only one who had gotten unanimous praise from the New Haven critics, had been fired. Abe had replaced him with a friend of Hermione's who had been hanging around since our rehearsals in New York. He was a vulgar and campy performer, no more suited to the subtleties of Jane Austen than his patroness. Chubby's performance had been so good and he was so well loved that most of the company was outraged at this change. That evening I heard a new overture for the first time. In an effort to sound more contemporary, Abe had thrown out Hershey Kay's lovely period arrangements, and had tarted up our overture to no good effect. I love a good, jazzy overture. *Gypsy*'s thrills me every time I hear it, but Gypsy Rose Lee and Jane Austen . . . well, there's no comparison. That night, at the end of the new overture, the fan closed and a dancer got stuck onstage and was nearly crushed by our lovely hedges, at which point he turned upstage and started to scream while beating on the scenery. The stage manager dimmed the lights and helped the dancer offstage, and the men in white came to take him away.

The Philadelphia reviews were slightly better than those in New Haven. This encouraged a false sense of security in those who thought our show was getting better. I didn't and decided to get into it with Abe before the next rehearsal. Since we could not have our conversation in the basement, where we would have an all-too-attentive built-in audience, he and I went into the men's room downstairs at the back of the theater to talk. We were soon "talking" at the top of our lungs. I held nothing back, and when I stomped up into the theater, I was startled by a solid round of applause. A large contingent sitting at the back of the darkened theater waiting for a dance rehearsal to begin, had heard every word.

My only pals in the cast, since Jimmy had understandably become a black cloud, were Donald Madden, who played Mr. Bingley, Darcy's best friend, and Marti Stevens, who played his sister, Caroline. Marti was a Schenck, the behind-the-scenes royalty of the movie business. Her father, Nicholas, and his brother Joe were two of the richest men in America in the 1930s. They ran United Artists, Metro-Goldwyn-Mayer, and Loews Inc. Marti grew up in a family that dominated the movie business, but when she decided that she wanted to be an actress, her father disinherited her. She just wanted to be on the stage, as I did. Devastated but undeterred, she pursued her dream. Fortunately, her Uncle Joe supported her dream. Marti and I became friends soon after we met.

Marti knew about an elegant little hotel off Rittenhouse Square in Philadelphia. Since no one else in the company was staying there, we three moved there in order to distance ourselves from the constant creative chaos that was going on nightly at the theater and also to be able to drown our sorrows and commiserate about a good idea that was being painfully dragged in all the wrong directions.

On Broadway

Ready or not, it was time. We moved to New York to prepare for our Broadway opening at the Alvin Theatre. The theatre had approximately 1,300 seats, a perfect size for a musical. It took a couple of days to load the production in, set up the scenery, and get everything in working order. Of course, I went down there early on Monday morning to check the place out. Several days later, the company received its official first call. More than getting the show in, up, and working had happened since Monday morning.

My geographical memory of the dressing room layout may be a bit hazy, but what had been done to them still shines brightly in my mind's eye. Polly Bergen was then married to Freddie Fields, an agent I had known in Hollywood, who had always called me "Kirk Baby." Freddie, also a successful producer, was with MCA, one of the most powerful agencies in show business. Possibly that gave Polly a little extra clout with our producers. In any case, she had taken over what had always been the chorus dressing room downstage left. The room was meant to accommodate eighteen or more people. It had been converted to a suite for one, carpeted and decorated all in white, with gorgeous period antique furniture that included a white-tiled Swedish stove. Everything had an MCA sticker on it. A red carpet ran from the stage door, past Hermione's small dressing room on stage right, all the way across the back of the stage up to Polly's dressing room door on stage left.

The first number that Polly and I did together in the show, "A Perfect Evening," took place at the Assembly Dance, where my character and Mr. Bingley, the other desirably wealthy newcomer, played by Donald Madden, are introduced to Mrs. Bennet and her five daughters. Elizabeth and Darcy were dancing at the moment when we began to sing; we were downstage center, arm in arm, facing the audience. On musical cues we could link arms to circle around to come to a stop facing in opposite directions. When Polly sang out to the audience confiding how she really felt about Darcy, I faced upstage, and then we reversed positions for me to sing privately to the audience. Polly had the first line in the song, and on opening night, she quite clearly and loudly sang "A Poifect Evening." When we reversed for me to sing my line to the audience, she hissed in my ear, "Did you hear what I said!?" I not only heard her, the conductor was looking up in shock and there were a couple of titters from the audience. I almost choked on my reply, "Ah, yes."

Our reviews, two favorable, one mixed, three unfavorable, and one pan, did not lead to long lines at the box office. I came off well, but the show was judged to be a failed attempt to repeat the success of *My Fair Lady*. Aside from unanimous criticism of a weak score, it was Hermione who received the hardest knocks. Richard Watts Jr. in the *New York Post*, then a serious and well-respected newspaper, wrote: "In a recent interview, Hermione Gingold said she was no admirer of Jane Austen, and it saddens me to report that she proved it last night." That sentence was merely a jumping-off point for his criticism.

For some reason, Abe Burrows took to hanging out in my dressing room. I remember him sitting there shaking his head and saying, "I don't know what happened . . . I thought she [Hermione] was the critics' darling."

Almost immediately after we opened, Polly began to complain about vocal problems. From that moment on, we hardly ever performed the same show twice running. We all had to check the call board before each performance to see which of Polly's numbers was being cut for that show.

A week later, at a matinee performance, I noticed the ensemble was paying less attention to the conductor during their numbers than usual. For the most part, they all seemed to be focused on someone in the theater. After one of our exits, I grabbed a dancer and said, "Who the hell is out there?"

She answered breathlessly, "Don't you know? Marlene Dietrich is in the audience."

I'd never met Miss Dietrich, but knew that she and Marti Stevens were friends, so it made sense that she would come to see our show. I sneaked a quick peek the next time I was onstage, but I couldn't spot her, so I forgot all about it.

Back in my dressing room after the show, I had gotten out of my costume and was cleaning off my makeup when my dresser burst into the room hyperventilating. I turned to ask him what was wrong as he blurted out, "Miss Marlene Dietrich is outside and she wants to see you." I finished cleaning up and told him to show her in.

As I stood up, in she came, looking very glamorous. I held out my hand, but she walked into my arms and gave me a big warm hug. Then she held me back at arm's length, looked deep into my eyes, and said, "Oh, Fahley, Fahley, where did you get those twousers? Your twousers are wonderful! I must know where to get them!"

She walked over to where they were hanging on a costume rack and proceeded to caress them. At one point she held them to her cheek. I explained that they had been designed by Alvin Colt and made by Madame Karinska, the world-famous costumer. She thanked me and backed out of the room still looking longingly at the twousers. She never mentioned a word about my performance or the show.

I was telling Marti about it sometime later when the lightbulb went on. Miss Dietrich was getting ready to make her first appearance in Las Vegas, and at one point in the show she appeared in top hat, tails, and . . . you guessed it.

That evening a notice on the board said that Polly was out of the show . . . permanently. I ran up the two flights of stairs to Ellen Hanley's dressing room. Ellen had been playing the part of Charlotte Lucas and was Polly's understudy. Even though we had not had a chance to rehearse, I knew that she was going to be a lovely Elizabeth. I wanted as much as possible, under the circumstances, to put her mind at ease and let her know how happy I was about the prospect of working with her. The rest of the company felt the same way and were incredibly supportive. That evening everything clicked, and the audience response was terrific. The show just got better for the rest of our run. We closed at the end of two and a half months.

If at First You Don't Succeed . . .

I was convinced I'd never work again, but not too many months later I received a call from a director named Warren Enters. Warren was directing a new play by Joe Masteroff called *The Warm Peninsula.* It was a comedy/drama about the comings and goings and entanglements of four young vacationers all staying at the same boardinghouse in Miami Beach.

The play was being produced for Julie Harris by her husband, Manning

Gurian. It had been touring the provinces for seven months, undergoing rewrites and tune-ups until he decided it was in good enough shape to bring to New York. When it closed out of town, Manning decided that he wanted an all-star cast. He fired the three leads with the obvious exception of Julie, and I was brought in along with June Havoc and Larry Hagman. He also brought in Ruth White, one of Broadway's most beloved character actresses, to take over the part of the landlady.

I was very happy about the prospect of working with Julie again. I had not seen her since *The Heiress*. In some ways, working in the theater is like playing a one-on-one sport: the better your opponent, the better you perform. Working with Julie in television had been both a challenge and a thrill. I couldn't wait to begin the rehearsal process with her in a play. She pulled me aside after our first few days of rehearsal and said, "You've obviously been working hard, Farley. I'm very impressed by how much you've grown."

That was a big compliment coming from Julie, who took her acting very seriously and is one of the most nominated and award-winning actresses of our time.

June Havoc was a multitalented artist, a good actress, a good writer, and, along with her sister, Gypsy Rose Lee, a survivor of a life that began in vaudeville under the iron fist of the quintessential stage mother, portrayed by Ethel Merman in *Gypsy*. Larry was also a theater brat. His mom, Mary Martin, who created leading roles in *Lute Song, One Touch of Venus, South Pacific, Peter Pan,* and *The Sound of Music,* was well on her way to becoming a musical theater legend. Larry played June's love interest in our play, and Julie and I were the other lovers. One evening Larry confided that June was driving him crazy in one of their scenes by being a little too hands-on. She was fussing with him, arranging his tie, fixing his hair, and brushing imaginary lint off his suit. He wanted to stop it without saying anything that might hurt her feelings. I had a wonderful, wise, and funny dresser who came up with the perfect solution when I mentioned this to him. Just before the scene, he put a spool of white thread in the breast pocket of Larry's jacket and just barely pulled the end of it through his lapel buttonhole. Larry worried that she might miss it, but we reassured him. June went for it like a trout for the right fly. In their scene, she gave it a little pull and then a bigger one. The more she pulled, the more it kept coming. Finally she cracked up and ran offstage. She never fussed with him again for the rest of our run.

We were playing at the original Helen Hayes Theatre, which became the center of controversy in 1982 when hundreds of New Yorkers, led by prominent members of the acting community, fought in vain to save it from the real estate developer's wrecking ball. While we were there, Mary Martin, opened across Forty-sixth Street at the Lunt-Fontanne Theatre in *The Sound of Music.* When their show loaded into the theater, Larry took me over to say hello to his mom.

She was seated on her dressing room floor surrounded by a huge pile of black lace-up boots from which she had to choose the correct ones for the show. She held her arms out to Larry, who leaned over for a hug and kiss, and welcomed me before he could make any introductions. Miss Martin remembered meeting me with Helen Hayes when she was playing *Peter Pan* for NBC in Brooklyn. She apologized to us for not having seen our show, but we all knew how hectic it was opening a Broadway musical. Larry and his mother seemed to have a nice easygoing relationship, so I don't want to imply that having his mom, one of the biggest stars of the musical theater, playing across the street made Larry nervous, but his intake of one preshow martini increased to an icy shaker-full by the time she opened. I still wish I had taken the opportunity of our proximity to get to know her better. Another image of *The Sound of Music* that I will always carry with me is walking past the Lunt-Fontanne's stage door and seeing nuns from the chorus hanging around with their skirts hiked up, smoking cigarettes and flirting with the guys passing by.

We opened on October 20, 1959, to fair reviews. The critics were kind to the four young lovers, unkind to the play, and unanimously in love with Ruth White, who deserved every rave. After two and a half months, we closed on New Year's Day. This was my second Broadway show and they both had almost identical two-and-a-half-month runs. I was developing a case of short-run paranoia.

Rita & Bertolt

With the decline of the anticommunist fever of the early 1950s, Buddy and Ethyl had decided to come home from Europe. Buddy was still in Spain working on a film, and Ethyl was in New York looking for an apartment for them. We had already seen each other several times when she called me one afternoon. Rita Hayworth was in town, knew no one, and Ethyl thought it would be nice if we took her out that evening for dinner and maybe the theater. I had only met Miss Hayworth one time briefly at Gene Kelly's after they had made *Cover Girl* together. She had seemed to be rather shy and very sweet.

Her screen persona, which had been set forever by *Gilda* and *Down to Earth,* was that of a screen siren who was improbably good beneath her veneer of dangerously seductive beauty. In *Gilda,* she immortalized the black satin strapless dress forever when she sang "Put the Blame on Mame" to torture her confused lover, Glenn Ford. In *Down to Earth,* she played the goddess Terpsichore, who danced her way into a Broadway musical. She was quickly baptized "America's

Goddess of Love" by the press. The men aboard the *Enola Gay,* the plane that dropped the atom bomb on Hiroshima to hasten the end of World War II, are said to have taped Rita's famous *Life* magazine wartime pinup to the bomb.

Ethyl got three tickets to an off-Broadway production of Bertolt Brecht's *The Good Soldier Schweik.* It was a great choice for Ethyl, who had worked in Germany and knew all about Brecht and his unusual technique of using alienating effects to encourage audiences to think rather than become emotionally involved. I was not too sure it was a great choice for either Rita or me. It was about a soldier who obeyed orders so scrupulously that he messed up everything with which he was involved.

I arrived at Rita's hotel in time to pick her up to meet Ethyl at Sardi's for a drink before the theater. She came out of the elevator looking gorgeous in a dark green satin dress with a white mink stole. I don't think Rita had any awareness of the effect she had on people. As she crossed the lobby to meet me, everyone stopped dead in their tracks to follow her with their eyes. She gave me a warm and friendly hug, and I was a goner.

We met Ethyl in the small downstairs bar at Sardi's and left for the theater after a couple of quick drinks. Rita had the same effect on the customers and also on the actors that she had everywhere: she took focus.

I remember nothing about the play, how good it was, whether or not I got it, nothing at all. Rita, on the other hand, had a swell time and at the curtain calls cheered the cast with lusty *olé*'s.

From there, we went off to the St. Regis for supper and lots of Champagne. After not too long, Ethyl begged off because she was meeting apartment brokers early in the morning. Rita wanted to dance, and that we did for what seemed like hours. At first I felt like a klutz, but she was such a feather, I soon relaxed, and started feeling like a pro. Rita was indefatigable. After an hour or so, the wine, which was going to her head, was going to my feet. I was getting tired, and she was tipsy. I paid the check and escorted her back to her hotel, where it took a few minutes for me to assure a suspicious room clerk that I was just seeing Miss Hayworth to her room. In the elevator she began to fold. I got her into her bedroom and on the bed. She did not want me to go. I slipped off her shoes and her dress and got her under the covers. She was like a lost little girl who was afraid to be left alone. I sat with her, holding her in my arms, until she went to sleep.

Ten years later, in Hollywood, Ethyl called to ask if I would mind picking Rita up for a dinner party she and Buddy were having. I had not seen her in the intervening years, and I said I would be delighted. I called for her at her new house behind the Beverly Hills Hotel. She was slightly heavier, but in her late forties she was still very beautiful. The house had an unlived-in air about it. What little furniture there was seemed to have been placed at random with no thought as to how it functioned. Even though Rita had been there for a while, there were a number of unpacked boxes and unhung pictures scattered about. She took me out by the pool so that she could point out Glenn Ford's house in the near distance. Ford had been her leading man in *Gilda,* the film that made her a superstar in 1946. He also co-starred with her in *The Loves of Carmen* in 1948, and in *Affair in Trinidad* in 1952 after her four-year marriage to Aly Khan broke up.

In the course of that evening, Rita's moods shifted unpredictably and swiftly from sweet to angry to frightened. At the time, we all thought that her behavior reflected the toll taken by disappointments in her personal life, as well as those exacted by her life as a contract player for one of the crassest of the old-time moguls, Harry Cohn. It was years before the world became aware that Rita was beginning to suffer the cruel ravages of Alzheimer's disease.

R & H & I

Not too much time passed before I got another call about a musical from my agent. A director named John Fearnley wanted to meet with me to discuss an upcoming project. We met in Charley's, a long-gone unpretentious bar in the theater district, and hit it off at once. He wanted me to play the king in a revival of *The King and I* that was opening the spring season at City Center. I was flattered, but not sure that I was old enough, or right enough, or anything enough for this part. He assured me that I was exactly who he wanted for the part. Barbara Cook was playing Anna, and he saw the king and Anna as a young couple whose sexual chemistry the audience could buy into. That sold me. I'd seen Barbara in *Plain and Fancy* and *Candide.* I thought she was delicious, a charming actress and the best soprano voice in the American musical theater. Gertrude Lawrence, who played Anna in the original production, had been very ill when she did it on Broadway and had neither the strength nor the voice to do the lovely songs justice.

It turned out to be one of the happiest productions in my life. Barbara was trying to make her failing marriage to David LeGrand work for the sake of their young son, Adam, so we never took our relationship to the next level, but oh, did we love each other, as well as working together and working with John and the superb cast. Barbara and I also fell in love with the twelve adorable kids who played the king's children. I've never had a more joyous experience on the stage.

At our final dress rehearsal John came back to tell us that Rodgers and Hammerstein would be in the house. It was one of those rehearsals when, magically, since we were on such a tight schedule, everything clicked and the invited audience was on its feet for the curtain calls.

When the knock came on the dressing room door. I jumped up to say "Come in," and John entered with R & H. Hammerstein came over to me, swept me up in a great bear hug, and said, "Thank you. You were wonderful." As he released me, Rodgers stepped in, pointed a finger and said, "*Babes in Arms!*" I was totally thrown for a moment, then I remembered that night I met them in Paris. Somehow their reactions backstage summed up the difference between the two men for me. Hammerstein was warm, loving, and totally open. Rodgers was smart, always on his game, and a bit guarded.

On opening night, I had a drink with Hal Prince and Mary Rodgers, Richard Rodgers's daughter, after the show. Mary went on about how much more her father loved our production than the original. I think it must have been because he had never heard his songs sung as beautifully as Barbara did them. I was on cloud nine. I picked up Barbara and we went off to a party that two old friends, Tom Morrow and A. T. Hannett, threw for me in their spectacular old wooden Federal house on Ninety-second Street. The reviews came out, and they were excellent. The party was full of the contagious high spirits that a hit show or a major sports event win can engender. It went on till dawn.

Each night the week after we opened, well-known Broadway producers started showing up at City Center. We all knew what that meant: we might be transferred to Broadway. The only dark cloud threatening what might be was an impasse between Actors' Equity Association and the League of Broadway Producers over contributions to an actors' pension and welfare fund. We were all confident, despite producer David Merrick's "war-like posturing," that the problem would be resolved. We were held over for two additional weeks, and it looked as if Rodgers and Hammerstein themselves were going to move us to a Broadway theater. Then, contrary to all expectations, the actors' strike struck. The lockout went on for several weeks before it was settled by Mayor Wagner. By then the momentum to move us to Broadway was gone. We discovered that Oscar Hammerstein was seriously ill. There is no way I can describe how devastated Barbara and I were by how quickly our high hopes were crushed. We had been ready to move to a Broadway house and open in a week.

Shortly after the lockout ended, we received an offer to do *The King and I* for a month, and for very good money, at the Carter Barron Amphitheater in Washington, D.C. John Fearnley kept as many of the City Center cast as possible, actually most of it, and, hoping to recapture some of the joy we had felt while performing in New York, Barbara and I agreed to do it.

The Carter Barron is a 3,700-seat amphitheater in a beautiful part of Rock Creek Park in D.C. On clear, moonlit, starry nights it could be magical, despite its overadequate size. We were rained on or out for almost the entire run. After a week straight of hot, steamy wet weather, there was nothing left to do but laugh and try to slosh through it when possible. The hardest hit—it seems they always are—were the poor dancers. If it was too wet, we cut the ballet *The Small House of Uncle Thomas.* It was just too dangerous for the dancers to try to maneuver on that vast stage. As miserable as the performance situation was, Barbara and I pulled out of our respective New York funks and managed to have a good time together.

We were invited for tea to Margaret Landon's house. Miss Landon wrote the book *Anna and the King of Siam,* on which a movie of the same name starring Rex Harrison, Irene Dunne, and Linda Darnell was based in 1946. She told us fascinating stories of being in Siam before World War II. While there, she heard rumors about an Anna Leonowens, an English governess at the Siamese court in the early nineteenth century, but every time she asked about her, she ran into a stone wall of silence. No one would speak about her. It was as if the woman had never existed.

When World War II broke out, she and her husband were sent back home to Washington, D.C. One afternoon, while browsing through a secondhand bookshop in Georgetown, she came across a book, *The English Governess at the Siamese Court,* by Anna Leonowens. She told us that she felt that if she picked up that book, her life would change forever. She did. It did.

As soon as I got back to New York, I wrote Rodgers and Hammerstein a short note explaining how much doing their show meant to me and how much I respected them. I had it hand-delivered to Mr. Rodgers. The next day, he called to say he had gotten the note and how much he appreciated it. He also said that he was going to read it to Oscar that evening. I was so pleased by his reaction that the implication of what he said didn't really register. That evening, after dinner with some friends, I came home, turned on the radio, and heard that Oscar Hammerstein had died. Even though it did not come as a complete surprise, a loss of that magnitude takes time to sink in. All I could think of was how much I hoped that Rodgers had been able to read my note to him.

On the Road

Actors did revivals at City Center for love, and for the opportunity to do parts that might not usually be offered to them. The pay was Actors' Equity minimum, which just about covered cab fares and food. Aside from the Carter Barron fiasco, which was short-lived, I had not been making a lot of money. Foolishly, since I was too naïve to understand what a bus-and-truck tour entailed, I allowed myself to be talked into going on one for the money.

Advise and Consent was the play. It was to star Chester Morris, a well-respected older actor, and me, and was being produced by a boyish entrepreneur named Martin Tahse who was a protégé of Maurice Evans. I felt that it might not be smart to leave town for eight months so soon after the success of *The King and I,* but I allowed myself to be talked into it by my agent, who not only got me a handsome salary but a percentage of the take as well. Financially it was a very good deal. It took almost no time at all for me to realize what a mistake it was.

The cast was a group of older, not-well-paid character actors playing senators and not doing it well. For the first couple of months, I was too depressed to leave my hotel room except to perform. I got a lot of worthwhile reading done. The original Broadway producers of the play were Fryer and Carr. Word must have gotten back to them about how unhappy I was, because Bobby Fryer came to see me in Cincinnati. He brought with him an extremely good-looking young man and suggested I might have a better time if I kept him, even though he behaved erratically every once in a while. I couldn't speak. I just got up, held the door to my dressing room open, and gestured at them to get out. I slammed it so hard, it splintered the door frame.

When I was in Detroit with this tour, I saw that Bette Davis was in town in a pre-Broadway tryout of Tennessee Williams's *The Night of the Iguana.* I stopped by her theater to say hello. As I expected, they were rehearsing, and she was there. She seemed delighted to see me and suggested that we get together for dinner after our respective shows. There was a wonderful roadhouse outside the city limits that she and Gary Merrill had discovered. Our curtain came down first, so I walked over to her theater to pick her up. She had a stretch limo waiting, and we took off into the night. Her co-star in the show was an English actress, Margaret Leighton, who, although a critic's darling, had a reputation as cold and technical with her fellow players. Bette mixed us both a drink, sat back in her seat, a drink in one hand and a cigarette in the other, and lit into Maggie: "She's impossible!" *(puff)* "I can't take it!" *(puff . . . puff)* "She's nothing but a *(puff)* technician!" *(puff . . . puff)*

All of this was delivered in her own inimitable technical fashion. Although I fought the impulse with every fiber of my being, I finally started to laugh, and for a moment I thought I was in serious trouble. She just stared at me with those enormous eyes, and then she started to laugh along with me.

Several months later, after we had opened in San Diego, Martin Tahse, our boyish, deceptively innocent-looking producer, came to pay us a visit. He asked me to have breakfast with him the next morning. First, he went on at length about how good he thought I was in the show. Then he talked about how important it was to keep the show running and how difficult it was with the payroll for such a large company. Then he waxed tragic about the fate of so many older actors if we had to close. Then he asked me if I would give up my percentage in order for him to be able to keep us going.

Now, even though math had never been my strong point, I knew full houses from empty houses, and I had been periodically checking the weekly take as we went along. We had been doing consistently good business all along, a fact that could be attributed to my movie name. I refused to take a cut and told him that if he wanted to replace me in the part I would be very happy to let him off the hook, but he would have to continue to pay me until the show closed. His true colors showed when he hit the roof. He said that he would go back to New York and spread the word to all of Broadway about how I refused to help the show, and I would never work again. I said, "Feel free," threw a couple of bucks down on the table, "for my coffee," and walked out.

Later, I asked Chester Morris if Tahse had asked him to cut his salary. He looked at me as if I'd lost a few marbles and said, "Of course not. Why on earth would I do that?" That confirmed my instinct that Tahse had hoped I would not know any better. We went on to a very successful engagement in San Francisco and another one in Los Angeles, and at last we closed.

Home Again

I returned to New York and fired my agents. I signed with Milton Goldman, who handled a number of English actors and had a reputation for doing first-rate things. I settled down and started enjoying life in New York again. I vividly remember the first big theater party I attended back in the city. It was at Ethel Merman's spacious East Side apartment during the run of *Gypsy*. It was a Monday evening, when all the Broadway theaters were dark, so just about everyone in the theater would be there to pay tribute to Merman. Marti Stevens knew her well and had asked me to accompany her. In the cab on the way we were discussing what a perfect show *Gypsy* was and what a high point it was in Merman's great career. She said that Ethel was having a great time doing it, with one exception; for some reason she couldn't stand Sandra Church, who was playing Gypsy. "Uh-oh," I said. "I wonder if she knows that I was the one who introduced her to Jule, which indirectly got her the part." Marti gave me a deadpan look and then laughed as she said, "For your sake, I hope not." We got there and the place was jammed. The entrance to her sunken living room was several steps up. As we came in, it was as if we were being presented. I spotted Ethel surrounded by a crowd of celebrities across the room just as she spotted us and waved. "Get over here, Farl," she sang out in that voice that could bounce off the back wall of Broadway's largest theater, "I wanna talk to you about that cunt!" We became great pals that evening. She was every bit as much larger than life in real life as she was on the stage.

I went to all the theater, opera, and ballet that I could cram in. I went to Stella Adler's master class and began to feel good about myself again. There I met an actor named Steve Hill. Steve will now most likely be remembered as the original D.A. on the television series *Law & Order,* but those of us who had the good fortune to see him onstage will always remember him as an actor of immense depth and range. Steve was directing his own adaptation of a Dostoyevsky short story at the Bucks County Playhouse, a prestigious summer theater with enough ties to Manhattan to be thought of almost as we think of off-Broadway today. Steve asked me to be in his play, and I gladly accepted his offer.

Unfortunately, the play didn't work. It was long, and the more Steve worked on it, the longer it got. Somewhere near the end of the third act, I had a scene in which I fought with my mother's lover, knocking him through the living room window. I then sank to the floor, head in hands, and cried out, "Oh, my God! What have I done. . . . What have I done?" One unforgettable evening, a deep voice boomed out from the back of the house: "You've kept us up till eleven-thirty . . . That's what you've done!"

NRT

Milton called me to say that two young producers, Michael Dewell and Frances Ann Dougherty, were starting a national repertory theater and wanted me to be a member of the company along with Eva Le Gallienne, Denholm Elliott, and possibly Julie Harris. The plays to be performed were Chekhov's *The Seagull,* Arthur Miller's *The Crucible,* and a third play yet to be chosen. I was intrigued, but when Milton told me that it would mean touring for nine months before coming to Broadway, I said, "No way!" Milton asked me to at least meet with the producers, and I finally agreed.

I went to meet them at Frances Ann's townhouse on Beekman Place. Michael Dewell was a graduate of Yale's renowned drama school. He was passionate, articulate, and obviously the driving force behind the company. Frances Ann Cannon Dougherty was a smart Southern beauty who had been engaged briefly to Jack Kennedy in the late 1930s. Her father, James W. Cannon, had nixed the marriage because no daughter of his, pampered and brought up at White Oaks in Charlotte, North Carolina, was going to marry a Yankee Catholic whose father was a bootlegger. Of course, it didn't occur to him that as a nouveau rich textile baron who founded and owned Cannon Mills, he and young Jack's father probably had a lot in common. She eventually married the writer John Hersey, but always had wonderful memories of her time with Jack, and they had remained friends. She had recently divorced Hersey, and as a member of the board of Theatre Inc., which was the governing body of the Phoenix Theatre, set out to satisfy her creative needs in the world of theater. Enter Michael Dewell, who had the passion, the ego, and a solid scholastic background in theater. A partnership was born. He had push and a driving need to get ahead, and she had ties to the social, literary, and political worlds that would prove invaluable for the creation of a national theater.

In 1959, Michael and Frances Ann became partners and formed the National Phoenix Theatre to send out touring companies of the Phoenix Theatre's more successful productions. Everyone thought they were crazy that first season to send to the provinces a company performing Friedrich Schiller's *Mary Stuart,* directed by Tyrone Guthrie and starring Eva Le Gallienne as Elizabeth I and Signe Hasso as Mary Stuart. It was conventional wisdom in the theater community that one did not tour the classics. It was hard enough to get an audience for them in New York. Everyone was proven wrong. The tour played to packed houses in San Francisco, Los Angeles, St. Louis, Chicago, Boston, Philadelphia, and Washington, D.C., plus a handful of smaller cities sprinkled in as connective stops. It opened in Los Angeles, where the *Los Angeles Times* critic said, "The fires that burned on the stage of the Biltmore Theatre last night were brighter than those of the brush fires in the canyons that threaten to engulf the city." From there, it went on to get unanimous rave reviews all across the country. Now, two years later, they formed a new company, the National Repertory Theatre, which was no longer affiliated with the Phoenix. They were in the process of assembling an acting company to tour with three plays in rotating repertory. Michael said that a friend of mine, Julie Harris, was seriously considering joining them.

I admired their ambitious plans to the extent that I said I would be both flattered and pleased to be a part of their company at some point, but I was still convinced that it was too soon for me to be away from New York for another Broadway season. They begged me not to rule anything out until I had met and talked with Miss Le Gallienne.

I had seen Le Gallienne on the stage at the Phoenix Theatre in their production of Schiller's *Mary Stuart* in 1958. It was a lean new adaptation of the 1801 play, and it had been directed by one of the theater's greatest men of the twentieth century, Tyrone Guthrie. Miss Le Gallienne had played Elizabeth I to Irene Worth's Mary of Scotland. The production was jet-fueled. Once started, it roared to its conclusion without giving the audience time to relax and breathe.

Irene Worth was a beautiful and moving Mary Queen of Scots, and Eva Le Gallienne gave the most riveting and complex performance I've ever seen on a stage.

I agreed to go up to Wilton, Connecticut, where Frances Ann lived, to meet her, but first I called Julie Harris. Julie invited me over for drinks. I knew she had apprenticed with Le Gallienne, and I also knew that, like stage stars of earlier generations, Julie felt strongly about the importance of touring. I wanted to know if she was seriously considering joining NRT.

She was. She adored Le G, as she called her, and thought that acting with her in a repertory of good plays, as well as being directed by her, would be the best of all possible worlds. That was why she had thought it over for so long, but she had decided she had to stay in New York just then. She and Manning Gurian had been going through some difficult times in their marriage, and she felt that it was very important, particularly for their young son, Peter, that she not leave New York. She understood my hesitation to leave New York for two seasons in a row, but felt that the opportunity to work with one of the major talents in the American theater was one I had to consider very seriously.

Just then, Manning came home. We all had a drink and a few laughs about the trials and tribulations of *The Warm Peninsula.* Manning then brought up June Havoc and told Julie that June was working on a play based on her memoirs, *Early Havoc.* She was interested in Julie playing the lead. We all knew that June had not been happy with the way she was portrayed by her sister, Gypsy Rose Lee, in the musical smash *Gypsy*. It sounded as if she was preparing to set the record straight. Julie asked if June had sent him anything to read. He said she hadn't, but she would if the idea appealed to Julie. She had read and liked the book and said she would love to see June's dramatization. She did the play on Broadway the following year and it was a very interesting flop.

When I left, Julie walked me to the door, where we stopped as she gave me a warm hug and whispered in the Irish lilt that crept in when she was being intensely serious, "Artists should never marry, Farley."

Le G

Eva Le Gallienne was born in England in 1899. Her father, Richard, was a renowned poet, and her mother, Julie Norregard, was a well-known Danish journalist and feminist. After three years, her parents divorced, and Eva spent half her time in London with her handsome, man-about-town father, and the other half in Paris with her pioneering feminist mother. Le G, as her friends called her, was fluent in Danish, Norwegian, French, and English. She and her mother sailed for America in 1915, where Eva pursued her ambitions as an actress. In 1921, she became an overnight star on Broadway playing Julie to Joseph Schildkraut's Liliom in the Hungarian playwright Ferenc Molnar's play of the same name. Many years later, in one of the rare instances when an adaptation outshone the original, Rodgers and Hammerstein based *Carousel* on *Liliom.*

She once told me that Pepe—her pet name for Schildkraut, whom she truly loved—could be very naughty and was always trying to break her up onstage. During a scene in *Liliom* where she had a heartbreaking monologue over Liliom's dead body, he kept tickling her breast with his upstage hand. She begged him to stop. When he didn't, she issued one last warning and threatened to make him pay if he did it again. He didn't. So the next time he "tickled her tittie," she lifted his hand to her lips as if to kiss it and bit through to the bone. She roared with laughter as she said, "He never tried *that* again."

Molnar was so enchanted by the young actress playing Julie in *Liliom* that he wrote his next play, *The Swan,* for her. In 1923 she was the toast of Broadway. Rather than following the path that most young actors would have taken to capitalize on her success, she turned her back on Broadway and founded her own theater company, the Civic Repertory Theatre, at 14th Street and Sixth Avenue, in 1926. There she gathered a group of dedicated actors and proceeded to introduce the classics and new plays in rotating repertory at prices that the general public could afford. The top-price ticket at the Civic Rep was one dollar. The productions were fully realized and first-class. The actors included some of the top names in the theater. She introduced the great European playwrights Ibsen and Goldoni to America. She was not the first one to present Chekhov in this country, but she was the first to popularize him. She also did most of her own translations of these plays, specializing in those of Ibsen and Chekhov.

Although she was an outspoken lesbian, she had tempestuous affairs with the actors Joseph Schildkraut and Basil Rathbone and managed to remain close to them throughout her life. In 1927 she had an affair with the married actress Josephine Hutchinson. When Hutchinson's husband sued for divorce, he named Le Gallienne as co-respondent, which was quite the public scandal, one she faced with her usual fearlessness.

During the Great Depression, President Roosevelt offered her the directorship of the Theatre Division of the WPA. She turned him down and struggled to keep the Civic Rep afloat. Her theatre closed in 1932, a victim of the Depression. Shortly after that, a gas furnace in her Connecticut home blew up in her face. Her hands, which she had instinctively held up in front of her face, were seriously disfigured, and her facial burns were bad. Years of painful plastic surgery followed.

In 1946, she and the English director Margaret Webster founded the American Repertory Theatre in an effort to revive Miss Le Gallienne's original idea. It lasted only two years. Now, in 1962, Michael and Frances Ann were trying it again with Le Gallienne as their figurative leader.

The producers of NRT drove me up to Miss Le Gallienne's home in Weston, Connecticut, the next afternoon. It did not take long for me to fall under her spell. The stories were true. Her passion for the theater and particularly for repertory theater was contagious. She convinced me that an actor had not lived until he had done repertory, where the creative juices stirred by one play spilled over to enrich the work in the others. She infused me with her enthusiasm for the benefits to an actor of being able to do great works rather than having to be limited to potentially successful commercial works. We also talked about some ideas for the third play. I remembered a comedy by Jean Anouilh that I saw in London with Claire Bloom called *Ring Round the Moon.* I suggested it as a play that might bring a nice balance to the other two more serious plays. She loved the idea, and said that Claire Bloom might be an ideal leading lady for the company. I realized that I had just committed myself to another tour.

Four Parts in Three Plays in Twelve Cities

Claire Bloom was interested but had conflicting film dates. The producers were also talking to Anne Meacham, who had impressed the Broadway critics that season in *A Passage to India.* Anne and an ingenue fresh out of Carnegie Tech, Kelly Jean Peters, were the last two pieces to fall into place. We began rehearsal in September in New York on *The Crucible,* directed by Jack Sydow, and *The Seagull,* directed by Miss Le Gallienne. After three weeks, the entire company moved to the University of North Carolina at Greensboro, where we continued rehearsing for three more weeks, adding *Ring Round the Moon,* also directed by Jack, to the other two plays.

Including a week of performances, we were there for four weeks as part of a program for drama students who observed the entire process. We lectured to classes and rehearsed each day. The schedule was exhausting. The sheer bulk of the lines that had to be memorized sometimes seemed overwhelming. In the Anouilh, I was playing two parts, the twins Hugo and Frederick, along with Konstantine in the Chekhov and John Proctor in the Miller play. In the same order of plays, Denholm was playing Patrice, Trigoran, and Reverend Hale; and Anne was playing Lady India, Nina, and Goody Proctor. Miss Le Gallienne urged us to drop thinking about one play when we moved to another. She always said the first would cook in our subconscious like a pot of soup on the back of the stove. Sometimes I could not avoid giving in to the jumble in my head. When that happened, I started to get agonizing cluster headaches.

The company and the producers stayed in a hotel in downtown Greensboro. The directors, the technicians, the designers, and the production staff all stayed at a motel adjacent to the campus in order to be closer to the theater. Their rooms were enormous, with multiple beds, probably to accommodate visiting families of students. They also had kitchens. Bob Calhoun, the production supervisor, and I had become friends in the course of rehearsal in New York. He was very good at what he did. We shared a love of the same kind of movies, music, dance, and theater, as well as tennis, sailing, and being beach bums. When the headaches hit, he suggested that I use his room nearby to lie down, in the dark, and relax till they passed. It was easier than getting a car downtown to the hotel and seemed to help the bouts pass more quickly. We were aware of a growing mutual attraction. Not only did we not act on it, but we didn't even speak about it. I guess we were trying to keep things simple, but like all the best-laid plans . . .

At the end of the three weeks, we began performing the first two plays to paying audiences. At the end of the third week, we added the Anouilh. By the time we had all three plays on their feet, the headaches were slowly replaced by a feeling of overwhelming elation. By no means did everyone feel that we were on top of things, but wow! we were doing it. The tour began.

After getting wonderful reviews in our first two cities, Cincinnati and Cleveland, Frances Ann decided to contact President Kennedy about the National Repertory Theatre and the great success it was having, and to ask if he could do anything to help establish NRT officially. After some thought and deliberation, he agreed to attend opening night at the National Theatre in Washington, D.C., and the gala afterward. He was going to anoint NRT as America's national theater and have it read into the *Congressional Record.* Needless to say, Frances Ann, Michael, and all of us involved were ecstatic.

Tragedy Intrudes

A number of weeks and several cities later, at the beginning of November, we opened to rave reviews in Philadelphia. I was flying high. This was theater! Le G, which she had finally asked me to call her, was a joy to work with, as was Kelly Jean, and I had as much fun with Denholm onstage as I had with him and his lovely young wife, Susan, offstage. Anne Meacham, who played my wife in one play and the unrequited love of my life in another, could be standoffish and neurotic offstage, but she was a consummate professional and rock-solid on stage. We were all having a wonderful time in Philadelphia and looking forward to our big opening night in Washington, D.C.

One Wednesday matinee of *The Crucible* was filled with inner-city high school kids whose admission had been free thanks to NRT and a local arts organization. At first the actors were a little nervous. This was not your usual polite "ladies who lunch" audience, but a bunch of rowdy teenagers who were not used to attending any theater, much less theater with a capital T. The auditorium was bedlam, but as the house lights dimmed and the curtain went up, they settled down very quickly and got with us. Soon you could have heard a pin drop. They didn't hesitate to interact with the characters: to warn their favorites of what they could see coming, to tell the ones they hated what they thought of them, to whistle, or to boo and hiss. They broke every conventional rule of audience behavior, and it was thrilling. The curtain calls were not accompanied by applause or standing ovations or bravos. We were met with pure sound, screams and whistles or boos and hisses. I hope we touched the hearts and souls of those kids the way they touched ours.

The Girl Who Came to Supper, a musical comedy version of Terence Rattigan's play *The Prince and the Showgirl* was the other big show in town. Noël Coward had written the music for it, and I was looking forward to seeing him again. The philanthropist and art collector Henry McIlhenny threw a party for both companies at his gorgeous mansion on Rittenhouse Square. Bob and I arrived late to the party because he had taken me to do a television interview after our show. We arrived at the mansion, and I was standing in the foyer admiring a Degas bronze ballerina when a familiar voice behind me said, "Mr. Granger, it's Noël."

Without turning, I said, "Noël who?" and he burst into laughter.

He pulled me off into a quiet corner where we sat and talked about the theater for a long time. He had read our reviews and told me how proud he was of what I was doing, which made me feel very good indeed. He knew Le G and admired her greatly. He also knew Denholm, who had acted in the great British wartime movie that Coward had written and co-directed with David Lean, *In Which We Serve*. We went in to join our host and the rest of the guests, and in no time at all Noël was as captivated by Denholm's wife, Susan, as everyone else always was. As the party began to slow down he pulled Bob, Susan, Denholm, and me aside to invite us back to a late-night party on an English battleship that was at anchor in Philadelphia. It seems that the admiral was a great pal of his. I'm not sure who the killjoy was who had the good sense to turn that one down. It probably was Bob, allowing the cautious and sensible side of his stage manager's nature to overrule our party instincts.

It was our last weekend in Philadelphia. Denholm, Susan, and I had arranged to go to see the Barnes Collection on Friday. It was a half-hour drive outside the city, so we got a cab. After spending at least two hours at the spectacular art collection, we decided to go back downtown for lunch. We got another cab and took off. After a few minutes, the driver said, "Did you hear the President's been shot."

We waited. "Okay," said Susan, "what's the punch line?" The driver said, "No punch line, that's it."

"Well, that certainly isn't very funny," I said.

"Another cabbie told me," he said. "That's all I know."

We didn't know what to think, so we just sat in silence. As we began to get into the center of the city, we saw people spilling out of the buildings. Around City Hall right in the center of the city, traffic jammed up. "I think I have to get out of this cab," I said. Denholm and Susan agreed.

The streets were now becoming filled with people. We paid the driver, got out of the cab, and began to run toward the hotel. I got to my room just as word was announced that John Fitzgerald Kennedy had been pronounced dead. I sat on the bed trying to comprehend what had happened. The phone rang. It was Bob calling from the theater. Had I heard the news? The show would be canceled tonight. He would see me as soon as he could get away. I didn't know what to do. I just lay on the bed and watched the news over and over.

The president was dead. John Kennedy was dead. How could that be? He was so young, so popular. He and his beautiful young wife and "Camelot" had brought so much promise to us all. Bob called again. Things were crazy at the theater. No one knew what to do about Saturday's two performances.

Bob and I met later for dinner in some famous old restaurant, I can't remember its name. I do remember running into Harry Kurnitz there with a contingent from his show, *The Girl Who Came to Supper*, which included José Ferrer, Florence Henderson, and, of course, Noël Coward. They were trying to figure out how to write a new opening for their show, which opened with an attempted assassination of the prince. They invited us to join them, but we knew they had work to do and we did not want company that evening.

Bob and I had something to eat and plenty to drink, although we both remained dead sober. We left the restaurant and walked in silence in the bitter cold for hours through the historical part of the city that was the first capital of the United States. We stopped at Independence Hall and the Liberty Bell, at Congress Hall and Declaration House. We walked until we were too tired and cold to walk anymore. We went back to my hotel. That night that he and I moved past our resolution to keep our friendship uncomplicated and became lovers.

The next morning I woke to an empty bed. Bob had gone off to the theater early to deal with performance and transportation schedules. I turned on the TV and watched the shock and dismay of the entire world reacting to the news. Bob called from the theater. Saturday's performances had definitely been canceled, and the company was leaving today for D.C. We were opening in Washington, D.C., on Monday. Oh, God!

Le G had been asked to read one of John Kennedy's favorite poems by Robert Frost in a memorial program that was to be televised live from Independence Hall on Sunday morning, and she wanted me to be there with her. Bob agreed to stay behind and drive us Washington after the ceremony on Sunday.

Bob was at his hotel packing, and I was doing the same. Both of us had our TV sets on, as I imagine most of the country did. We were watching in stunned disbelief as Jack Ruby shot Lee Harvey Oswald on camera. It felt as if the entire world as we knew it had gone mad.

Sunday morning was very cold and windy. I sat alone in Independence Hall. Four large TV monitors were there, and I watched as JFK's casket was taken to lie in state at the Capitol rotunda. Suddenly there was a flurry of activity as the dignitaries arrived, and the camera crews prepared for the ceremony. Bob came in with Le G and we took our seats on the platform.

Washington

After the ceremony in Philadelphia, we left as quickly as possible and sat lost in our own reflections for most of the two-and-a-half-hour drive. We dropped Le G and her companion off at the Willard and went to the Jefferson, where we, the Elliotts, and Michael and Frances Ann were staying. At the desk there was a note from Denholm and Susan asking us to meet them at an Italian restaurant downtown. We dumped our bags and left immediately. We needed friends. When we got there, it was like a reunion. We ate some pasta and drank a lot of wine. How on earth were we going to open the next night at the National Theatre with *The Crucible,* a play about senseless hysterical violence? It was almost midnight when we got up to leave. Outside the restaurant Denholm stopped, turned to us, and said, "Let's go." We knew what he meant and left immediately for the Capitol.

We walked there and got in a line that seemed to snake for miles to the rotunda. It was bitterly cold and brilliantly clear. The bright white Capitol dome looked two-dimensional, almost like marzipan, against the night sky. There was no wind, which was merciful, since so many of the people in line had children and infants with them. We were struck by how silent it was. Even with all those children and infants, there was no noise, no crying, just thousands of people waiting patiently in cold silence. About thirty minutes later, a guard who recognized me came up and said, "Mr. Granger, by the time you get to the Rotunda, the President will be gone. The line is too long, and they are removing his body to St. Matthew's Church at six A.M." We thanked him, and we left after a few minutes.

We had to open as scheduled on Monday with *The Crucible.* It was too late to cancel the party that had been planned for after the show. The theater was more than half empty. Of the many who had accepted the invitation, the only government dignitary in attendance was an elderly Supreme Court justice and his very young wife. Our gala, in the lobby of the National Theatre, was even more sparsely attended than the performance. This was a very difficult time for our producers, Michael and Frances Ann. They could feel their dream of launching a national theater slipping away from them as well as experiencing the grief we all felt at the loss of our young president. In Frances Ann's case, all those feelings were compounded by the fact that John F. Kennedy had been her first young love.

On Tuesday morning, the funeral mass for JFK was held in St. Matthew's Church, which was only a block away from our hotel.

Our reviews were very good, but under the circumstances that was small comfort. For the entire run in Washington, we played to half-empty houses. The assassination had pulled the rug from under what could have been the defining moment for the establishment of a national theater company. We were too involved with the common grief shared by the country at the time to think about this, but in the subsequent years, NRT slowly lost its impetus. It lasted for only three more years, when an attempt to establish it as the resident company at Ford's Theatre in Washington,. D.C., succumbed to political infighting.

Liberated

Christmas was rapidly approaching when we finally closed in D.C. and left for Boston. We felt so liberated to be out of Washington that some of us actually kissed the ground when we got off the plane. We were booked there for a month. We received great reviews and got back to the joy of performing on-stage. The company stayed at a turn-of-the-century hotel, the Touraine, which was in the center of Boston's small theater district. Unfortunately, like so many of the older buildings that gave character to our cities, it has since been torn down and replaced with a bland postmodern cube.

I had a corner suite, which overlooked the Boston Garden and the Common. My living room had a large bowed window, which was a perfect place for a Christmas tree. Bob and I walked to the old Faneuil Hall public market and bought a ten-foot tree, which we carried back to the hotel through the snow. Exchanging Christmas greetings with smiling Bostonians along the way was almost like an antidote to the pain that was still with us from Washington. I threw a Christmas party and invited the company, suggesting that everyone bring ornaments to dress the tree. Everyone came, even Le G, who usually stayed away from any and all company social activities. The director in her came out as people began decorating the tree. She stayed until the last ornament was placed to her satisfaction.

Kelly Jean was convinced that she was being stalked by the Boston Strangler. She had received several strange phone calls, and suspicious notes were being left for her at the hotel. The police took this very seriously and security was placed at the hotel and at the theater. Fortunately, nothing happened before we closed and left for New Haven, where Kelly Jean did have a problem.

One of the major plot points in *Ring Round the Moon* involved a ball gown worn by Kelly's character, Isobel, in the second act. It was an elaborately draped pink and blue chiffon gown that accomplished its purpose admirably by turning the plain young girl into the princess with whom Hugo and Frederick, the twins I played, fell in love. The night after *Ring* opened, the Shubert Theatre in New Haven was broken into. All that was missing was the dress. A scramble to find a replacement took place the next day because there was no time to make another one. Kelly took the train to New York and she and Frances Ann found a flowing pale green and blue chiffon gown at Bergdorf's that looked even better on her than the original. The New Haven police did their best to track down the original, but came up with no answers.

Also playing in Boston while we were there was *Funny Girl* in its out-of-town tryout. My old pal from my Navy days, Kay Medford, was playing Fanny Brice's mother. This was the first time I had seen Kay since we were in Hawaii when World War II ended. She said that their show was a mess but that the girl playing Fanny Brice, although she could be a major pain, was also a major talent. Everyone was working furiously to pull it together. The work paid off. When the musical opened in New York in March, it was a huge hit, and Barbra Streisand was on her way to megastardom. Kay and I laughed about the fact that she seemed doomed to play mothers: Amanda in *The Glass Menagerie* in Hawaii and Japan in her early twenties, Dick Van Dyke's mother in *Bye Bye Birdie* in her early thirties, and Streisand's mother in *Funny Girl* before she hit forty.

Our tour continued to be a great success, and we ended it by coming to New York for several months. Once again, the reviews were excellent . . . but only for *The Crucible* and *The Seagull.* We were not able to put on *Ring Round the Moon* because it had been optioned to be adapted into a musical and could not be performed anywhere within a fifty-mile radius of New York City. Its absence hurt us because it was the light comedy in our repertory of three plays, and it helped to display the diversity of styles we were able to handle.

Incidentally, Kelly's stolen ball gown was found in use at a rowdy New Haven party just before we opened in New York. The party was a drag ball, and the gown was again serving its purpose, this time turning a young man into a princess.

A high point of our Broadway run was when Bob came backstage after a matinee of *The Crucible* to tell me that Arthur Miller had been in the audience and wanted to meet me. He came to my dressing room, and we talked for at least ten minutes. He said to me, "This is what I always wanted my play to be." I think he felt the original Broadway version had been overproduced. He then said he would like to meet the rest of the company.

I went to find Bob, who, anticipating the moment, had assembled everyone onstage. Mr. Miller shook hands with each person and thanked them for the way they had fulfilled his expectations. Jack Sydow, who had directed *The Crucible,* was also there that afternoon. Mr. Miller told him that he was extremely impressed with the clarity of our production. A taciturn man, Arthur Miller had a reputation for not being easy to please. We were all aware of that, which made his praise very important to all of us.

NRT—Second Tour

Out of loyalty, I stayed with NRT for another season, which kept me out of New York for the third season in as many years. We did Ibsen's *Hedda Gabler* with the Swedish actress Signe Hasso in the title role; Sheridan's *She Stoops to Conquer,* and Molnar's *Liliom* with me in the title role. The tour was successful, but it was not as good as the first one, and did not come into New York. If I had worries about being absent from Broadway for two years in a row before the first tour, going on the road again made very little sense. It was a combination of several things that made me decide to do it: Bob had been made associate producer and would be traveling with the company in order to try and set up committees to support NRT in each city; my loyalty to Frances Ann had no limits; and Le Gallienne would be directing me in two of her signature plays, *Liliom* and *Hedda Gabler.* I had never done Restoration comedy and this might be my only chance, with Jack directing *She Stoops to Conquer.* After seven months, when we were preparing to close in Chicago, my agent suggested that I think about going to Hollywood to explore the opportunities presented by television, which was now almost exclusively shot on the West Coast. I promised I would think about it.

Once back in New York I could not resist the lure of Broadway. Hal Holbrook, Carol Rossen (Robert Rossen's daughter), Jo Van Fleet, and I were offered the parts in *The Glass Menagerie.* It had been opened with Maureen Stapleton as Amanda. When Maureen had to leave, the producers decided to put in a whole new cast. The only problem was that there was almost no time for rehearsal. The director did his best in the little time he had, but it was learn as you go. As a result, Hal, Carol, and I bonded quickly and became fast friends. I must admit that Hal stole the show. He was the best Gentleman Caller I have ever seen. Jo Van Fleet could be a wonderful actress in the right part, but her lack of whimsy did not help her interpretation of Amanda.

Just a Long Weekend

Not too long after *Menagerie* closed, Bob and I were having dinner with Tharon Musser, Broadway's top lighting designer, who also did the lighting for NRT. Tharon's partner, Dina, was on tour with the national company of *Funny Girl* in the Kay Medford part. Bob had finished a season with the Dallas Civic Opera and I had no new show in sight, so we all spontaneously decided to go to Los Angeles, surprise Dina, and see *Funny Girl.* We planned to stay for about a week, but for Bob and me, it turned into four years.

Shortly after we got to L.A., my West Coast agents called to say that I had been offered a guest shot on the popular series *Run for Your Life* starring Ben Gazzara. Bob had been observing at NBC on a brand-new daytime series called *Days of Our Lives* when he was offered a job as production supervisor for a new theater that was opening in the Los Angeles answer to New York's Lincoln Center, the L.A. Music Center. A friend of his, Gordon Davidson, had been hired to run the Mark Taper Forum, which was the Music Center's equivalent of the Vivian Beaumont at Lincoln Center in New York. He in turn hired Bob to help him get it up and running. So we rented a great house in Malibu, got two Airedales and two cats, and went to work.

My part on the TV series was that of a movie star who had seen and done it all and wanted to experience the thrill of fighting a bull. There were two Mexican matadors there to coach me with the bullfighting moves. When the day for my big scene arrived, we were on the back lot of Universal where they had set up a small bullring. A large van arrived and they unloaded several bulls. They were light gray with large humps on their backs. There was a moment of dead silence, then everyone roared with laughter. Everyone, that is, except the Mexican matadors. One of them went up to the stunned director and said in Spanish the equivalent of "I ain't going in no ring with that animal." With that, he gestured to his pal and they walked off the set. The director sent all the actors home with instructions to report back the next morning. The next day I got into costume and makeup and reported for duty. There in the ring was a large black bull with a large black hump. They had taken one of the Brahma bulls and somehow spray-painted it black. I was about to repeat the Mexican matador's phrase when the director hurried over to tell me there was nothing to worry about because the bull and I would never have to be in the ring at the same time. He would shoot us separately and cut it so it looked like we were. That was my first experience back in Hollywood.

For the next three years Bob was kept very busy at the Mark Taper Forum, while I did a variety of guest-starring roles on episodic television. It was nothing at all like the live television experience I had grown to love so much in New York. The material rarely rose above mediocre. There was never enough time to discuss anything with the director or fellow actors. The focus on the set was always on the technical, never on the performances. The work was usually done in the midst of chaos. I had grown up on quiet soundstages, gone on to quiet TV studios in live television, and graduated to theater, where rehearsals and performances were organized and focused experiences. This was a new way of doing things, and not only could I not get comfortable with it, I quickly grew to loathe it.

Our life in Malibu was idyllic. The dogs took to the ocean like seals. The cats littered the entire living room with fish one moonlit night when the grunion were running. We had friends over for weekends and beach barbecues. Except for the fact that Bob was off at work all the time, it was perfect and I was miserable.

At one Hollywood party or social gathering or another, I ran into some of the movie directors I had known and worked with in the early 1950s. They were all delighted to see me, all happy that I was back, all saying that I looked better than ever, but none of them ever called to ask me to do a film.

My close friend Alex North, the film composer who had introduced jazz to movies in *A Streetcar Named Desire* and had scored such memorable films as *Viva Zapata!, Cleopatra, The Rose Tattoo, Spartacus, The Long Hot Summer, Unchained, Who's Afraid of Virginia Woolf?,* and countless others, lived two houses down the beach from us. When I was talking to him about my predicament one evening, he said, "Farley, when you bought out your contract, Goldwyn put out the word not to use you. Zanuck didn't care about anything Goldwyn wanted, so he did use you. But when you refused to do one of his biggest productions . . ."

I interrupted him: "Alex, *The Egyptian* was a world-class stinker!"

"You don't have to convince me," he explained. "I've been there. I also know times have changed, but a lot of the old prejudices still exist. Some of the hard-liners out here probably feel that since you turned your back on Hollywood, they are not going to let you back into the club that easily." I knew he was making sense, and I had expected some of this, but from people I had considered friends it hurt, and it made me angry.

The Princess

During the 1950s a number of the live TV shows I had acted in were produced by David Susskind. Now, in 1966, he called to offer me a part in a TV version of *Laura.* It was a new adaptation by Truman Capote, who had written it for his friend Princess Lee Radziwill, Jackie Kennedy's sister. The other people cast in it were Robert Stack, George Sanders, and Arlene Francis, and it was to rehearse and shoot in London.

I accepted.

We gathered in London for the first reading in a studio in the Duke of York's Barracks, where each morning we had to pause while the Queen's Guard piped whatever it was they were piping. George, Arlene, and I hit it off immediately, as we all realized that we were stuck in an archetypical vanity production. I'd hesitate to call Robert Stack dumb, but he had no sense of humor. George used to bait him mercilessly. Most of the time, it went right over Bob's head. The actors all lunched together most days at a little Italian restaurant nearby on Kings Road. Stack never failed to ask us if we needed our receipts . . . every day. George observed wryly that the poor chap may have had tax problems.

One day at lunch George leaned over to me and whispered, "Farley, Ray Milland is over there in the corner booth. I think he would appreciate if you went over and said hello." Ray had played Stanford White in *The Girl in the Red Velvet Swing* with me. I had not noticed him when we came in, but I knew that Ray had not worked in a while. I went over to say hello, and he seemed quite touched. That was the real George Sanders, thoughtful, caring, and considerate.

Arlene Francis was my closest friend, my drinking buddy, and my salvation during this entire production. She was warm without being gushy, sharp without being bitchy, and a trooper who never let any of the daily trials and tribulations that we all went through, trying to make a princess look like an actress, get her down. After rehearsal we usually went to a nearby pub to unwind and recap the day's events, a process that almost always began with "Did you see what she did when . . ." I asked George to come with us several times, but he confided that his wife, Benita Hume, was quite ill and he needed to spend as much time with her as possible. As difficult as that must have been for him, he never let any of it show at work.

Arlene and I spent as many evenings as possible going to the theater. We saw *Rosencrantz and Guildenstern Are Dead,* which heralded the amazing talent of Tom

Stoppard. We saw Laurence Olivier in Strindberg's *Dance of Death* at the National Theatre after hearing the rumor that he was gravely ill with cancer. Not only was his performance magnificent, but he beat the cancer!

One day at rehearsal, Lee came up to me and said, "You take Arlene out all the time. How come you never ask me to do anything?"

So, like a good boy, I asked her out. We went to the theater and had supper afterward at a nearby seafood restaurant. Lee spent the whole evening complaining about the script and how Truman had done her in by not showing up. Two martinis, two Dover soles, and some very good white Bordeaux later, we poured ourselves into a cab and went back to her house in Chelsea for a nightcap. When we got there, I had a brainstorm. "Why don't we call Truman?" I suggested. She loved the idea and had a bunch of numbers for him. The hunt was on, but he was nowhere to be found. Knowing Truman, I would not be a bit surprised if he had heard that things on *Laura* were not going well and was avoiding this particular phone call. After an hour or so we gave up, and I went home. *Laura* turned out to be no one's finest hour, but at least I had the good fortune to get to know George and Arlene. George's wife died shortly after our production, and two years later, after a brief fourth marriage to Zsa Zsa Gabor's sister Magda, George killed himself, leaving a note that said, "I am leaving because I am bored. I feel I have lived long enough. I am leaving you with your worries in this sweet cesspool. Good luck."

The State Department

Bob and Eddie Parone, a talented New York director who helped launch Edward Albee's career, had gotten a Rockefeller Foundation grant to produce a program called *New Theatre for Now* at the Taper. It was a big success and the State Department had approached Gordon Davidson about sending two evenings of new American plays to India, Iran, and the capitals of Eastern Europe. Davidson had agreed to do it and had submitted the plays for approval. As is always the case, this bureaucratic decision was taking a very long time. Bob had never been to Europe, and I thought this was the perfect time. He needed a vacation and at least he would have some of his shots and a passport if his tour came through. Selfishly, I would have the pleasure of introducing him to places I loved, most of them in Italy.

We went first to Munich to spend some time with Alex North and his young German wife, Anna. There we rented a car and drove to a small town called Fussen to visit Ethyl and Buddy. Ethyl's daughter, Judy, had married Hal Prince, who was directing a film there. His studio was an inflated dome in a field at the foot of the mountain peak that mad King Ludwig's fairytale castle, Neuschwanstein, perched on. Coming upon the site for the first time was as surreal an experience as rounding a corner today in Bilbao and seeing Frank Gehry's titanium-sheathed Guggenheim Museum.

After a couple of days, we left for Italy, crossing the Alps via the Brenner Pass. We arrived in Verona in the middle of the night. The next morning over *caffè latte* and pastries in the main square, Bob fell in love with Italy. Our next stop was *La Serenissima,* Venice. We stayed in La Fenice et des Artistes, the small hotel next to the opera house. The first thing I did was look in the phone book for my old friend and drinking buddy, Peggy Guggenheim. She was there and invited us to come over for lunch. We did. It had been fourteen years since I had seen her, and she was every bit as lively as I remembered. After lunch she asked if I would like anything else. I said I was perfectly content. She raised her eyebrows and said, "Have you forgotten?"

I still didn't get it. She said, "Not even a little grappa?"

Then I laughed. We had ended many cold winter evenings with "just a little grappa." Then she took us through the museum to show me the improvements that had taken place in the fourteen years since I had last been there, including a small downstairs gallery devoted to the paintings of her daughter, Pegeen, who had killed herself in 1967 after a number of attempts. A couple of days later, we met for dinner at the Taverna La Fenice and spent a marvelous last evening in Venice with the woman the Venetians called "the Last Duchess."

The following morning we headed for Rome. After checking in at the Hotel de la Ville, we ran into Mickey Knox in the bar. I'd known Mickey slightly in Hollywood during his acting days. After becoming one of the early victims of the blacklist, he had moved to Paris and now lived in Rome. He was married to Joan Morales, whose sister Adele had been stabbed with a pen knife by her husband, Norman Mailer, during their tempestuous marriage. Adele, who was not critically wounded, had refused to press charges. The sisters had a Cuban mother and a Peruvian father. Joanie was a completely down-to-earth young woman whose Brooklyn accent could be cut with a knife. She was crazy-funny, and one of the most beautiful women I've ever seen. She, Bob, and I bonded immediately. Through Mickey, who was working nonstop as a dialogue director in the Italian film world, I met Roger Beaumont, the representative in Italy for Creative Management Associates, one of Hollywood's most prestigious talent agencies at the time. Roger and Mickey began trying to convince me to remain in Italy because of all the film work still going on there.

Meanwhile, Bob received a telegram from the Mark Taper Forum. Two one-act plays that he had directed had been chosen as part of a two-evening program of new plays to be sent to India, Iran, and the capitals of Eastern Europe. He had to return immediately for casting and rehearsals. I decided to stay in Rome and explore the film possibilities about which Roger seemed so positive.

I settled into a small hotel in the heart of Rome. The two people who best helped keep my loneliness at bay were Joanie and Gore Vidal, who had an apartment in Rome as well as his mountaintop villa on the Amalfi coast. He invited me to dinner and then on a weekly basis to his Sunday gatherings, where he would collect a few of the most interesting people in town at that moment for drinks and dinner.

Bob was in rehearsal back in Los Angeles, and our phone bills began to mount. Franco Zefferelli heard I was in town and called to invite me to a party he was giving at his villa on the Appian Way. He said that Luchino would be there, and it would be just like old times. I arrived and didn't know a soul. The hit of the evening was Franco's new ice-making machine. It was sitting front and center in the living room like an honored guest.

After Franco and I hugged, I was left on my own feeling like an out-of-place wallflower. Then Monica Vitti came over to talk with me and changed all that. She knew and loved every frame of *Senso* and was also a big Hitchcock fan. She could not have been more gracious. I had only known her, as most Americans do, as the glacial, elusive leading lady in Antonioni films like *L'Avventura* and *Red Desert.* In the 1960s she was the only female star in Italy whose name would guarantee the money for a film. She was also their number-one comedienne, and after seeing several of her other films, I knew why. She was an Italian combination of Carole Lombard and Carol Burnett, equally at home doing high style or low comedy. If you ever get a chance to see her in *Dramma della Gelosia,* or *The Pizza Triangle,* as it is called here, along with Marcello Mastroianni and Giancarlo Giannini, or *Polvere di Stelle,* a k a *Stardust,* with Alberto Sordi, you will see what I mean.

Late in the evening, Visconti made his grand entrance with his latest find, Helmut Berger, in tow. I was concerned that he might still be angry because I had been unable to return for the execution scene in *Senso.* But he seemed as genuinely glad to see me as I was to see him. Helmut Berger, not a very good actor, was perfect as Ingrid Thulin's decadent son in Visconti's disturbing film about pre–World War II Germany, *The Damned.* Luchino went on to make one more cinematic masterpiece in 1971. It was his film of Thomas Mann's famous novella, *Death in Venice,* starring Dirk Bogarde in an unforgettable portrayal of Gustav von Aschenbach. Visconti's last major film, *Ludwig,* in 1972, starred Hemut Berger as the mad king of Bavaria. Berger was merely adequate opposite the delicious Austrian actress Romy Schneider as Empress Elisabeth of Austria. One of Ludwig's follies was building my favorite castle, Neuschwanstein.

The next day I got two job offers. Roger had gotten me the lead in an Italian film that was being shot in Egypt, and my agent in Hollywood called to say I had been offered a leading role in a prestigious film being made for TV. The cast included Uta Hagen, Marty Balsam, Cloris Leachman, and Johnny Rubenstein as my son. I stalled them both and called Bob.

He told me that the United States Information Agency had finally read the plays that had been submitted for the tour months ago. They did not approve of their political content and had canceled the State Department tour, citing unrest in the Middle East as their reason. Bob urged me to come back and do the TV film in L.A. Then we would pack up the Malibu house, take the dogs and cats, and move to Rome. It was a plan.

I was delighted to be in rehearsal again. I had worked with the director, Paul Bogard, before and thought he was top-notch. Uta was as much fun to work with as she had been to play with in Paris. Marty was a rock-solid old pro. Johnny Rubenstein, the great pianist's son, was a gifted young actor who was obviously going places. Cloris Leachman was playing my wife. She had put her career on hold to raise a family and be supportive of her husband, the director George Englund. Since she was playing my wife, we sat together for the first reading. All she did that day was complain about how old she looked and how tired she was. Obviously Paul was not appreciative of her lack of focus on the part or the script. The next day she was not there. A couple of years later Cloris won an Oscar for *The Last Picture Show* and appeared on *The Mary Tyler Moore Show* and her own spinoff, *Phyllis.* Our star-studded TV movie, from which she was fired on the first day, played to good reviews and sank without a trace. This is an example of the crapshoot that is show business.

Soon it was Christmas. Bob and I gave a party to say good-bye to all our friends. The lease was up on the beach house on January 1, so we packed up, put everything in storage, took Luke and Molly, our two Airedales, and the two cats, and left for Rome right after the first of the year in 1970.

Italy Again

After a month at the Cavalieri Hilton, which had grounds where the dogs could run, we rented a beautiful rooftop apartment with a terrace in a fifteenth-century building in the heart of old Rome. It soon became obvious that Roger, my agent, and Mickey, my friend, had exaggerated the amount of quality work available in the early 1970s. I was offered a lot of projects but, especially since I had done a film with Visconti, none of them was remotely interesting or challenging. In the four years we spent in Rome, I averaged two films a year, none of which were worth writing home about. One of them, *Lo Chiamavano Trinità* or *They Call Him Trinity,* a comic book of a movie, was one of the highest-grossing films ever made in Italy.

In 1975 the bottom fell out of the Italian film industry and film production came almost to a complete halt. Also, Watergate and its repercussions were looming large in America. It was time to go home. We packed up the dogs and cats, gave away the furniture, and left for New York and then California.

Hollywood or New York

My friends Ethyl and Buddy were going to Mallorca to spend a month with Judy, Hal, and their grandchildren at Hal's mountaintop villa in Pollensa. They suggested that Bob and I use their house in Beverly Hills while we were deciding whether or not to stay in L.A. To complicate this decision, things were not going well between Bob and me.

I began accepting guest-starring roles on episodic TV again. There were a lot more opportunities, but if anything, the quality of the material and the lack of time for preparation had gotten worse. I was not happy. My agent knew how I felt and called to say that I had been offered a lot of money to do a soap opera in New York. He said that many respectable New York theater actors worked in soaps in order to make enough money to live decently in New York and to be available to work in the theater whenever the right part came along. I said that I needed time to think about it and accepted an offer from the Seattle Repertory Theatre to play one of the leads in Noël Coward's *Private Lives.*

The production was a smash hit with both the public and the critics, and I had the time of my life playing Elyot. When it closed, I returned to Hollywood and episodic television, which seemed even more banal after Noël Coward. When my agent said that the soap, *One Life to Live,* in New York was still interested in me and had upped the money, I returned to New York. Bob stayed in California.

New York, 1977

Back in my favorite city, I stayed with Shelley, who was in a big prewar apartment on Riverside Drive. We sat up until the wee small hours having the same old discussions about acting and planning things that we could do together in the theater. I found an apartment with a magnificent view looking east across Central Park. At sunset, all the windows of the East Side high-rises turned a brilliant shiny copper. It was just a short walk to the ABC studio where I worked. When Shelley saw my apartment, she fell in love with it. Never warm enough, even in the dog days of summer, she said that the winter winds coming down the Hudson River were killing her over on Riverside Drive. She called Jay Julien, our trusted mutual lawyer and business manager, and he was able to get her an apartment in my building, four floors below me.

Shelley had her apartment redesigned, making the master bedroom and living room into one large space with wall-to-wall windows on two sides. The views were spectacular, but seeing all that expanse of Central Park made her cold, so she covered them with heavy insulated drapes that were always drawn. When that didn't work well enough for her, she bought several of the largest portable electric heaters that could be found, plugged them all in at the same time, and plunged her wing of the building into complete blackness. After that was sorted out, she purchased a lot of cheap mattresses and leaned them over the drapes as another layer of insulation. The end result was that it was impossible to visit her for too long a time because it was like being in a sauna.

I thought I disliked episodic TV, but the soap was worse. Soap acting requires certain skills that I have never been able to develop: the ability to be a very fast study, the ability to concentrate in the middle of complete chaos, the ability to learn material that is the same but slightly different each day, and always, the need for instant acting with little or no rehearsal or preparation time. I have nothing but admiration for the many fine actors who have mastered these skills. For young actors it is an invaluable technique to acquire for a limited period of time. I couldn't master any of these necessary abilities. It took me many painful years and two additional tries to realize this.

At the time I thought, maybe my mind is going. Maybe my ability to memorize lines has deserted me. I was able to memorize three plays simultaneously for repertory and couldn't remember three scenes for a soap. Maybe I had early-onset Alzheimer's. I went to doctors, to hypnotists, to acupuncturists, to people who supposedly knew how to teach acting technique for soaps. Nothing worked. I developed a spastic colon. My gut had always spoken for me when I was unhappy and felt unable to do anything about it. I had memories of it speaking out in meetings with Mr. Goldwyn, or at formal dinner parties in my young movie star days, but this was getting more serious. I was in danger of perforating my intestine.

One day, in an effort to stop the mental and physical pain, I just walked off the set, went to my dressing room, got my things, and left the studio. I didn't go back. I didn't answer my phone for days. I just slept. When I started to feel a little better, I went to see Jay Julien. Jay handled everything. My colon stopped complaining, and I began to feel whole again. I needed to work in order to prove to myself that I could work.

I went into a bad dinner-theater production of *The Sound of Music* and had no problem at all memorizing the lines, which erased a huge worry. It paid very well, but I quickly realized that dinner theater was not for me. I then toured summer stock in a bad production of "the original" *Dracula.* At one theater a handsome young apprentice came up and introduced himself to me. He said, "Hi, Farley, I'm Sam Goldwyn's grandson, Tony." I was taken completely by surprise. I'd liked and felt a certain kinship with his father, Sammy Jr. Even though life with my father was far from ideal, I knew that Sammy's was no day at the beach either. I felt an almost personal sense of pride about the good things Sammy had been doing in the movie business. Tony has distinguished himself in both theater and in films as a triple threat: actor, director, and producer.

Shelley and I finally got to do a play together. We were offered two of the parts in a limited run of *Kennedy's Children* in Chicago. The play consisted of six actors in a bar doing long intersecting monologues that define them as children of the 1960s. Once again, I proved to myself that learning lines was not a problem for me. Shelley did have an occasional problem with her lines. I'll never know whether or not it had to do with her love of improvisation, but I always knew she was up when she would pause for a moment and say, "I remember when I first met Eleanor Roosevelt . . ." The estimable wife of FDR had never been mentioned in the play by the author. The original production had not been a success in New York, but the subject matter had enough appeal for enough people, including me, that it continued to be performed all over the country for several years. It's a hard piece to pull off and we didn't fare any better than most. The only person in our company who came off well, and deservedly so, was the talented and too infrequently seen actor Al Freeman Jr.

Bob and I had kept in touch. He came to New York for a monthlong trial run to explore producing and directing for a soap. It would mean a significant increase in income, and he decided that if he received an offer to direct he would accept. The offer was tendered, he did accept, and he moved, with the

Airedales, Luke and Molly, into an apartment across the hall from me. At the time, it was the best of all possible worlds.

The next project I worked on was with a close friend, Shirley Kaplan. Shirley is a very talented director who just happens to also be a superb painter. She was involved in developing projects at Playwrights Horizons. She was working with Carol Hall, who had composed the music and lyrics for *The Best Little Whorehouse in Texas.* This project was tentatively titled *Sweet Main Street.* It was an effort to create the *Saturday Evening Post,* Norman Rockwell world of pre–World War II small-town America. Shirley was designing the sets as well as directing. We worked on it for almost a month. It was a good idea that never came together. But we all had fun trying to make it happen. Frances Ann, my producer with NRT, loved it and tried to get the funding that would enable Shirley to continue developing *Sweet Main Street,* but that never happened.

Two Strikes

Michael Kahn was a member of the McCarter Theatre Company in Princeton, New Jersey. He had been artistic director of the American Shakespeare Festival in Stratford, Connecticut, and he is currently the artistic director of the American Shakespeare Festival in Washington, D.C. Michael asked if I would be interested in coming to the McCarter to be in the classic comedy about amateur theater, George Kelly's *The Torch Bearers.* Some of the other actors in it were Peggy Cass, Dina Merrill, and, last but never least, Tovah Feldshuh. Tovah was young, talented, and defined the tasty Yiddish word *chutzpah.* I've watched her grow through the years into a very accomplished actress and singer. I don't know how good our production was, but I had fun, especially with Peggy, whose tart Boston Irish sense of humor kept everything in perspective.

While performing in Princeton, I was invited to Mel Gussow's house for an after-theater Christmas party. Mel was a drama critic with *The New York Times.* He had been a major force in the evolution of off-Broadway, and he had also written many superb books with and about the most important playwrights in modern theater. It had been a long snowy drive back to New York from Princeton, and like most actors after a performance, I was starving. I jumped out of the car in front of the Gussows' town house in Greenwich Village, hoping there would be some food left. As I started up the steps, the front door burst open and out came a sobbing Jessica Tandy followed quickly by her husband, Hume Cronyn. Jessie rushed down the steps, and Hume sputtered out a "Merry

Christmas, Farley" as he rushed after her. Inside, in front of the fireplace, nose to nose, stood Joe Papp, the artistic director of the Public Theater, and Edward Albee, one of America's foremost playwrights, screaming obscene insults at each other. I felt a hand on my arm and turned. Mel's wife, Ann, was standing there. She said sweetly, "Welcome, Farley. I'm so glad you could come. Why don't we go downstairs and get you something to eat." With a quiet smile she took me down to the kitchen and got me a drink and some food. As she sat down with me, we heard the front door slam with such force that it shook the house. She gave me a nonplussed look and shrugged. As I was taking my first bite, I heard heavy, determined footsteps coming down the stairs behind me. I glanced at Ann, whose look had become mildly apprehensive. Edward plunked down beside me and glowered at me. I took another bite and looked at him. He was still glowering and narrowed his eyes slightly. As he started to say something, I said quietly and slowly, "Go away."

He looked a little surprised but continued to stare. So I repeated, a little louder and very slowly, "Go away!" He did. And as I heard him clumping up the stairs, Ann stood and said, "May I freshen your drink?"

I've gotten to know Edward through the years, and every time we meet, he is warm, friendly, and a complete gentleman.

About a month after *The Torch Bearers,* Michael Kahn called again. He was directing Turgenev's *A Month in the Country* for the Roundabout, now one of the most important theater companies in New York. Then it was a relatively low-profile group with a large theater or two down in Chelsea. I loved the play and Michael was assembling a first-rate cast that included Tammy Grimes, Jerome Kilty, Phil Bosco, Boyd Gaines, and Amanda Plummer. I had liked working with Michael, so I jumped at the chance.

The read-through went very well, but after several days of rehearsal, a dangerous pattern began to emerge. Tammy was monopolizing the rehearsal time. A director always has to head off this possibility at the pass, but Michael went along with Tammy's never-ending need to discuss her character's motivation and purpose. The days were slipping away, and a lot of the other scenes and people were not getting the attention they needed. The part I was playing, her lover, was a bit of a wimp, but with a little help from the director I had hoped to make a choice that could change that, for the good of the play. As it turned out, I was barely given enough time to discuss my blocking, much less my character. At one point, quite close to the opening, I discovered that Michael and Tammy had done *A Month in the Country* together before. I was furious. It is the director's responsibility to guide all of the actors into a cohesive whole to realize a particular vision of a play. Indulging one performer's need for attention while neglecting the rest of the cast can produce very uneven results. I was not good in the play when it opened. By the time we were several weeks into the run I had pulled together a relatively decent performance, but that was several weeks too late.

Next I appeared in an off-Broadway revival of *Outward Bound,* directed by an old pro who lived across the street from me, Harold F. Kennedy. Through the years we had run into each other frequently and had often talked about working together. Harold called one evening to ask if I would be interested in his newest project. He had put together an interesting cast, which included two comic geniuses, Imogene Coca and Henry Morgan. The result was disappointing, but the people were fascinating. Imogene, who came to fame as Sid Caesar's sublimely funny partner on television's *Your Show of Shows* in the 1950s, was actually one of the most painfully shy and insecure performers I have ever known. Henry Morgan, one of radio's last big stars during the same period, was known for being snide, sarcastic, and just plain mean. He was actually one of the most polite and pleasant people with whom I've ever worked. The show did not fare as well as I did with the critics. *The New York Times* called it "a leaky dramatic vessel." Of me they said, "Mr. Granger skillfully follows his predecessors, Alfred Lunt and Leslie Howard, in the central role as a self-destructive prodigal with a strong sense of decency."

Harold Kennedy, our director, also just happened to write the funniest book I've ever read about summer theater. If you ever come across it in some used-book bin, buy it. The title is *No Pickle, No Performance.* If it doesn't make you laugh out loud, I will buy it from you. I can never find enough copies to give my friends.

The Right Part

I went into the long-running Ira Levin play *Deathtrap.* It had been on Broadway for four years, and four different actors had played the leading part of Sidney Bruhl. Two members of the original cast had remained the same: Marian Seldes as my wife, Myra, and Elizabeth Parrish, a protégée of Stella Adler's, as the psychic, Helga ten Dorp. William LeMassena, who been a member of the Lunts' company, played Porter, my lawyer. The other new member of the cast, who had been there for a few months, was Steve Bassett, a young actor fresh from Juilliard. Steve played Clifford, the ambitious and unscrupulous young writer who was my lover. They were all rock solid and extremely good. The producers were Alfred de Liagre Jr. and Roger Stevens, both men with good reputations. I only saw de Liagre, and I assumed he was now running the show since Roger Stevens was the head of the Kennedy Center in Washington, D.C. I also assumed that de Liagre was obviously not prepared to spend any more money than necessary to keep *Deathtrap* alive. Perhaps he thought it had run its course. He said he would pay for only two weeks' rehearsal. My character never left the stage and never stopped talking. The amount of tricky stage business was mind-boggling. If ever a play demanded a full rehearsal period, this was it. I loved the play and I knew what fun I could have with the part. I agreed to do it.

We began rehearsal, just the stage manager and I. By the time we finished that first day, I knew I was in deep trouble. He was not the original stage manager, and therefore had not been a part of the original creative process, when a cast and director find the truth that works for them. He was going to be no help at all. He wanted a robot, or an unquestioning understudy who would mimic the actor currently playing the lead. He could not deal with the fact that I had ideas about the part. I asked him when the director was coming in to work with me. He said, "Oh, he's too busy. He won't be coming in."

I don't know which reaction was stronger, anger or the sinking feeling in the pit of my stomach. In any case, I held them both in check and went to the theater to talk to the assistant stage manager. He was an intelligent young man who without saying a word against his boss let me know that he understood my dilemma. We made a plan for him to come to my apartment and work with me on the QT. I don't know that I would have gotten through this period without his help. In the second week of rehearsal, he let a little bit of information slip that saved my life. It seems that another name actor had turned the part down before it was offered to me. He had told them that he would not consider doing this part with less than three weeks' rehearsal. That was all I needed to hear. I told the stage manager to notify the producer that I would not go on unless I had another week of rehearsal. Mr. de Liagre did not come in from East Hampton, but Jay Julien's phone was very busy for a few hours. Jay stuck to my guns and got my third week.

Business began to pick up as soon as I went into the show. A short time later the play was re-reviewed in *The New York Times.* The review was excellent for me and the show. Sales picked up even more, and we ran for almost another year and a half. At one point during our run, Mr. de Liagre received a special award for his contribution to the the theater. There was a ceremony at Sardi's across the street, and we were all encouraged to attend. When I entered the private dining room upstairs, Mr. de Liagre came up to me and said, "Who did you have to pay to get that review?"

I smiled and moved on. Then the director, Robert Moore, whom I had never met, came up to me and said, "Hi, I'm Bob Moore. I hear you're in a hit." I bit my tongue, smiled, and moved on.

I enjoyed doing *Deathtrap* so much that when it was time for a two-week vacation, I only took one week. Bob took a week at the same time, and we flew to London. We went to the theater every night, and met Susan Elliott after the curtain every night. Susan and Denholm had gotten a large apartment on Abbey Road just down the street from where we were staying with our friends Peter and Mary Noble. We never got home before 6:00 A.M. After this week of round-the-clock reveling, we flew back to New York on Sunday, and were back at work on Monday. We both felt as renewed and refreshed as if we'd spent a month on a deserted beach.

Sailing

I met Betsy Crawford when she was working as Shelley Winters's assistant in New York on theater-related projects. For years, Betsy had been involved in various aspects of the theater. She was currently involved with a small off-Broadway company that was struggling to stay alive and had come up with two one-act plays. Louise Lasser, Woody Allen's second wife, was still hot as a result of the cult hit TV series *Mary Hartman, Mary Hartman*. She had agreed to star in the one-acts. Betsy sent me the plays to read and I loved one of them. *Sailing* was written by Michael Shurtleff, one of Broadway's most important casting directors. It was a two-character play about an older well-to-do couple at their summer home on a bluff overlooking a beautiful bay. The husband, an avid sailor, is a cynical, overly articulate curmudgeon who never stops complaining about the decline of civility and manners in today's society. His wife has long ago learned to tune him out and concern herself mainly with the trivia of their existence. Their marriage has little substance left, and they no longer communicate on any meaningful level, but they are stuck with each other.

The companion piece was an outrageous sex farce. After the first company read-through, I realized two things: I was wrong for the farce, and Louise was wrong for *Sailing*. Louise was a unique talent, and I would have loved to work with her, but these two plays were not the right vehicles for us to co-star in. I went to Betsy, and she confided that both directors agreed. Happily, she was able to talk the producers into making the change. Louise got a new leading man, and I got a new leading lady. Together we got great reviews, and our little theater was packed every night, mostly with theater people.

Talley & Son

Almost immediately after *Sailing* closed, I received a call from Marshall Mason, the head of the Circle Repertory company. He was a longtime collaborator of Lanford Wilson, one of contemporary theater's more original voices. Marshall wanted to send me Lanford's new script to read. Would I be interested? I said, "Yes."

I read the play as soon as I received it, and called Marshall immediately. I knew at first reading that the play, the man, and the words were as right for me as I was for them. Now all I had to worry about was the audition.

Although some rare and courageous actors love the process of auditioning, most of us hate it and feel that we come off badly. The number of choices for the approach to any material are so numerous that we always worry that whatever we choose may be different from what the director wants and will scuttle our chance at getting the part. I know that I'm not putting enough faith in the director's imagination, but it is the only plausible reason I can come up with to explain the number of really talented actors who do not work nearly enough.

When I called Marshall with my reaction to Lanford's play, he said, "Good. Then you've got the part."

"When do you want me to audition?"

"Farley, we saw you in *Sailing*. You don't have to audition."

Talley & Son is the third play in Lanford's trilogy about the Talley family, which includes *The Fifth of July* and *Talley's Folly*. It takes place in 1944, during World War II, in the Talley house at the same time that *Talley's Folly* is taking place down at the dock. *The Fifth of July* is set in 1977, after the Vietnam War.

Our company was rehearsing and opening in Saratoga, a beautiful town in upstate New York, famous for its racetrack. The theater there was an old proscenium house. Our award-winning set designer, John Lee Beatty, had designed the set so that it would only have to be reconfigured slightly when we moved into the Circle Rep's much smaller multipurpose space in the heart of Greenwich Village.

My wife was being played by Helen Stenborg, a member of the Circle Rep and a superb actress, who was married to actor Barney Hughes. There was a small college near the theater that had donated two dorms for the company to use. After a couple of nights in the men's dorm, I decided that it might be a little quieter and more conducive to learning lines if I stayed with the women. So I moved to their dorm. The women were worse than the men. I went back to where I had been assigned . . . with earplugs.

After the first read-through of the play, Marshall told us how he planned to rehearse. I didn't like his idea at all. He wanted us up on our feet at once and planned to go though the play sequentially, a specific number of pages at a time. He would spend several days on each section until we were all comfortable and starting to absorb both movement and words, then he would move on to the next section. After two days, it felt like the most natural way to learn the material and was a method of rehearsal that I quickly grew to love. Instead of stopping repeatedly to discuss problematic moments, we let the momentum carry us through them. By the time we got to the end of the section, most of our questions had answered themselves. Lanford's words had a unique rhythm that was tasty and inevitable. I had not felt this comfortable with any text since doing Chekhov.

We opened to full houses and appreciative audiences, and settled in happily for our two-week pre–New York City run. Helen had a car with her, so we explored Saratoga and its environs. She took me to visit Yaddo, a community for artists on a beautiful 400-acre estate in nearby Saratoga Springs. One of Yaddo's alumni was Patricia Highsmith, whose first novel was *Strangers on a Train.*

We also passed a few peaceful hours at the Saratoga racetrack watching the horses work out. All in all, breaking in the play was not the usual hectic effort to get the rewrites in, up, and working. It was, instead, a rewarding time during which we polished and deepened the material before opening in New York.

We moved into the Circle Rep's home on Sheridan Square, and within a short period of adjusting to a different stage and a much more intimate theater, we were ready to open in New York. Our reviews were generally good, but some critics preferred the other two plays in the trilogy. Happily, my reviews were excellent. Even the potentially caustic John Simon was complimentary. I know a lot of actors say that they don't read reviews. I can't make that claim, but I don't seek them out. The good ones make me feel good and the bad ones make me feel bad. Touring the country's major cities with the National Repertory Theatre helped me put reviews in perspective. When you open in ten cities in three plays over a number of months and are reviewed by critics in at least two papers in each of those cities, there are so many different points of view to choose from, quite often in direct contradiction to each other, that the easiest thing to do is enjoy the good reviews and forget the bad ones. In my lifetime there have been a few critics I've read to learn from. Elliot Norton in Boston was one, and Mel Gussow in *The New York Times* was another. Their intelligence and their wealth of theater knowledge, as well as their ability to be objective, made their criticism helpful. Otherwise, I feel that it is easiest to let the reviews fall where they may.

Giving It Another Try

During this time, Bob had progressed from director and line producer on two NBC daytime shows to executive producer at CBS on his fourth soap, *As the World Turns.* It took him nine grueling months, but he finally met the head writer with whom he could transform the eighth-ranked show into a winner. Within six months, he and Doug Marland had moved the show into first place, and it went on to win a Best Show Emmy Award for the first time in its thirty-five-year history.

Against Bob's instincts and, even though I was tempted to take on the challenge of mastering a technique which had up to this time eluded me, against mine, Doug persuaded him to persuade me into signing me for the show. Immediately after signing a three-year contract with mutual out clauses for *As the World Turns,* I was offered a part in a movie, *The Whoopie Boys,* that would reunite me with my old friend Denholm Elliott, as well as Carole Shelley, Michael O'Keefe, and a host of other good actors. We discussed the shooting dates with Douglas, and it looked as if I could finish the film before I was needed to begin on the soap. The movie company kept changing its start date, and Bob finally had to exercise his right to say no to the movie since I had signed with him first. When they got around to making the movie, it was a disaster. For some strange reason I still get credited with being in it. The soap is another story.

Eileen Fulton, whose singing still continues to charm supper club patrons in Manhattan, has played Lisa, the resident vixen on *As the World Turns,* since shortly after the show went on the air. She was chosen to be my love interest on the show. Eileen was helpful, caring, a consummate professional, and in general a delight to work with. Lisa also happened to own the one restaurant/club in Oakdale, the fictitious Midwestern city somewhere near Chicago in which the show took place. Doug Marland was a master at writing scenes at this restaurant/club, the Mona Lisa, where a large number of the show's leading characters supped, drank, plotted, and crossed paths. In this way, he was able to spread information quickly, and dramatically illustrate its effect on the various people involved. The technique worked wonderfully, but these scenes were the most difficult and time-consuming to stage, rehearse, and tape. Whenever the cast saw a heavy day scheduled in the Mona Lisa, we knew that we would be lucky to finish before midnight.

On my first day of work, I had an early-morning call for some of the intimate scenes that introduced my character to Oakdale as well as an afternoon call to play a number of see-and-be-seen scenes at the Mona Lisa. The morning scenes were finished by around 11:00 A.M. I went back to my dressing room, where I sat until my next call at ten-thirty that evening. It was complete chaos in the studio, and everyone was tired. I could not remember one word.

I tried, oh, Lord, I tried. I had a recliner put in my dressing room, kept to myself, and studied my ass off. By the time I was called to the set, I always knew my lines perfectly. The moment I hit the studio, even for the simplest of scenes, the normal noise and chaos of daytime television—sets being changed, last-minute lighting adjustments, the cameras and boom microphone platforms working out traffic problems—blew my concentration. I would tense up and the words would desert me.

There were not enough hours in most days to allow the actors a quiet run-through or two on the set. Whenever we were able to have one, I could remember lines and come up with a performance. But those opportunities were extremely rare. More often than not, the dress would be taped in hopes of getting something good enough. The producers, the directors, the technical staff, and almost all of the other actors could not have been more supportive and encouraging, but it wasn't enough. I still couldn't master the technique of tuning out the surroundings. I knew it and everyone else did, too. I was miserable. By this time in my life, I knew I was a good actor, but that knowledge also made it possible for me know how bad I was in this particular situation. I kept trying for over a year, partially out of loyalty, partially out of stubbornness, but my health began to suffer. I tried new diets, meditation, acupuncture, hypnosis, and whatever else anyone recommended. Nothing helped. Things did not improve. After a few more months, old reliable, my colon, started to act up for the second time since my battle to get out of my contract with Sam Goldwyn.

I was diagnosed with spastic colitis brought on by stress. I asked what I could do about it because it was obviously the soap and I had eighteen months left on my contract. My doctor's answer was, "You have no time left. A perforated colon is an extremely serious problem. It is also one you will be facing soon, if you do not stop what is causing your colitis."

I went to Bob the next day. He said that he knew how unhappy I had been, but had no idea that it was making me sick.. He called Doug immediately, and they discussed replacing me with another actor or writing me out of the show in a way that would be dramatic and serve the plot.

Within two days, Doug Marland had figured out how to write me out of the show, but he needed a month. He agreed to keep my performance schedule as light as he could without damaging the story line. As soon as I heard that, I started to shed some of the tension that was making me ill. After several days, people at the studio started complimenting me on how well the scenes were going. Bob called me into his office and said, "Do you have any idea of how much better you've gotten since we agreed to release you from your contract?" I said that I hadn't, but I did acknowledge that the scenes seemed to be getting a little easier to do. At that point he said, "Maybe you won't have to leave the show." As I quickly turned to leave his office, he yelled after me, "Just kidding."

I got a call from Marshall asking me if I would accept being made a permanent member of the Circle Repertory Company. I was pleased and flattered and said yes. A week later, I received a notification in the mail that I had been nominated for a *Village Voice* Obie Award for my performance in *Talley & Son*. I was pleased, of course, but I knew very little about the award. In fact, I was scheduled to be working at the studio in one of our Mona Lisa marathons on the afternoon of the award ceremony, so I put it aside and forgot about it.

Shirley Kaplan, who had directed me in *Sweet Main Street*, was the first of my friends to call to congratulate me on the Obie nomination. In the course of our conversation, I mentioned that I didn't think that I would be able to make it to the ceremony. She started in about how important it was, but I told her that I had no time to discuss it, because I was studying my lines for the next day's taping. Within the hour I got a call from Mel Gussow. Mel was a very polite and soft-spoken gentleman. I could tell that he was upset. "Farley, Shirley called to tell me that you are thinking of not attending the Obie Award ceremony. Is that true?"

I explained that I would be working at the studio that afternoon, and I was sure that we would go late into the evening. He asked if I'd talked to Bob about getting out early.

"No." I didn't say that I knew nothing about the awards, but he must have sensed a lack of enthusiasm on my part, because he went on to tell me about them.

The Village Voice, the alternative to New York's mainstream papers, had founded the Obie Awards in 1956 under the direction of theater critic Jerry Tallmer. Through the years, they had grown in importance as off-Broadway had grown in importance. Mel, one of the strongest supporters of off-Broadway, felt that the Obies were every bit as important to the theater as the Tonys. For one thing, they represented the world of theater that was there for a younger and broader audience who could not afford Broadway prices. For another, they represented that aspect of New York's theater world where chances could be taken on new writers, actors, directors, and experimental work. It was not nearly as dependent on commercial success. In essence, off-Broadway was the future. Of course, I knew this was true; I had just been preoccupied with my own problem of getting through the last few days on the soap. Mel said, "Farley, please try to attend."

"Yes. Of course I will," I responded.

At the studio the next day, I stopped by the office of the associate producer in charge of arranging the rehearsal and taping schedules. We did not rehearse or tape in sequence. It was done out of order depending upon which sets were standing and which had to be replaced for the next day. When I told her about the Obie Award nomination, Susan Strickler chided me gently for not coming to her sooner about such an important thing and agreed immediately to rearrange the shooting schedule in order to get me out early. When I said that I hadn't wanted to bother her, because everyone was constantly pestering her for early outs, she laughed, "Farley, bothering me is trying to get out early for a party or a ball game. This is something that really is important. Most of the good things I see in theater are off-Broadway. You will be finished in the A.M. session. Go win an award." She waved me out of her office as I tried to thank her.

The Obie

I was impressed by everyone's enthusiasm about my nomination, and feeling a bit stupid about my lack of knowledge of the award, since I had worked off-Broadway several times and loved it. I called Janice Rule, with whom I'd done my first off-Broadway play, and asked if she would attend with me.

We arrived at the downtown club where the awards were being held. It was small and dark, with a bar and a somewhat central raised performance space. Not knowing anyone officially associated with the Obies, Janice and I headed for the bar. Drinks in hand, I spotted Helen Stenborg and her husband, Barney Hughes, waving at us from a small table. Helen, who played my wife in *Talley & Son,* was also nominated for an acting award. We threaded our way through the crowded space, saying our hellos to the actors each of us recognized, and joined Barney and Helen. Shortly after we got seated, the lights brightened on the performing area and the ceremony began. It was all very informal and relaxed.

I was getting up to get us another drink when I heard my name being called out. This was so unexpected that I just stood there frozen until Janice took the glasses out of my hands and pushed me toward the stage. I made my way through the applauding crowd to the lighted area where I was presented with a plaque signed by six critics as Best Actor of the Year for my performance in *Tal-*

ley & Son. I was still in a state of shock when I made it back to our table and a barrage of hugs and kisses. When I heard them call out Helen's name as Best Actress, my happiness for her brought everything back into focus. I had never won anything in my whole life. Now, at a moment in time when my self-esteem needed it most, I had been publicly honored for my work in a play that I had loved doing.

After the awards had all been handed out and after meeting and thanking the critics who had voted for me, Janice and I slipped away to a small Italian restaurant we both knew in the Village and digested the evening along with some terrific pasta.

We reminisced about working together at the Phoenix, which had been my first onstage appearance in New York. After that, she had married Ben Gazzara, whom she had met in a play produced by Ben's and my lawyer and business manager, Jay Julien. They kept an apartment in New York, but moved to Beverly Hills to make it in the movies. Instead, she had become a highly respected psychoanalyst who left the Coast when their marriage fell apart. I, too, had bounced back and forth, including a four-year stint in Italy. But unlike Janice, the only times I had been really happy in my work was when I was onstage.

I had realized my ambition to become a real actor, and had been lucky enough to do some extremely good things in each of the three golden ages I worked my way through: movies, live television, and theater. The Obie Award was much more to me than an affirmation of work well done, it was proof that the world I fell in love with when I saw Ethel Merman hold an audience in the palm of her hand during my first trip to New York was where I belonged.

Epilogue

I never thought that one of Goldwyn's most famous malapropisms would apply to me so accurately that I would one day quote it as the title for my memoir.

I'm sure he was smart enough to realize that celebrity and talent are not necessarily one and the same. I don't know if he was sensitive enough to realize *I* was smart enough to have figured this out from the beginning. I wanted to develop my talent. I had no interest in becoming a household name or in playing by the rules of the game to become a movie star. When I bought out my contract, Goldwyn thought I was escalating my rebellion to a crazy level for some ulterior motive. I was following my heart and doing what I had to do.

It worked. To this day I cannot forget the thrill of getting my first laugh onstage, the joy of dancing and singing "Shall We Dance?" onstage with Barbara Cook, the sense of accomplishment when the curtain came down on the plays with the National Repertory Theatre. I loved the excitement of creating a character in a new play with the playwright's collaboration, and I will never forget the pride and happiness I felt for receiving an award for doing something I enjoyed so much.

I owe Sam Goldwyn for creating the circumstances that forced me to include myself out. Thanks, Mr. G.

INDEX

FG stands for Farley Granger.